GLOBALIZATION: THE INTERNAL DYNAMIC

GLOBALIZATION: THE INTERNAL DYNAMIC

Edited by

PAUL KIRKBRIDE
and KAREN WARD

ASHRIDGE

JOHN WILEY & SONS, LTD

Chichester · New York · Weinheim · Brisbane · Singapore · Toronto

337
656292

Copyright © 2001 by John Wiley & Sons, Ltd,
H   Baffins Lane, Chichester,
West Sussex PO19 1UD, England

National   01243 779777
International   (+44) 1243 779777
e-mail (for orders and customer service enquiries): cs-books@wiley.co.uk
Visit our Home Page on http://www.wiley.co.uk
or http://www.wiley.com

All Rights Reserved. No part of this publication may be reproduced, stored in a retrieval system, or transmitted, in any form or by any means, electronic, mechanical, photocopying, recording, scanning or otherwise, except under the terms of the Copyright, Designs and Patents Act 1988 or under the terms of a licence issued by the Copyright Licensing Agency, 90 Tottenham Court Road, London W1P 9HE, UK, without the permission in writing of the publisher.

Other Wiley Editorial Offices

John Wiley & Sons, Inc., 605 Third Avenue,
New York, NY 10158-0012, USA

WILEY-VCH GmbH, Pappelallee 3,
D-69469 Weinheim, Germany

John Wiley & Sons Australia, Ltd, 33 Park Road, Milton,
Queensland 4064, Australia

John Wiley & Sons (Asia) Pte Ltd, 2 Clementi Loop #02-01,
Jin Xing Distripark, Singapore 129809

John Wiley & Sons (Canada) Ltd, 22 Worcester Road,
Rexdale, Ontario M9W 1L1, Canada

British Library Cataloguing in Publication Data

A catalogue record for this book is available from the British Library

ISBN 0-471-49941-2

Typeset in 11/14pt Bembo by Dorwyn Ltd, Rowlands Castle, Hants.
Printed and bound in Great Britain by Biddles Ltd, Guildford and King's Lynn.
This book is printed on acid-free paper responsibly manufactured from sustainable forestry, in which at least two trees are planted for each one used for paper production.

CONTENTS

University Libraries
Carnegie Mellon University
Pittsburgh, PA 15213-3890

PREFACE

Since 1959 Ashridge has earned the reputation of being one of the world's leading business schools. Through all our activities, from executive education and post-graduate qualification programmes to research and consulting, we combine leading-edge thinking with a strong practical focus. We believe that learning must be involving, challenging and above all real, so that it does make a significant difference when applied in the workplace. To this end we have reinforced and built upon the philosophy of our founders: that business needs to inform and reflect the environment in which it operates. Our work with clients and business school partners from all parts of the world endorses this still further.

We know that globalization is not an isolated subject, as it integrates with all organizational activities and as such creates fascinating business and development opportunities. Our faculty's expertise in globalization has developed from research, observation, hands-on experience and passion for the subject. We are therefore delighted that our faculty members are able to share their learning and insights more widely by contributing chapters to two complementary books published by John Wiley & Sons.

I hope you find that these two books *Globalization: The Internal Dynamic* and *Globalization: The External Pressures* help you address your own particular issues and I would be pleased to hear your thoughts and comments on Ashridge's approach to globalization.

Leslie Hannah
Chief executive

ACKNOWLEDGEMENTS

The original idea for this book and the companion volume (Kirkbride, P.S. *Globalization: The External Pressures,* Wiley, 2001) came from Kate Charlton, then Director of Corporate Development and Paul Pinnington, Stream Director for Tailored Programmes. Kate and Paul were convinced that Ashridge had a wealth of talent that could be brought to bear on the topic of globalization and so the resulting works owe a debt to their vision. They had initiated discussions with publishers and Paul Kirkbride's role, as newly appointed Research Fellow, was to bring the books to fruition. Paul was solely responsible for the first book but managed to recruit Karen Ward to help edit the second book.

Editors of a collection such as this owe a debt of gratitude to the individuals who volunteered to provide chapters, often having to fit writing into a very busy teaching or consulting schedule. Thanks therefore to Paul Pinnington, Karen Ward, Bob Westwood, Samreen Khan, Andrew Ettinger, Cath Redman, Stefan Wills, Phil Hodgson and Randall White for their sterling contributions.

Paul would like to thank the following:

- My secretary, Tracy Bowdrey-Long, for her usual efficient work and for her calming influence;
- Rachel Oakley, from the Ashridge Graphics Department, for her excellent work on the Figures for the book;
- Leslie Hannah, Chief Executive, for his support and encouragement;
- Karen Ward, for her involvement in the development of the book and her constant encouragement and support despite the competing time pressures of her pregnancy and subsequent maternity leave;
- Claire Plimmer and her team at Wiley for their expert advice and assistance;
- Staff at the Australian Graduate School of Management (AGSM) in Sydney, especially Dr Robert Westwood, for providing me with a peaceful and relaxing venue to complete my own chapter contributions while teaching a summer school in January and February 2000;
- My many international clients, and the global managers within them, who have shaped my view of globalization and the global organization;
- My children, Daisy, Holly and William, for support and encouragement (as long as my writing did not intrude too far upon family activities!)

Karen would like to thank the following:

- Paul Kirkbride, for somehow getting me involved in this great project despite the fact I was already too busy and for chasing me for deadlines in the gentlest way possible;
- David Findley, former HR Director GlaxoWellcome, who had the courage to give me my first global role and the wisdom to help me learn from that experience;
- Claudia Heimer and Kevin Barham for all the lunchtime and late night chats about how the world really is in these global organizations;
- My wonderfully supportive husband, Martin, without whom I could not balance a global job and being a mum to my boys Rian and Matthew;
- Last, but certainly not least, all the global leaders and their teams whom I have had the pleasure of working with. Without you and all we have learned together there would be nothing to write. Thank you.

Paul Kirkbride   Karen Ward
Reading, August 2001   St Albans, August 2001

EDITORS' INTRODUCTION

Paul Kirkbride and Karen Ward

If the shelves of airport bookstalls are any indication, the 1990s were the decade of globalization. Whether in the fields of business, management, economics, information technology or e-commerce, the word appeared to be on everyone's lips. As a leading international business school, Ashridge was not immune from such trends. The start of the decade saw Ashridge adopt a clear strategy of internationalization, if not globalization. It extensively expanded its work in continental Europe as well as in Asia-Pacific and the United States.

In parallel with this move were several other trends within Ashridge. Obviously, 'globalization' began to be taught more frequently on development programmes as a special topic, but also other parts of the 'curriculum' began to take on a more global dimension. Members of the Ashridge faculty were increasingly working with more 'global' clients and researching more into various aspects of globalization. For example, in 1993 Paul Kirkbride organized the Third Conference on International Personnel and Human Resources Management at Ashridge (Kirkbride, 1994). The theme for this conference was 'Human Resources Management in the New Europe of the 1990s' and it dealt with a number of globalization issues, including the role of national cultures, the developments in the European Union, the growth of Eastern Europe, and the creation of pan-European managers. Karen Ward spent the late 1990s researching and working with international project teams. This research project culminated in the production of a new model of international team working (Canney Davidson and Ward, 1999). Ashridge also began a deliberate process of 'internationalizing' the faculty that led, by the end of the decade, to a faculty with very diverse cultural origins and working experiences.

However, part of the role of a high-quality business school is its ability to take an objective and critical look at topics and processes that might simply be passing managerial 'fads'. Our view is that innovations in terms of new concepts tend to go through two distinct phases. In the first phase, which we term recognition, the new concept attracts a great deal of attention. Many people jump on the conceptual bandwagon and rush into print with books and articles seeking to elucidate the concept. Managers rush to seminars and conferences to learn all about the new concept and the implications for their own organizations, often fearing that they may be missing out on something important. At the end of this phase the concept is high in the popular consciousness. Everyone has heard of it and has an opinion on it. However, while much heat has been generated in the discussions and debates around the topic, there is often not quite so much light. There are a number of examples of this process in recent years, ranging from 'lean manufacturing' to 'business process reengineering' to 'emotional intelligence'. Our argument is that globalization is yet another example of this trend. Indeed, we would argue that globalization is a particularly good example, as the globalization debate tended to get caught up within a more general '*fin de siècle*' or 'millenniumist' debate that saw globalization as the arrival of a new epoch in the twenty-first century.

The second phase of dissemination, which we term understanding, is more sober. Here the concept is held up to critical inspection and evaluation in an attempt to distil its real elements. The protagonists are not naïve supporters of the idea but objective observers. It is our contention that the concept of globalization is ripe for such a critical reappraisal. This notion, plus the fact that many from within the

Ashridge faculty had been doing research, either pure or applied, into aspects of the topic, led to the suggestion that they should pool their thoughts in a book on globalization. As this idea was debated, two distinct books emerged. The first, *Globalization: The External Pressures*, was edited by one of us (Kirkbride, 2001), while we worked together to write chapters for, and edit, this second book on the internal aspects of globalization. Both books are the products of authors who are full-time Ashridge faculty, recent Ashridge faculty and/or Ashridge associates.

This volume, *Globalization: The Internal Dynamic*, focuses on what it really takes to become a global organization. We essentially argue that, despite the rhetoric, few organizations are really global or transnational. This volume thus seeks to understand what such organizations would look like and the potential barriers to true global status. It offers practical advice in terms of what organizations would have to do to be really global in nature. The companion volume, *Globalization: The External Pressures* (Kirkbride, 2001), seeks to examine the concept of globalization and the existence of global financial and labour markets. It looks at the pressures towards globalization and at how organizations are responding on a macro scale and, in terms of their external interfaces, with an increasingly global environment.

PLAN OF BOOK

In Chapter 1 Paul Kirkbride, Paul Pinnington and Karen Ward, all from Ashridge, seek to examine whether the much hyped 'global' organizations exist in reality or are simply a myth fed by hyperbole and an overexcited managerial literature. They suggest that a number of the supposed drivers of this process are found to be wanting under a critical spotlight. They also challenge whether companies are really global and whether the much vaunted 'global mindset' exists in global organizations as well as in the global managerial literature. In opposition, they assert that the cultural origins of specific country business models are stronger than the 'globalists' would seek to suggest. Thus most 'global' organizations are dominated by their home-country mindset. This chapter also identifies the high human and personal cost of global leadership roles.

Kirkbride, Pinnington and Ward then go on to list and describe a number of problems and issues that companies face when seeking to globalize, before concluding by trying to examine critically the nature and complexion of a truly global organization. Here they outline a new model of global organization that would allow companies to audit themselves and see how far down the road to globalization they have progressed.

Chapter 2 tackles the issue of designing your organization for globalization. Karen Ward, from Ashridge, draws on her consulting experience to identify the key barriers to global design. These include the tendency to overelaborate; the tendency to promote similarity; the inability to deal with conflict constructively; and the prevailing mechanistic view of organizations. Karen then goes on to describe how to design organizations for global success. This involves a careful consideration of the key design 'choices'; ensuring alignment to strategic intent; the ability to live with the tensions of a multi-focus design; the building of an organization that is customer facing and yet has clear internal accountabilities; and the ability to achieve sufficient flexibility to allow the organization to adapt to future changes. Karen illustrates her argument with a number of examples and cases drawn from her consulting work.

In Chapter 3 Paul Kirkbride, from Ashridge, and Robert Westwood, from the Australian Graduate School of Management, seek to explain the concept of culture and assess the degree to which culture is really a barrier or problem for companies seeking a global presence. Drawing extensively on the existing literature, their own research work and their practical experience in cross-cultural settings, including the Asia-Pacific region, they identify ten core dimensions of cultural difference. These dimensions are illustrated, where appropriate, with real-life cultural vignettes that serve to illuminate the practical nature of some of the cultural barriers. Paul and Robert conclude by describing how global organizations, and the global managers within them, can develop greater cross-cultural understanding and sensitivity. They also address the perennial argument of convergence versus divergence of cultures, concluding that, while it is impossible to predict the future, culture and cultural difference will continue to be a significant issue and problem. Organizations will have to address cultural issues in a much more comprehensive way if they want to be truly 'global' in scope and nature.

Is organizational change different for global organizations? In Chapter 4, Paul Kirkbride argues that the global nature of some organizations raises *a priori* problems for the successful management of change: problems that have been overlooked in the rush to globalize. He identifies two main sets: the problem of scale and the problem of cultural differences. In relation to the first, he uses structural inertia theory to argue that any large organization, such as a multinational, will find it very difficult, if not impossible, to meet global changes in its environment by internal transformations as advocated by the popular management literature. In relation to the second problem, he raises a number of questions. Can a single change approach work across cultural boundaries? Can particular changes, such as total quality management (TQM) or business process reengineering (BPR), be equally applied in all cultures? Are change tools and techniques transferable? And is change a universal truth? Using his own extensive research experience and data from the Asia-Pacific region as examples, Paul identifies problems in answering in the affirmative any of these questions. He concludes by offering some advice to global organizations faced with a change agenda.

Chapter 5 moves on to consider the issue of organizational learning. Samreen Khan, from Ashridge Consulting, argues that in order to achieve learning that supports and reinforces the strategic direction of the business, organizations have both to define the individual learning needs of their staff and to understand how culturally diverse staff learn. Unfortunately, she argues, these two prerequisites are often in conflict in the global organization. Samreen argues that the processes of defining the learning needs of individuals and allowing them to drive their own learning form a paradox. She begins her analysis by considering the key challenges for a global learning organization before analysing the learning process from an individual perspective. She then turns her attention to the paradox that she raised at the start of the chapter and suggests ways in which existing assumptions can be challenged and transcended in an attempt to dissolve the paradox.

In Chapter 6, Cath Redman and Andrew Ettinger from the Ashridge Learning Resource Centre approach the issue of organizational learning from a rather different perspective. Their focus is on the rapid expansion of global e-learning processes and systems. They describe how organizations are using new technology to create e-learning systems that serve to link distant parts of global corporate empires. They identify a number of trends, such as the expansion of the Internet, the learning organization, knowledge management and intellectual capital, which can be integrated through e-learning systems. Cath and Andrew start by describing what is meant by a global e-learning environment and discuss the rationale for developing such an environment. They then spend time, using their extensive practical knowledge, in describing how to create the best e-learning environment for the learner. After a discussion of the pros and cons of corporate universities, they conclude by outlining their key success factors for global e-learning.

Karen Ward, from Ashridge, has spent the last few years studying complex and virtual teams in multinationals. In Chapter 7 she shares some of her experience and conclusions. Karen starts by establishing why teams are so important to global organizations before moving on to describe how to create successful teams in such organizations. She introduces her four-phase model of team development, which charts in detail the start-up, first meeting, strategic 'moments' and completion and review phases of the team. Karen describes for each phase a number of examples of best practice and illustrates each phase with vignettes and mini-cases taken from her research and consulting work.

In the early 1990s Stefan Wills was the joint author of an Ashridge Report into the nature and competencies required by international managers (Barham and Wills, 1993). This report identified a number of key things that international managers had to 'do' but, more interestingly, also identified the types of personal characteristics required by successful international managers. These were grouped under the headings of cognitive complexity, emotional energy and psychological maturity. Eight years later, Stefan reflects in Chapter 8 on these original findings and his subsequent work in this area. In doing so, he develops the original ideas and focuses on what he now terms the 'head', the 'heart' and the 'soul' required by potential global managers in their leadership role.

In Chapter 9 Phil Hodgson, from Ashridge, and Randall White, from Executive Development Group and the Fuqua School of Business, Duke University, also consider the issue of global leadership, but adopt a slightly different trajectory. They note that global leaders over the ages have prized three forms of clarity: clarity of purpose, clarity of external operation and clarity of internal operation. Phil and Randall identify a further core leadership issue, the ability to handle the uncertainty you face as a leader when tackling the increasing level of ambiguity found in today's external environments. They then proceed to identify and explain eight behaviour enablers that they claim allow leaders to cope with ambiguity and feel less uncertainty in the process. As they suggest, 'global leaders will need to lead their organizations effectively towards uncertainty [and] this ability . . . is perhaps the most important clarity of all'.

Chapter 10 represents the last of our three chapters on global leadership. In this practical case study chapter, Paul Kirkbride considers how Pirelli, a large Italian tyre and cable multinational, has begun to deal with the issue of developing a global leadership capability. The case focuses on the Pirelli Leadership Path, a programme rolled out throughout the company's worldwide operations during 2000/2001, and, in particular, its implementation in the UK. Paul explains the Full Range Leadership Model on which the initiative is based and then outlines how the leadership path, involving training courses, 360 degree feedback and personal coaching, was organized and delivered. Paul concludes by trying to evaluate the success of the initiative and how this leadership programme potentially links to the other components of the 'six-ball' model of global organization outlined in Chapter 1.

References

Barham, K. and Wills, S. (1993) *Management Across Frontiers*, Berkhamsted: Ashridge Management College Report (AMRG 929).

Canney Davidson, S. and Ward, K. (1999) *Leading International Teams*, London: McGraw-Hill.

Kirkbride, P. S. (1994) *Human Resource Management in Europe: Perspectives for the 1990s*, London: Routledge.

Kirkbride, P. S. (2001) *Globalization: The External Pressures*, Chichester: John Wiley.

GLOBALIZATION: WHERE IS YOUR ORGANIZATION TODAY?

**Paul Kirkbride, Paul Pinnington
and Karen Ward**

CHAPTER 1

GLOBALIZATION: WHERE IS YOUR ORGANIZATION TODAY?

As identified in the introduction, the primary purpose of this volume is critically to examine the globalization phenomenon from an internal organizational perspective and to explore whether there is substance behind the much hyped 'global' company. This first chapter will look at global organizations in practice, explore the key characteristics of a global organization and provide a framework for assessing the extent to which your organization is moving towards, or has become, truly global. Subsequent chapters will explore particular aspects of global organizations in more detail.

However, the first challenge to pose is whether global organizations exist in reality rather than merely in the PR machines of the world's multinational companies (MNCs).

GLOBAL ORGANIZATION: MYTH OR REALITY?

As noted by Rhinesmith (1996), 'globalization has arrived in the world, but not in most of the world's organizations'. To explore his assertion, we need to identify the different trends that are influencing globalization and examine the extent to which these are affecting the way in which organizations operate. Behind Rhinesmith's comment is a view that while the external drivers of globalization are well documented (Kirkbride, 2001), their impact on actual business practice is more limited. This will be the focus of this first section.

Pick up most business newspapers or magazines and somewhere in their pages will be an article or comment on how the world is shrinking, how we all live in one global community, how we need to work faster and smarter in this virtual marketplace. In our companion volume (Kirkbride, 2001), we have labelled these views as 'globalist' and critically contrasted them with the dissenting views of the 'sceptics', 'transformationalists' and 'anti-globalists' (Kirkbride, Pinnington and Ward, 2001). Even 10 years ago multinational companies (MNCs) accounted for almost a quarter of world trade and a quarter of the world's GNP (Bartlett and Ghoshal, 1999). Today, global business continues to be dominated by the 500 largest MNCs. They account for 90 per cent of all the world's foreign direct investment and over half its trade. Over 40 per cent of the global market for US organizations such as Coca-Cola, Gillette, Lucent, Boeing and GE Power Systems is in Asia (Prahalad and Lieberthal, 1998: 78). If we glance into the future, McKinsey estimates that over the next 30 years truly global markets will produce and consume more than 80 per cent of the world's GDP versus 20 per cent today (Bryan and Fraser, 1999).

Over five years ago, the Institute for the Future, in its book *Global Work* (O'Hara-Devereaux and Johansen, 1994), identified four 'fault lines' that were driving organizations inexorably towards a global reality: the globalization of consumerism; the transformation of the traditional hierarchy into a global network of interconnected roles; the fragmentation of work and creation of global jobs; and the ascendancy of knowledge as a primary global product. Since the publication of that study, the fault lines have become deeper and the emergence of the Internet has significantly speeded up the pace of the changes. So what have been the organizational responses to these changes in the external environment and how have they contributed to the notion of the global organization?

Bigger Is Better

As organizations have faced the changing demands of consumers and the pressure to deliver cost-effective, high-quality products and services to multiple markets, one of the responses has been to buy global capacity and scope through mergers and acquisitions. Recognizing that organic growth was not going to give them economies of scale and access to new markets quickly enough, many of the world's top 500 companies have been involved in mega mergers as industries consolidate into a handful of global players. Examples include the automotive industry, pharmaceuticals, white goods and soft drinks. The rhetoric that accompanies the announcements of these consolidations usually talks about access to extended customer bases across the globe, global economies of scale that reduce costs and risks and being able to access the best people from the global talent pool to develop innovative global products and services, thereby giving the impression that the key driver behind this consolidation is the intent to become a truly global organization.

However, behind the newspaper headlines and the much-hyped press conferences to the global analyst community, the practice for many companies is very different. Although on paper the consolidation gives them extended global reach, the reality of integrating two or more diverse organizations globally with highly developed and distinct structures, processes and mindsets proves to be a complex challenge. They are so focused on trying to make the new organization work effectively that they take their eyes off the external marketplace and provide space for local and regional competitors to steal market opportunities. Three examples from different industries illustrate some of the challenges of assuming that 'bigger is better' when it comes to playing on the global stage.

A good example of the power of the strategic hype over the reality of integration and implementation is the DaimlerChrysler merger that is currently disappointing shareholders. The initial reaction in the financial communities to Daimler-Benz's bold move was overwhelmingly positive. Many commentators at the time heralded it as the beginning of the next era of global automotive players. Yet, although in theory the initial merger and the subsequent integration of Hyundai and Mitsubishi create a global giant in the automotive industry, the jury is still out as to whether the cost of making such different organizations work together effectively will outweigh any of the global strategic benefits that drove the initial consolidation. Integrating German, American and Japanese norms, values and beliefs into one common global culture is not something that will happen overnight, particularly when the mindset of the senior managers is predominantly rooted in the German culture.

In some industries the preferred route to global expansion has been through creating global alliance networks rather than through mergers and acquisitions, yet integrating these global alliances has proven equally challenging. For example, in the airline industry, the **one**world and Star alliances face a number of issues, such as should they move to full code sharing agreements or looser contractual arrangements; how can they harmonize service levels with alliance partners (e.g. Lufthansa, Singapore Airlines and Thai Airways); and how does the alliance develop a global mindset rather than a German or Anglo-American mindset. Even more challenging is how you create a common customer experience across carriers from national cultures with fundamentally different perspectives on customer service. Yet the espoused aim of these alliances is to provide a seamless service for the globe-trotting executive.

A recent study by the management consulting firm A.T. Kearney concludes that merged pharmaceutical companies create significantly less economic value than independent pharmaceutical

> players, challenging a dominant belief in the industry that global
> reach is the key determinant of success (*The Economist*, 1998).

So although globalization appears to have driven industry consolidation, it has not necessarily resulted in the creation of effective global
organizations.

Global Brands

One of the most visible signs of globalization to managers consists in
the increasingly familiar products and services that appear to be present
in every city: we pick up the same model car from our preferred rental
company, drive to check in at the hotel chain where we have a frequent stayer account and order a meal from a room-service menu that
offers a 'global' standard range of dishes. Similarly, to the average
person on the street, globalization is the changing face of some of the
familiar products they put into their shopping baskets each week. For
example, in the UK market there is currently a massive advertising
campaign on television and in print to let consumers know that a
cleaning product formally known as Jif has been changed to Cif. The
purpose of the name change was for the manufacturer to have one
common brand name across the European market.

Identifying which brands are local and which should become
regional or global is a crucial decision for a global company. Not only
does it educate the consumer to accept regional or global products, but
it can be the route to significant cost advantages. For example, Volvo
has achieved significant premiums by substituting its brand for acquired
brands. Similarly, Interbrew has decided that Stella Artois, Hoogaarden
and Leffe are to be global brands offering scope for economies of scale
in product development, production and marketing. On the other
hand, Electrolux has determined that in Europe, Electrolux, Zanussi
and AEG will be positioned as regional brands to take into account
local preferences. And despite Coca-Cola being known for its 'global'
domination of the soft drinks market, CEO Douglas Daft recently

announced that world-wide decision making would be pushed down to the local level. Coca-Cola would embrace local brands and flavours and move away from American advertising, for example using Bollywood stars in India. This has led to 6000 employees losing their jobs in the global headquarters in Atlanta.

The implementation of a global brand strategy lasts for decades, not years, in many industries and has to take into account the different positioning in individual markets. On a recent global brand manager development programme, the participants were asked to bring examples of their global products. In one case a cleaning product that was a leading 'global' brand for the organization had 14 variations to accommodate various regional markets – and those were only the examples that made it to the course. So the reality is often very different from the media myth created in the eyes of the consumer: even global giants have to accommodate changing consumer preferences.

How Global Is Global?

Despite all the talk of global reach and global brands, when you take a closer look at the source of sales revenue of even the bigger multinationals, it is usually concentrated in the developed world and in a few key markets. Most multinational enterprises (MNEs) have a global presence but are organized on a regional basis in the triad markets of North America, Europe and Asia. In addition, most of the decisions in development, marketing and production are made at a regional level because of different government regulations and consumer needs. For example, 95 per cent of all the motor vehicles produced in Europe are sold in Europe.

Table 1.1 illustrates the comparative global market shares for Volkswagen and Electrolux in 1996 and 1999/2000. Despite both organizations shifting their sales away from their home markets, for VW the growth has been concentrated in the rest of the European market and North America, with very modest growth in Asia-Pacific and a reduction in the Latin American markets. Electrolux, on the other hand, while reducing its reliance on its European home markets, has only grown in non-EU Europe and North America and declined in all other markets.

Table 1.1   Global sales revenue by region (% of total global market)

Volkswagen	1996	2000	Electrolux	1996	1999
Germany	63.9	28.7	EU	52.4	42.7
Rest of Europe	17.7	39.8	Rest of Europe	7	7.5
North America	2.8	19.8	North America	27.2	39.9
Latin America	14.2	6	Latin America	6.4	3.8
Other countries	1.4		Asia	4.2	3.7
Africa		1.2	Middle East	0.9	0.6
Asia–Pacific		4.5	Africa	0.9	0.9
			Oceania	1	0.9
Total	100	100		100	100

Source: Electrolux and Volkswagen annual reports.

Yet does activity in these key markets reflect a truly global organization? A range of evidence would suggest not. First, we can explore the extent to which consumers in Europe, Japan and North America are representative of consumers globally. An e-mail that has been circulating on the Internet recently paints quite a different picture of how the world is actually shaped today.

The Harter E-mail

If we shrink the current population of the globe to a village of precisely 100 people, with all the existing human ratios remaining the same, the village would be populated by the following people:

- 57 Asians, 8 Africans, 21 Europeans and 14 from the remaining western hemisphere – north and south
- 52 women and 48 men
- 70 non-whites and 30 whites
- 70 non-Christian and only 30 Christian

- 6 of these people would possess 59 per cent of the entire world's wealth and all 6 would be from the USA
- 70 would be unable to read
- 50 would suffer from malnutrition
- 1 would have a college education
- 1 would own a computer

Source: *Fast Company*, 2001.

As this e-mail dramatically illustrates, the majority of the world does not live in the western hemisphere in the developed consumer markets of existing global companies, but rather in the developing world with emerging markets.

Organizations have been slowly waking up to the fact that the future for many industries does not lie in existing markets but in the rapidly growing emerging markets of China, India and Brazil. The *Financial Times* (FT) list in 1999 of the world's top 500 companies based on market capitalization includes only one company from India and none from mainland China. This will definitely change over the next 10–20 years. As Prahalad and Lieberthal (1998) note, 'a vast consumer base of hundreds of millions of people is developing rapidly', which offers significant potential for the so-called global players in each industry.

Yet evidence from the last two decades indicates that emerging markets can be a nightmare for global companies. For example, despite being a leading player in the global white-goods industry, Whirlpool has recently lost $100 million in China. Some of the more obvious hurdles companies face as they try and enter these new markets include:

- Legal and political constraints, e.g. an insistence on local joint ventures, a lack of legislation to stop copying of intellectual capital, a legal system that fails to support contracts.
- Difficulty in obtaining market data.
- High transportation costs as a result of poor infrastructure.

- Complicated distribution channels dominated by local relationships.

However, some more subtle barriers are also at play, which stem from the imperialist mindset of the current dominant 'global' players. There has been an assumption among global executives that their organizations could export their current business models around the world – often with significant negative consequences.

One key misunderstanding has been the analysis of the size and nature of business opportunity in these emerging markets. Wooed with tales of a growing middle class starved of consumer choice and ready to spend their new-found wealth, global players have been falling over themselves to gain a share of this apparently limitless market potential. The reality has been a much more sobering experience.

Global segments in emerging markets have proven to be much smaller than initial estimates and local competitors more aggressive than expected. Global players have failed to segment the new consumer base appropriately and have assumed that consumers would behave in similar patterns to existing markets. After 20 years of studying these markets, Prahalad and Lieberthal (1998) have concluded that there are some significant differences, as indicated below:

- Consumers, although more affluent than 10 years ago, are not affluent by western standards. For example, in China only 2 million consumers have purchasing power over $20 000, while 330 million have purchasing power of between $5000 and $10 000.
- A relatively small number of consumers are attracted to 'global' brands and have the money to afford these products and services. For example, 7 million consumers fall into this global segment in India, whereas 125 million potential consumers are still loyal to local products.
- The 'luxury' or 'global' segment begins at a much lower price barrier. For example, to avoid the 'luxury' car market in emerging markets products need to be positioned well below $20 000.

■ Consumers are more focused on the price–performance ratio than are their western counterparts.

The net result is that in many emerging markets, all the global players are concentrated in a small high-value niche segment, constricted by local competitors dominating the other segments. For example, Revlon competes for 3 per cent of the Chinese market, whereas Tahoma, its local competitor, aims at half the market. Similarly, the Chinese premium beer market accounts for approximately 15 per cent of total beer consumption. Yet Fosters, Lion Nathan, Heineken, San Miguel, Asshir, Interbrew, Anheuser-Busch and South African Breweries are all fighting for a share of this sector, with Coors Carlsberg and others waiting in the wings for an opportunity to enter. All the global players, with one exception, are currently making losses in their Chinese operation.

Besides competing in a small global segment, the arrival of foreign global players stirs the local companies to action. Aggressive local players have been able to restrict and in some cases reduce the size of the global opportunity, as shown in the following examples.

Jollibee foods in the Philippines overcame an onslaught from McDonald's by upgrading service and delivery standards but also developing value menus customized to local tastes. Along with noodle and rice meals made with fish, Jollibee created a hamburger seasoned with garlic and soy sauce, allowing it to capture 75 per cent of the burger market and 56 per cent of the fast-food business in the Philippines.

Bajaj Motors forced Honda out of the Indian scooter market by strengthening its distribution and investing more in R&D specifically targeted to the local market.

> Kellogg's spent a fortune trying to get consumers in India to buy its products, only to be undercut by local competitors who started to make breakfast cereals based on more familiar flavours.

Similarly, there are 'local' players in the emerging markets who are not content to stay as such and will soon be taking on the current 'global' players at their own game. For example, the list of Chinese contenders includes Boshan Iron and Steel (steelmaking), Haier Group (appliances), Sichuan Changhong (television), North China Pharmaceutical (drugs), Peking University Founder Group (computer software) and Legend Holdings (personal computers).

Having dominated the Chinese market, the Haier Group has now launched in the US white-goods market and its global ambition is clear.

Indian contenders will come initially from the software industry, for example Infosys Technologies, which in 1999 became the first Indian company listed on the NASDAQ, Satyam Infoway, WIPRO, NIIT, and the HCL Group. Examples from other industries include ICICI in financial services, Ranabasey in pharmaceuticals, Reliance Industries in petrochemicals and the diversified Tata Group. Indian companies are now buying western brands. For example, Tata Tea has acquired Tetley, the inventor of tea bags, market leader in the UK and Canada and No. 2 in the US market. Its vice-chairman was quoted in the *Financial Times*: 'This is a first step in globalisation. Tetley brings sophisticated tea blending skills and quality control which are essential if we are to secure global leadership for Indian tea' (Merchant and Pretzlick, 2000).

A recent European study that tested the extent of true globalization within global organizations also backed this narrow definition of 'global'. It concluded that 'global managers are less in evidence than is commonly believed and that in fact regional management is far more widespread' (Roure et al., 1993). Prahalad and Lieberthal conclude that if multinationals are seriously going to become true global players by participating fully and effectively in current emerging markets, then they will have 'to develop a new mindset and adopt new business models to achieve global competitiveness' (1998: 79). The next section explores this issue of mindset and prevailing business models.

Global Mindset: Does it Exist?

So what is meant by a new mindset to lead global organizations and why is it important? Rhinesmith (1996) notes that 'the real vulnerability [of organizations going global] may lie in the lack of a global mindset'. Bartlett and Ghoshal (1999) also comment that a global mindset is a prerequisite if companies are going to evolve to a transnational operating model for competing effectively in the global marketplace.

A mindset can be defined as a predisposition to see the world in a particular way – a filter through which to look at the world. It is often seen as a way of being rather than a specific set of skills, although many researchers have tried to document the underlying characteristics of effective global managers (Barham and Wills, 1993 and Wills, Chapter 8 in this volume). The definition used by Rhinesmith in his book for global managers is 'an openness to other cultures that facilitates international dealings and decisions', yet he also notes that this sensitivity to cultural diversity is something that 'few people possess naturally' (1996: 32). Commentators seem to agree that a global mindset is desirable and should be prevalent in global organizations, yet what is the evidence?

Our experience working with a number of 'global' corporations indicates that unless they actively seek to introduce diversity into the organization, a monocultural mindset can dominate long after the business conditions have become global. Is this so surprising? As individuals, we are all conditioned by the cultural norms, values, beliefs and assumptions of the world in which we grew up. We have been influenced by the dominant assumptions of the national psyche in which we were educated and have worked. Hofstede (1999) goes as far as to state that those cultural values are shaped in our early experiences, so that 'after the age of 12 . . . such values . . . are hardly changeable'. While other commentators may disagree with such a prognosis, there is much research to support Hofstede's view that national cultural values will fundamentally affect an organization's attitude and ability to operate globally. Just like individuals, companies have roots and often a strong cultural heritage that grows from their national origin. Examples would include IKEA from Sweden, Volkswagen from Germany and Glaxo-SmithKline from the UK. Their approaches to structure, funding, technology transfer and research and development may differ due to the different values of their countries of origin. These also create different blind spots for each organization as it moves into new global arenas.

One indicator of the extent to which a company is likely to possess a global mindset is to conduct an analysis of its top team. In too many cases the originating culture predominates: Germans run German companies, Swedes run Swedish companies and so on, even where the company is present in multiple locations around the world. Recently there has been some evidence that this is changing, however. Prahalad and Lieberthal (1998) predict that if boards are to reflect the markets where their companies operate, in ten years' time up to 30–40 per cent of the top team should come from countries like China, India and Brazil. Unilever is leading the way with the appointment of Keki Dadiseth, chairman of Hindustan Lever, as a Unilever main board director. However, as globalization accelerates, the need becomes greater for all levels of the organization and not just senior managers to develop a global mindset. A systems analyst in Italy may interact on a daily basis with a software programmer in India. A sales manager in Germany or the UK might be part of a global Wal-Mart account team and be working together with their American colleagues on a regular basis.

The key to a truly global mindset is deep self-awareness: the ability to know what informs your way of seeing the world and a knowledge that your way of seeing is only one of a myriad of valid alternative perspectives. It is a recognition of your blind spots and an openness and curiosity about differences. As Rhinesmith (1996) points out, 'the more you know about, and the less you are restrained by your own cultural attitudes, the more effectively you can contribute' within a global organization. Although seemingly obvious in theory, our experience is that actual practice is less common. As Hofstede (1999) notes, many managers of global organizations have been raised in cultures where self-awareness or reflection has not been encouraged or valued. Indeed, in many global companies the emphasis is on action, doing and busyness.

Creating a global mindset will not happen by accident, it requires concerted effort over a sustained period. Heimer (1994) has demonstrated that selection on to the boards of global companies is largely determined 'by tradition rather than innovation', with incumbent CEOs selecting new board members by 'operating within their own networks'. If these networks are predominantly monocultural, the profile of the senior team will not change dramatically and any external appointments are likely to be rejected, as the dominant mindset of the other board members is too similar and unable to see the world differently. Prahalad and Oosterveld (1999) also note that 'senior managers, against all good advice and their better judgement, entrust new tasks to old friends who may not be prepared for it'.

Some organizations are trying to manage this issue actively. To accelerate the development of a global mindset in ABB, for example, former chief executive Goran Lindhal asked a group of Asian and Indian managers to work on the 'ABB bible'. That was to produce a set of values that would be acceptable to the Indian and Chinese cultures and religions, as well as the Christian values that underpin the original 'ABB bible'. Electrolux, Volkswagen and Philips Semiconductors all run cross-cultural, cross-functional development programmes for their global high-potential managers (see Kirkbride and Westwood, Chapter 3, this volume). Some nations see the issue as more critical than others: there are an estimated 50 000 Japanese business people in New York with good English, compared to a mere 500 US business people in Tokyo with good Japanese. Although the theory of global organizations developing managers with global mindsets is an attractive one, the barriers to achieving it in practice are therefore not insignificant.

Dominant Business Models

Another aspect of developing global mindsets within organizations is to examine the origins of the dominant models and theories of organization and management that inform the thinking of these global organizations. A quick glance at any undergraduate or post-graduate business syllabus reveals a significant bias towards texts originating from US or European authors. Yet if we explore the dominant cultural assumptions of these countries, it is highly questionable how globally appropriate some of these assumptions are (see Kirkbride and Westwood, Chapter 3, this volume). As Hofstede (1999) notes, management as a concept originated in Britain in 1776 and was then developed over 100 years later in the US, where it was promoted to a separate field of study. Both the US and Britain were 'strongly individualist societies' already and 'all theories of management that were developed subsequently betray their individualist roots'. However, the majority of the world's population, particularly in many emerging markets, does not share these cultural norms. Similarly, as Prahalad and Oosterveld (1999) note, over time companies develop sets of managerial routines and 'the more successful the firm, the more entrenched the managerial routines'. They also conclude that because managers are all socialized in the same organizational values and norms, they may not even 'have an intellectual understanding of (much less experience with) an alternate model of managing' a global organization. To illustrate how dominant mindsets can profoundly influence management practices, D'Iribarnes (1997) studied three identical plants based in France, the Netherlands and the USA, which belonged to one organization. He was able to control for organizational and technological variables, focus on the national cultural impact and vividly demonstrated that the working practices on the shop floor of each plant were fundamentally different. He refutes the 'universality of management fads by showing how life in each country follows a line of historical continuity'.

However, before we all get deeply depressed and conclude that if we do not currently have a global mindset we will never be able to develop one, take heart from the following. Even researchers working in the field of cross-cultural understanding are prone to the cultural bias of their own roots. Hofstede (1999) himself acknowledges that his initial research overlooked a critical cultural dimension (long- versus short-term orientation) on which the economic success of the developing Asian economies has subsequently been predicated. It took a team of Chinese researchers working with Professor Michael Bond in Hong Kong to see the gap in Hofstede's original study. Recent research by Bartlett and Ghoshal (1999) indicates that this dominant mindset can open doors for aspiring global wannabes from emerging markets. They can use their newcomer status to challenge the rules of the game, capitalizing on the inflexibilities in the existing players' business models. For example, BRL Hardy, Australian wine producers, have developed very innovative strategies that have helped them penetrate the established and mature UK market.

This discussion of developing global mindsets within global organizations is based on a fundamental assumption that could be tragically flawed: that employees around the world aspire to be global leaders working in global organizations; in other words, that there are enough individuals out there who are both willing and able to become global players. Yet there is increasing evidence in the global organizations with which we are working that managers should not take this for granted − unless they change the way they are currently implementing their global strategies.

Burn-out: Who Wants to Be a Global Leader Anyway?

Part of the ambivalence on the part of employees is due to the question of whether their organization is implementing its global aspirations in a sustainable fashion. Evidence from working with numerous global leaders indicates that while the strategic benefits of globalization to an organization are high, the costs of delivering these benefits in human terms may be unsustainable in the long term. Organizations are implementing globalization in a manner that will lead to individual and organizational burn-out, which will in turn affect their ability to attract and retain key staff.

Role modelling by senior managers is critical in setting the style of global working within an organization. If staff see senior managers continuously travelling, getting off the 'red eye', coming straight to the office and working through a full day, or using the weekends to travel to ensure that they are in an overseas office for a full working week, then it is not surprising that these organizations quickly have an escalating travel bill and an increasingly exhausted workforce. The following quote from one department typifies the usual pattern in organizations:

> Unfortunately our Divisional VP was too busy travelling to have much impact on our performance.

Part of the difficulty we see in many global organizations is due to the difference in lifestyle between some senior managers and the majority of staff who have to make global organizations work. First, the majority of senior managers we encounter are over 45, male and have followed their chosen career for a number of years. If they have children, these are usually adult and no longer living at home. Their model of global work is often the colonial expatriate cadre, who have chosen to spend their career moving every two to three years to far-flung parts of the world. The senior managers we encounter who are younger than this or are female have often made a conscious decision to put their career before their family and many are single, divorced or have partners in equally responsible roles. Employees around the world, on the other hand, can be of all ages and have very diverse family and personal circumstances. They may not have chosen to dedicate their career to one organization and may not be prepared to sacrifice their personal life for work to such an extent.

There is increasing evidence that a macho style of globalization (where executives compete to see who can notch up the most frequent flyer miles) is marginalizing whole sections of the global workforce. The most obvious group affected are parents, for whom long stretches away from home mean missing large chunks of their children's development. As one global brand manager commented: 'It's a great job if you don't want a life.' This expectation of being able to jump on a plane at a moment's notice tends to discriminate against female managers, who typically still have most responsibility for childcare.

This style of global management is a barrier to creating a culturally diverse management cadre and may create a 'glass ceiling' within the organization. While many Japanese, US and increasingly European managers seem to be resigned to this style of global working, many cultures around the world place far more emphasis on community and family values and it would not only be personally but also socially unacceptable to be seen to 'neglect' your community and family responsibilities in this way. The practice also acts as a significant barrier to recruiting younger generations of talent. Recent graduate surveys in a number of countries have highlighted that work–life balance and individual career paths are now at the top of their criteria when selecting prospective employers.

Even for experienced managers who seem to have found ways to balance a global role and family life successfully, the impact of this 'macho' style can be more subtle, as the following vignette illustrates.

A senior manager was appointed to a newly created global role, which required him to spend half his time overseas. Fortunately his children were grown up and his wife was about to take early retirement. He came to an agreement with his organization that instead of flying business class, he would fly economy and his wife would accompany him. This cost the company no extra money and it met the needs of the couple. In addition, there were intangible benefits for the company of the wife accompanying the executive, as they were often doing business in countries where family values are held in high esteem and the wife was able to act as an ambassador for the company with clients. This arrangement worked very successfully for all concerned for two years.

However, when the manager's company was subject to a takeover and the manager had to apply for a new role – again a global one – he was unsuccessful. One of the reasons given was that if he needed to take his wife with him, he probably was not up to the job!

Two years later members of the senior management team who took this decision were willing to admit privately that they had made a mistake, but only after the 'successful' candidate had lost them significant business due to his cultural insensitivities.

Our experience of this style of global leadership is that it is simply not sustainable in the long run, neither from a financial nor a human cost perspective. Senior managers need to demonstrate a more 'humane' way of being an effective global leader. They need to recognize that if someone is not prepared to make the same sacrifices as they have, it does not mean that they cannot make a valuable contribution as a global player. They can learn to use technology to support their global working, for example conducting effective meetings using phone or videoconferences, rather than clocking up the air miles. They can also explore ways of conducting international business that meets the needs of both the company and individuals, as the following example illustrates.

One organization introduced guidelines that all international team meetings had to be scheduled on Tuesday, Wednesday and/or Thursday, to enable all participants to travel during the 'core' business week. Scheduling international meetings during public holidays of any of the team members was also discouraged. This had the added bonus of encouraging team members to learn more about other members' customs so they knew what public holidays to avoid.

In practice, many managers chose to do additional personal local business when they were at a location for a team meeting and maximize their travelling time. However, this was their decision and if they needed to be back home for the weekend, international team business did not prevent that.

More importantly than developing and encouraging staff to widen their horizons and participate in global teams and assignments, senior managers need to consider how they are going to expand their personal experience of working globally. Seeing how it works in practice is often a sobering lesson for many senior managers exhorting the benefits of globalization.

Learning as a Source of Global Competitive Advantage

The final myth of global organizations to be explored in this section is the extent to which an organization can develop a unique competitive advantage by leveraging its global intellectual capital and bringing it to bear irrespective of location. The rhetoric argues that in global industries, traditional advantages in terms of access to a wider customer base, cheaper raw materials, alternative distribution channels and so on are breaking down and competitive advantage will increasingly be based on leveraging intangibles. One of the critical core competencies of a global organization will be how well it leverages its intellectual capital, which is a major intangible source of advantage. The ability to develop a learning organization underpins its capability for doing this. Many companies aspire to being a learning organization, but few achieve it. Even at the most basic level, balancing the tensions inherent in delivering global efficiency while simultaneously being locally responsive depends on the ease and skill with which organizations accumulate and distribute information internally. For example, ABB won a rail contract in the USA against the locally dominant GE by drawing on its European experience, technology and knowledge of similar contracts.

A good example of an organization that is attempting to transfer learning between key markets is Jollibee foods, the Philippines fast-food company that we saw earlier has successfully defended its home market against the onslaught of McDonald's by tailoring products to local tastes. It is now taking on McDonald's in that company's back yard since it entered the US market a year ago. Jollibee's US operation already sources chicken and beef supplies for US restaurants from South-East Asia, building on existing strong relationships with local Asian suppliers and offering significant economies of scale. Back in the home market, on the other hand, its Philippines stores have launched a cheesy bacon and mushroom sandwich originally developed for the US market.

Recent research by Doz, Santos and Williamson (2001) suggests that the companies with the greatest ability to learn are 'born in the wrong place'. By this they mean that their home market is too small to sustain growth for any length of time and they are thus forced early in their organizational life to look beyond their domestic borders for continued growth. Consequently as they grow, the revenue from their home market represents a very small percentage of their global turnover (examples include Nokia and Nestlé). These companies are almost forced to develop a competence in leveraging their intellectual capital across borders and boundaries. Others may be insulated or indeed protected from this pressure, if their home market represents 50–80 per cent of their turnover, as is the case for many American companies.

The critical issue for organizations if they want to make this approach work is to develop a culture that enables the best solution from one part of the organization to be transferred and modified to meet the needs of the rest of the organization; a 'not invented here' mentality is the death knell for many global organizations. For example, UK retail group Kingfisher has built its pan-European business around expertise in its French team. In the company's view, the French Darty operation has been so successful that it should be adopted as the role model for other European operations.

Global organizations develop a learning organization in two ways: technologically and by building personal networks. Clearly there must be an infrastructure that facilitates access to relevant and timely data and information, but too often organizations focus on the technological infrastructure at the expense of the latter. The two must work together. A leading-edge intranet won't build competitive advantage on its own – it needs to be used by staff who know what they need to access, and when. As Rhinesmith (1996) notes, 'to be global, a company . . . must have a corporate culture and value system that allow it to move its resources anywhere in the world to achieve the greatest competitive advantage'. However, experience of working in global organizations indicates that this is easier said than done. Building the personal networks that underpin a learning organization is not a short-term activity and requires some thought and investment from the corporate centre. The networks are built during such activities as cross-functional strategy meetings, international assignments and projects, international management development programmes and so on. As these activities can be expensive, they are often the first to be axed in times of recession, despite the fact that they are fundamental to building a global learning organization.

The initial discussion in this chapter has focused on the gap that often exists between an organization's espoused global 'strategic intent' and the reality of its 'strategy in action'. It has highlighted that even those players generally recognized as the global leaders in their industry are still heavily biased to home markets and certain regions of the world. The discussion has also sought to question the reality of implementing some of the taken-for-granted features of global organizations: that bigger is necessarily better; that global mindsets are integral to being a global leader; that global brands actually exist; that being a global leader is an attractive proposition to employees; and that knowledge and information can be a global commodity. Yet even when organizations recognize these challenges and proactively try to align their organizations with their global aspirations, there are still hurdles to overcome, as discussed in the next section.

PROBLEMS AND ISSUES ENCOUNTERED WHEN GLOBALIZING

Investing in the Future and Keeping Your Current Shareholders Happy

One of the greatest dilemmas facing leaders of organizations attempting to become global is how to deliver short-term goals and targets while simultaneously realigning and developing the organization itself. Developing a global business takes time. Building global brands, achieving significant shares in emerging markets, integrating acquisitions, developing new cultures, aligning organizational designs and processes and developing global leaders do not happen overnight.

The short-term pressure comes from two primary sources: internal and external. Many global organizations have their cultural heritage rooted in norms and belief systems where action and doing are valued over reflection and being (Hampden-Turner and Trompenaars, 1993). Time is considered to be a scarce resource and is valued at a premium. Hampden-Turner and Trompenaars identify these cultural assumptions as driving specific strategic and competitive behaviour, as illustrated in the following examples:

> A global automotive company, which had a very strong production and engineering culture, had a planning cycle that was a daily ritual and there was strong mistrust of any forecasts that looked further than three months ahead. This made it very difficult for the marketing function to explore car-buying trends over the longer term.

> A global IT company had incentivized its staff on sales of its existing market-leading product. They were so focused on the monthly and quarterly revenue, sales and market share data that fed into their incentive payments that they failed to notice that changes in the technology arena, e.g. the Internet, were eroding the long-term market for all their core products.

The organization's dominant cultural norms and beliefs may therefore predispose it to favouring the short term. Hofstede (1999) notes that the cultural dimension long- versus short-term orientation (see Kirkbride and Westwood, Chapter 3, this volume) has been a consistent predictor of economic success in the last couple of decades, with most of the strong Asian economies possessing a long-term orientation. Rhinesmith also notes that the improvement required to achieve sustainable global competitive advantage 'cannot be achieved without a capacity for reflection' (1996: 32). The short-term perspective adopted by many external stakeholders – analysts, fund managers and shareholders – then compounds this internal drive to the short term. The digital economy results in increased transparency so that the short-term performance of the organization is under intense scrutiny from all stakeholders. Therefore, global companies face the challenging task of managing the long term and the short term at the same time.

Superstitious Learning

The second dilemma facing aspiring global organizations is knowing when you are getting it right, because deciding you need to operate globally and actually implementing that decision do not always go smoothly. If you have only operated within your domestic market, you may make several initial tentative steps into overseas markets with varying degrees of success. Often these initial forays are opportunistic:

- You are thinking about operating outside your home market and you meet a senior manager of an overseas competitor at a conference or trade show. You get chatting and discover that the other company is looking for a joint venture in one of the countries into which you had been considering expanding.
- Your sales and marketing director is approached by a local distributor offering you first refusal on an exclusivity deal for an attractive market sector in his market.

Seizing these types of opportunity and experimenting with different approaches to going global are, in principle, positive activities. The difficulty arises if the organization does not view what it is doing as an experiment and therefore does not put in place processes to review the experiment and capture the learning.

What then happens in organizations is what we term 'superstitious learning'. An organization steps outside its domestic market and gets its fingers burned. For example, it fails to penetrate the market as planned, eventually withdrawing after having 'lost' significant sums. It fails to learn from the experience to help it build its global know-how for the longer term. The norms and assumptions of operating in its domestic market shape the mindset of management during this time. It therefore views its overseas experience through that filter, which may or may not be appropriate. Through this filter it may not understand what really happened and why it had problems, but draws conclusions based on its assumptions and beliefs, often inappropriately. For example, one organization that entered the Indian market 15 years ago, well ahead of the competition, lost significant money on the venture. This was primarily due to a lack of understanding of the distribution system operating in India at that time, which the experience highlighted. However, the board concluded that India was 'too difficult' and consequently the Indian market has been overlooked in all subsequent strategic reviews of potential markets. This is despite the fact that only one of the original board is still in post – the myth has won out over the reality of what really happened.

Attracting and Retaining Global Talent

The third problem was touched on in the previous section, but is so often raised by global leaders and management commentators that it is worth exploring further. One of the main problems faced by companies implementing global strategies is the lack of leadership talent with the experience and cultural sensitivity required to be successful, especially in emerging markets. Jacques Nasser, CEO of Ford, is a rare exception. He was born in Lebanon, grew up in Australia and joined Ford there, worked in the US, Latin America and Asia, returned to Australia, then became chairman of Ford Europe before moving to the US. Too many senior managers have risen to the top of their organizations without venturing outside their home market, and may therefore not see the value of establishing a diverse and culturally sensitive workforce.

The monocultural dominance in some organizations is a critical blind spot when it comes to attracting and retaining global talent. For example:

The pharmaceutical industry in the UK was increasingly worried about the pool of talented scientific graduates to staff its R&D functions and commissioned a study to see how to attract the best science graduates to its companies. The researcher hired to undertake the study had a global perspective on the graduate employment pool, having worked extensively outside the UK market. During the study it became very clear that the issue was not shortage of talent but a narrow perspective among management on where this talent could be found. They were looking to the higher education establishments where they had been trained and relying on contacts and networks with lecturers and professors they knew, without considering either how the education sector in the UK had changed since they were studying or what was happening in other countries.

The same blind spot affects 'old-economy' global players in the US. Read any human resources or business magazine in the last year and you can find interviews with senior managers bemoaning the fact that they are losing the 'best' MBA talent to internet start-ups. When you challenge their notion of the 'best', you discover that they are fishing in a very narrow pond consisting of a handful of US business schools. Considering that most of them are looking to hire the potential global managers of the future, one has to question whether this pool is relevant, let alone the most appropriate. Casting their net outside their domestic market and outside the MBA field for talent will open up a rich and diverse candidate pool.

However, as Prahalad and Lieberthal (1998) note, some organizations are recognizing the winds of change. ABB has reduced its European headcount by 40 000 while simultaneously growing by 45 000 in Asia and Philips estimates that it now employs more Chinese than Dutch employees.

Having attracted appropriate raw talent, the next big challenge is how to develop and retain them within your organization. Retention involves developing a career plan with high-potential people that prepares them for their future as leaders in a global world. At the most basic level, this will involve cultural and language training, then leaders will need to learn how to work and lead complex project teams in a cross-cultural and multi-functional arena and lastly some form of overseas assignment is likely to be necessary. None of these options is easy, but it is the last that historically has often given organizations the biggest headache. Failure rates for overseas postings of up to 70 per cent are not unknown, with companies reporting an average of between 15 and 25 per cent. However, within this there are big cultural differences, for example only 1 in 15 European repatriates fails compared to 1 in 3 Americans. Expatriates are expensive, with some estimates of $0.5 million for a senior manager, and Colgate-Palmolive estimates that the cost of expatriate managers is up to 400 per cent of those employed in the USA. When you consider that expatriates are still a dominant feature of emerging markets – there are an estimated 170 000 expatriates in China alone – these failure rates have significant consequences for the global ambitions of organizations.

Additionally, the changing demographics and social trends of dual-income families and the work–life balance aspirations of Generation X (those born in the 1960s and 1970s) look set to make this challenge harder rather than easier. Global organizations that wish to develop global talent are going to need to think beyond traditional expatriate solutions and develop tailored development and retention packages for each of their high potentials. The other critical period is at the time of repatriation. The key factor for successful re-entry is to find a role that fits the individual's career ambitions and helps to transfer their learning and perspectives back into the organization.

So before organizations announce new global aspirations they need to check the reality of implementing it. Do they have the right people in the right place or can they get hold of them when they need them?

Leading in Complexity

Finally there is the issue of how to make this all work on a day-to-day basis. Talking to middle managers in large complex organizations, their biggest complaints are often: Where do I fit in? Who do I report to? What impact can I have? Many are lost in the fog of three- or four-dimensional matrices. In many cases the efficiency advantages of global scale and scope are wiped out by the extra costs of managing complex global organizations. Many of these organizations, designed by consultants, are wonderful in theory but a nightmare in practice. There is a clear tension between central control and local accountability. The successful global companies manage to achieve central control in critical areas while leaving clear local accountability.

This process can involve moving away from the classical matrix to a global business unit structure. However, these global organizational designs often result in reduced local accountability. Country managers in this situation take on a more ambassadorial role for their company, with responsibilities for stakeholder relationships and co-ordination of country HR as well as legal and tax functions. Country managers and local general managers often feel disenfranchised by these changes, seeing a loss of power – and with it status and self-esteem – and may passively resist or actively sabotage the organization's shift to more integrated global working. Added to this loss of status is the loss of 'empire' as the various local functions, purchasing, R&D, logistics, marketing and sales often begin to report directly to the centre or to a global headquarters function. If these changes are not managed effectively, it can leave companies very vulnerable to strong local competitors who understand what customers value and have direct control of all the functions necessary to deliver it. Strategically if local managers do not stay committed to the organization's wider global objectives, it will be very difficult to reap the benefits of an integrated global strategic intent. There are several routes open to global leaders for designing their organizations more effectively so that complexity becomes a competitive advantage and not an Achilles heel (see Ward, Chapter 2, this volume).

The previous discussion has highlighted leaders' recognition that being 'global' is not a quick fix and it does not happen overnight – it requires long-term commitment and a willingness to change. Rhinesmith (1996) notes that being global requires us to 'challenge and change many of our views', which will 'require a long-term commitment for most large organizations simply to get moving'. Yip states that 'if a company cannot make the needed organization changes it should not even try to have a global strategy – *some companies are better off not trying to compete globally*' (1992: 166, emphasis in original). With this warning ringing in your ears, how can you make the judgement of whether you are one of those companies that should tread cautiously into the global marketplace? The final section of this chapter explores the key components of a global organization and provides a framework for assessing your status quo.

WHAT WOULD A TRULY GLOBAL ORGANIZATION LOOK LIKE?

In the rush to examine aspects of international, multinational, global and transnational organizations (Bartlett and Ghoshal, 1989; Kirkbride, 2001; Ward, Chapter 2, this volume), it is easy to forget that, despite the differences between these types and more domestic forms, they are all organizations at base and thus have certain common elements. Therefore our search for the core components of truly global enterprises must start with a basic model of organizations *per se*.

There are a number of well-known models of organizations, including Leavitt's diamond (organization, technology, tasks and people) and the McKinsey 7S framework (strategy, structure, systems, skills, staff, style and shared values). However, for examining the reality of global organizations, we propose to adapt a model that was developed a few years ago by Kirkbride and Schroeder (1998). Originally known as

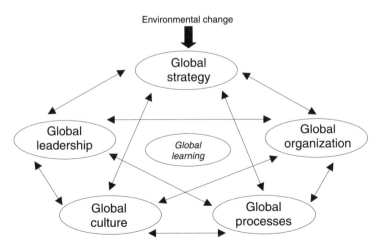

Figure 1.1 The global organization model.

the five-ball model, an additional dimension has been added making it a six-ball model.

Within this model, organizations are seen as made up of six different components: strategy, organization, processes, culture, learning and leadership. These six components are interactive and affect one another. Ideally they need to be in alignment with each other and with the wider external environment that the organization faces. Another way of looking at these components is as organizational 'lenses'. Here our analogy is with the theatre, where different coloured lenses are placed in front of powerful lights to bathe the stage in different colours. Thus the same physical space is seen differently in different lighting. Our argument is that organizations, and the managers within them, tend to use certain preferred lenses to view their own organizational reality. They therefore develop a 'one-dimensional' view of organizational reality and need to learn to view the organization through the other lenses to get a balanced view.

Each of these components or 'lenses' probably requires little explanation:

- *Strategy* refers to the strategic direction of the organization. It would thus encompass the mission of the organization and the organizational vision of the future. More mundanely, it would encompass the formal organizational strategic plans and objectives. Obviously it covers emergent as well as planned or directive strategy (Mintzberg, 2000). It would also cover the key 'qualitative features' of strategy as well as actual content. Thus we would need to consider the degree to which the strategy was aggressive or defensive; proactive or reactive; risky or safe; and future oriented or backward looking.
- *Organization* refers to the 'structural' features of the organization. It would thus encompass the formal organizational structure as laid out in organizational charts and the roles and responsibilities that go with the positions identified in such a structure. However, it would also cover the key features of the structure such as the degrees of formalization, centralization, standardization and specialization. It would also include the different types

of what Mintzberg (1992) has termed 'structural configurations' or ideal structural types. These types would include simple structures, functional structures, machine bureaucracies, professional bureaucracies, multi-divisional structures, matrix structures and 'adhocracies'.

■ *Processes* refer to all the formal and informal systems, processes and procedures within the organization. These would include both the processes by which the product or service is produced and internal processes by which the enterprise is organized. This heading would therefore cover the whole range of processes, from technological to financial to managerial. It would also encompass the more informal ways of working in the organization, including skills and competencies.

■ The next component is *culture*, which refers to the shared and common values, attitudes and behaviours exhibited by those within the organization. Thus culture is both 'what we do around here' and 'what we value around here'.

■ The fifth component is organizational *learning*. Organizations that desire to succeed and survive have to learn, both as an organization and as individual managers. This learning requires a number of mechanisms to be present in the organization, including a cultural acceptance of the importance of learning as well as processes for the transfer of best practice and the capturing of intellectual capital.

■ The final component is *leadership*. This refers not just to the highest level of corporate leaders, but also to all levels of leaders within the organization and to its generalized 'leadership capability' or competence.

These six components, which represent 'the organization', interact with the wider environment in which the organization is located. This environment can be seen as having political, economic, social, cultural, technological, legal and physical components. Changes in any of these areas can affect the organization. Thus another crucial factor to consider is the degree of environmental change experienced and how this affects the organization. Theoretically environmental change can have an impact on any of the six organizational components (balls), but an obvious starting point is strategy, which often has to alter to meet changing environmental pressures including new competitors, changing customer needs, new technologies or changing regulations.

To what extent:	Global strategy	Global culture	Global organization	Global processes	Global leadership	Global learning
Have you got clarity?						
Is it oriented to the future?						
Is it aligned globally and locally?						
Is it communicated and owned?						
Is it open to feedback and change?						

Figure 1.2   The global organizational grid.
Source: Adapted from Kirkbride and Schroeder, 1998

The first part of the model thus identifies key components of any organization. The second part identifies a number of key criteria that need to be used to assess the effectiveness of each of these components.

Clarity

A key issue for any organization is clarity. Obviously this is particularly true in terms of the organizational strategy. How clear is the strategic direction of the organization? To those charged with developing the strategy? And to those lower down who must implement it? Of course, in many organizations the strategy is very unclear. A major multi-national recently surveyed a number of its most senior managers and it was obvious from the results that many were completely confused about the corporate strategic direction, although they were clear about the strategy of their own particular unit.

We would argue that this criterion also applies to the other organizational components (balls). How clear, or well defined, is your current organizational culture? Or the organizational culture you are seeking to inculcate? How clear, or transparent, is your organizational architecture? Do organizational members understand the structure and the reasons for it? How clear and simple are your organizational processes? Do people know what knowledge needs to be shared with others? And finally, how clear is your leadership style? Is there an agreed form of leadership that is accepted and do managers understand what leadership style they should be adopting?

Future orientation

Organizations facing change have to move forwards. It is therefore important that the key organizational components are all forward facing rather than being rooted in the past. Thus the strategy, organization, processes, culture and leadership components all need to be future oriented. Obviously this is not always the case. In some organizations the cultural values and norms hark back to former glories. In others the current processes are not supportive of new strategies and challenges. For example, in a major utility where we were recently working, the new market-focused strategy and structure were being undermined by the lack of a suitable customer information system. The current information systems were rooted in past structures and systems and were extremely resistant to change.

Alignment

We have already noted that the six organizational balls ideally need to be aligned together. However, it is obviously important that they are also aligned to the realities of the external environment. We do not wish to get into a sterile academic debate about which factor aligns to which, as in the classic strategy versus structure debate. Our simple thesis would be that organizations with greater levels of internal alignment will find it easier to be successful in their markets if, and only if, these internal components are also aligned clearly to the external environmental situation.

Communication and ownership

We have often worked as consultants in organizations that at the highest levels have clarity of purpose, future orientation and good alignment, but unfortunately fall at the next hurdle. That is, they fail to communicate the strategy clearly to all organizational members and thus generate the levels of ownership and motivation that are required for successful implementation of the strategy. Indeed, in a couple of farcical situations, lower-level managers seeking clarity of direction and purpose from senior levels have been told that there is a strategy but that it is restricted or secret! We would argue that not only does the strategy need to be communicated and owned, but that this criterion also applies equally to the organizational, process, cultural and leadership components.

Feedback and change

Finally, we would suggest that each ball has to change over time to react to the changes in the external environment. Thus our final criterion is that each component must be open to feedback and change. This means that senior levels must be willing to take feedback from all levels of the organization concerning the strategy, the organizational architecture, the culture, the organizational processes and the forms of leadership. If this is not done, the organization will stagnate and become increasingly divorced from its external environment.

We are suggesting that this model can easily be applied to organizations that are trying to be 'global'. By this term we encompass organizations trying to be multinational, global and transnational, to use Bartlett and Ghoshal's (1989) terms. Each of the 'balls' now has a global dimension. Such organizations would have to have a global strategy, a global organizational architecture, global processes, a global culture, global learning and global leadership. And each of these would have to be clear, future oriented, aligned both globally and locally, communicated and owned, and open to feedback and change. We would suggest that such organizations have to ask themselves a number of questions in order to see in which 'cells' of the model they have problems and in which 'cells' they have achieved the required results.

Global strategy

- Have you got a clear strategy for globalization?
- Is your globalization strategy future oriented?
- Does your globalization strategy align both to your global environment and to your local business strategies?
- Is your globalization strategy communicated and owned around the whole organization?
- Is your globalization strategy open to feedback and change from any part of the organization (and not just from HQ in the home country)?

Global organization

- Have you developed a clear global structure designed to deliver your globalization strategy?
- Is your global organizational structure flexible enough to react to future and potential changes?
- Is your structure suitable for both the global environment facing you as well as for the local environments facing your strategic business units?
- Is your global structure communicated and owned by the organization?
- Is your global structure continually tested and challenged in response to changing circumstances?

Global processes

- Are your (global) processes clearly defined on a global scale?
- Are your global processes sufficiently oriented to the future?

- Do your global processes support both your global objectives and your global needs?
- Are your global processes widely understood and accepted throughout your global structure, in affiliates as well as HQ?
- Are your global processes subject to continual feedback, challenge and review?

Global culture

- Have you established a clear global identity and culture to integrate operations worldwide?
- Is your global culture oriented to the future?
- Does your culture support both your globalization strategy and the diverse business strategies of your business units/divisions?
- Is your global culture communicated and owned on a global scale?
- Is your global culture open to feedback and change?

Global learning

- Are you clear about what you have learned on an international and global scale as an organization?
- Are your learning processes oriented towards future action, rather than being rooted in historical analysis and fault finding?
- Does your organization learn on both the domestic and global level and leverage the learning from one to the other?
- Are the knowledge and intellectual capital derived from your learning processes widely disseminated and understood by those in your organization?
- As an organization, are you open to forms of feedback and challenge that lead to learning and creativity?

Global leadership

- Have you created a clearly defined cadre of global leaders or a global leadership system within the organization?

- Are your global leaders looking forwards or backwards?
- Is your leadership style aligned both to your global competitive environment and to your local market requirements?
- To what extent is your global leadership style clearly communicated throughout the organization and owned by employees worldwide?
- Are your leaders open to feedback and change from anywhere in the globe?

For a more detailed diagnosis of your organization and its progress on the path to globalization, see Appendixes A, B and C.

References

Barham, K. and Wills, S. (1993) *Management Across Frontiers*, Berkhamsted: Ashridge Management College Report (AMRG 929).

Bartlett, C. A. and Ghoshal, S. (1989) *Managing Across Borders: The Transnational Solution*, Boston, MA: Harvard Business School Press.

Bartlett, C. A. and Ghoshal, S. (1999) *Transnational Management: Text, Cases and Readings in Cross-border Management*, London: Richard D. Irwin.

Bryan, L. L. and Fraser, J. N. (1999) 'Getting to global', *McKinsey Quarterly*, 4, 68–81.

D'Iribarnes, P. (1997) 'The usefulness of an ethnographic approach to the international comparison of organisations', *International Studies of Management and Organisation*, 26(4): 34–47.

Doz, Y., Santos, J. and Williamson, P. J. (2001) *From Global to Metanational: How Companies Win in the Global Knowledge Economy*, Boston, MA: Harvard Business School Press.

Economist, The (1998) 'The mother of all mergers', 5th February.

Fast Company (2001) 'Please don't forward this e-mail! The story of an accidental web celebrity', http//www.fastcompany.com/invent/invent_feature/email.html, 18 March.

Hampden-Turner, C. and Trompenaars, F. (1993) *The Seven Cultures of Capitalism: Value Systems for Creating Wealth in the United States, Britain, Japan, Germany, France, Sweden and the Netherlands*, London: Piatkus.

Heimer, C. (1994) 'The principle of requisite variety and the composition of executive boards of international companies: implications for the internationalisation of the firm', unpublished MSc dissertation, Birkbeck College, University of London.

Hofstede, G. (1999) 'Problems remain, but theories will change: the universal and the specific in 21st century global management', *Organizational Dynamics*, 28(1): 34–44.

Kirkbride, P. S. (ed.) (2001) *Globalization: The External Pressures*, Chichester: John Wiley.

Kirkbride, P. S., Pinnington, P. and Ward, K. (2001) 'The state of globalization today', in Kirkbride, P. S. (ed.), *Globalization: The External Pressures*, Chichester: John Wiley.

Kirkbride, P. S. and Schroeder, H. (1998) 'The 5 Ball Model of Organizations', course materials for Strategy and Organization, Berkhamsted: Ashridge Management College.

Merchant, K. and Pretzlick, C. (2000) *Financial Times*, 28th February.

Mintzberg, H. (1992) *Structure in Fives: Designing Effective Organizations*, New York: Prentice Hall.

Mintzberg, H. (2000) *The Rise and Fall of Strategic Planning*, London: Financial Times/ Prentice Hall.

O'Hara-Devereaux, M. and Johansen, R. (1994) *Globalization: Bridging Distance, Culture and Time*, San Francisco, CA: Jossey Bass.

Prahalad, C. K. and Lieberthal, K. (1998) 'The end of corporate imperialism', *Harvard Business Review*, July–August, 76(4): 68–79.

Prahalad, C. K. and Oosterveld, J.P. (1999) 'Transforming internal governance: the challenge for multinationals', *Sloan Management Review*, Spring, 40(3): 31–9.

Rhinesmith, S. H. (1996) *A Manager's Guide to Globalization: Six Skills for Success in a Changing World*, New York: Irwin.

Roure, J., Alvarez, J. L., Garcia-Pont, C. and Nueno, J. (1993) 'Managing internationally: international dimensions of the managerial task', *European Management Journal*, 11(4, December), 485–92.

Yip, George S. (1992) *Total Global Strategy: Managing for Worldwide Competitive Advantage*, London: Prentice Hall.

DESIGNING
GLOBAL
ORGANIZATIONS

Karen Ward

CHAPTER 2

DESIGNING GLOBAL ORGANIZATIONS

A s identified in the introduction, many organizations across a range of industries espouse a desire to be global. They identify that changes in the external environment require different strategic responses; often words like flexible, responsive to customers, adaptable and innovative are used to describe their strategic intent. Yet take a closer look at these organizations and they appear to be designed with very different aims in mind: power is seated with strong country managers, budgets are allocated on national or regional lines, career progression is up through functional hierarchies and the senior team is white, male, middle aged with long service records in the industry. So why are so many global organizations suboptimally designed?

BARRIERS TO GLOBAL DESIGN

The critical issue to recognize when designing global organizations is that you are designing for diversity. You are looking to build complexity and dilemmas into your organization. Yet this goes against some basic tenets of human nature. This chapter explores these barriers to effective organizational design in global organizations and recommends some key steps to overcome these difficulties.

There are four key difficulties that seem to prevent leaders from designing optimal global organizations:

The KISS Trap (Keep It Simple, Stupid)

Ask many managers to describe their organization to you and they will initially produce an organization chart from their desk with neat boxes and lines apparently depicting the organization. These organization charts are replicated in annual reports to shareholders and in meetings to employees. If an organizational change is demanded by changes in the external environment, the initial response is usually a shuffling of the boxes and the lines and perhaps a relabelling of the boxes.

This desire to be able to simplify and describe a complex world on one sheet of paper is one of the challenges of global organization design. Senior managers often argue that the simplification is for the benefit of staff, so that they can clearly understand where they fit in the wider organization. Yet is this really what employees want? Talk to them about their experience of their organization and you get a much richer, complex dynamic picture with inherent contradictions and power struggles. They live in this world every day, dealing with customers and suppliers, and they know it cannot be summarized on one sheet of paper.

So if this desire for simplicity is not for the employees, who is it for? In many cases, it is for the leaders themselves. Some like to feel in control of the business unit they are responsible for and being able to describe it in simple terms with boxes and lines provides that level of comfort, even if the reality is somewhat different.

Other leaders get a sense of achievement through the size of the unit they lead – being able to communicate this readily to other leaders is an important reinforcement of their status and self-esteem. Seeing themselves at the 'top' of the organization chart bolsters their sense of importance. Unfortunately this ambition can lead to unproductive empire building and unwieldy organization designs just to satisfy the egos of managers.

A consequence of inexperience among the leadership of an organization can be a design with unnecessary multiple horizontal and vertical layers, leading to a 'silo' mentality and a top-heavy organization. Their inexperience leads them to want to be able to design their organization in 'manageable chunks' so that it does not become too complex for them. As one senior manager commented, 'I like to be able to get my arms around it.'

None of these reasons is a valid argument for retaining suboptimal organizational designs. Yet in too many global organizations, suboptimal designs are not being challenged, because the very people who should be challenging them have a vested interest in the status quo.

> *Key principle: Design the organization to make it more effective, not to make it easier to manage.*

Join the Club

The second factor that contributes to suboptimal design is our desire to be with people like ourselves. First, managers have a tendency to recruit and promote in their own image – it is human nature that unless we make a conscious effort to do otherwise, we are predisposed to prefer people who are similar to us and to reject those who remain different from us (Herriot and Pemberton, 1995: 9).

Unless there are specific processes designed into an organization to prevent this happening, it will soon be populated by similar types of people with a similar outlook on life. This 'club's' view of the world becomes so prevalent that the organization develops corporate blind spots. If the environment in that industry is relatively stable, with no new entrants redefining the boundaries of how business is done, this may not be a problem. But how many industries operating globally fit that description?

> Marks & Spencer's current woes are a classic example of the danger of a club whose entry criteria are restrictive. Often cited in the past as a benchmark for effective people management with a strong corporate culture founded on quality, its very strength has become its Achilles heel as the face of the retail industry has changed beyond recognition. It believed so strongly that its recipe was successful that it was unable to see the warning signs – until the eleventh hour. Some commentators still question whether the real implication of their plight is fully acknowledged internally – or whether the company's belief in the rightness of the club still prevails and it sees everyone else as out of step.

The biggest danger of the 'club' is its view of non-members. Patronizing at best, downright dismissive at worst, members reinforce their feeling of belonging and uniqueness by putting down 'outsiders'. Yet ignoring newcomers to the industry as inconvenient distractions or 'upstarts' – 'they cannot join, they don't meet our entry criteria' – has been the downfall of many industry leaders. This myopia makes it very difficult to challenge the status quo or implement changes to an organizational design that no longer delivers business benefit. Organizations become trapped in designs that reflect their past rather than prepare them for the future.

> *Key principle: Look to the future needs of your business, seek out difference and value diversity.*

If You Can't Stand the Heat, Get out of the Kitchen

The third factor that leads to suboptimal design is an organization's inability to deal with conflict constructively. Global organizations are inherently complex and meeting the needs of a myriad of customers across multiple markets isn't for the faint hearted. Often different parts of the business will have legitimate competing aims, born out of a desire to deliver value to customers in their local market. Conflict will always exist where you have a wide diversity of business and customer views and opportunities.

Needless redesigns and reorganizations happen because leaders cannot live with the tensions and dilemmas inherent in operating in a complex world. They naïvely believe that by reinforcing or moving the solid lines or the dotted lines on an organization chart, conflict will somehow disappear.

This is not to say that clarity of accountability is not critical to successfully designed organizations, as will be discussed later. However, we are challenging the often widely held beliefs that conflict is somehow a negative force in organizations and that the politics that often accompany conflict situations should be avoided at all costs.

To understand a different perspective, let's look at the original meaning of politics: stemming from the idea that when there are divergent views, society should provide a means of reconciling these differences through consultation and negotiation (Morgan, 1997). There is also the notion that a key feature in any strong democracy is the presence of a vocal and effective opposition. Following these ideas, one could argue that conflict and opposition to the dominant view within an organization are key characteristics of healthy and responsive organizations. This is particularly true of global organizations, whose external environments offer a plethora of competing opportunities. To capitalize on these business opportunities, effective designs for global organizations should therefore incorporate processes for constructive resolution of legitimate differences of opinion.

Key principle: Dilemmas are inherent in global organizations.

It Should Work like Clockwork

The fourth factor contributing to suboptimal design is the way in which many leaders view organizations. Although the 'machine' perspective of organization originates from the end of the nineteenth century, there is still a tendency for managers to view organizations in strictly technical terms. The way organizations are often depicted, as a series of boxes and lines, has much in common with an electrical wiring diagram. The assumption is that rewiring the components in an alternative configuration will lead to increased output.

This prevailing view of organizations as machines was further evidenced by the popularity in the late 1980s and early 1990s of reengineering, an approach dominated by machine and technical language. The failure of the reengineering movement to bring about the much vaunted process improvements led some managers to challenge this mechanistic view of organizations (Binney and Williams, 1995: 28).

One of the difficulties of viewing organizations from a machine perspective is that it assumes that the organization is a self-contained unit, separate from outside influence. A critical recognition in designing global organizations is that each company does not exist in such a vacuum and that the environment in which a firm operates plays a key role in its ability to be successful. This challenges us to see organizations as open rather than closed systems, interacting with their environment. This perspective invites us to draw on biological metaphors (organizations as living beings or complex systems) as opposed to engineering metaphors to gain insight into how we might design more effective global organizations.

A key design principle for global organizations is the principle of requisite variety (Morgan, 1997). If managers can understand this basic principle, it will enable them to see their organizations in a different light. This principle states that the internal processes of an organization must be as diverse as the environment in which it is operating and that 'only by incorporating required variety into internal controls can an organization deal with the variety and challenge by its environment'.

Furthermore, 'any organization that insulates itself from diversity in the environment tends to atrophy and lose its complexity and distinctive nature'. This principle would lead us to expect global organizations to be designed to maximize their internal diversity and mirror the rich diversity of the markets, customers and suppliers with which they interact. Yet as we saw at the beginning of this chapter, reality often paints a very different picture.

> *Key principle: Global organizations are open systems and interact with their environment. If the environment is diverse, greater responsiveness is required internally.*

DESIGNING FOR SUCCESS

The discussion so far has focused on four key barriers to effective design in global organizations. If these are such powerful drivers of current organizational behaviour, what can leaders do to change the status quo?

First, if leaders work from the premise that organizations are not closed systems, they will conclude that, to be truly effective, the design of an organization should reflect the external environment in which it is operating. As the environment changes the 'optimal' structure will change. This has significant consequences for organizations as they go global and their environment becomes more complex.

Let's be clear that by 'optimal' we do not mean 'perfect' structure. There are costs and benefits to all organizational designs. However, nor does this mean that all structures work equally well, or that it is simply a matter of preference or style. Some designs do work better than others in a given organization's context. The rest of this chapter will discuss how leaders can optimize the design of organizations operating globally.

There are five key parameters that global organizations need to keep in focus when designing themselves to operate effectively across the globe:

- Make sure that the key design 'choices' have been evaluated and considered.
- Ensure that the resulting design is aligned to the strategic intent of the organization.
- Be comfortable living with the tensions of a multi-focus design.
- Build an organization that simultaneously is customer facing and has clear internal accountabilities.
- Proactively design in sufficient flexibility to enable the organization to adapt to changes in its environment in a timely fashion.

These will be discussed in more detail below.

The Key Design Choices

Philip Sadler, an ex-principal of Ashridge and well-known management authority, has clearly outlined the key design choices facing any organization, global or local, in his 6C model (Sadler, 1998). These are perhaps best viewed as choices that the organization has to make in the design process and, depending on what choices are made, different organizational structures emerge. And yet for many organizations it appears that the word 'choice' would be a misnomer. The organizational architects seemingly fail to pose or answer these key questions and the resulting structures owe more to custom, what was there before or serendipity than to conscious design. What are these key choices?

Control

Control, as seen by Sadler, has two components: control over the information flows within the organization and control over organizational activities or outcomes. All organizations, when considering their structural design, need to decide how much control of these contingencies is necessary for organizational success.

These issues are of particular importance in the multibusiness company (Goold and Campbell, 1987; Goold, Campbell and Alexander, 1994) and in the large global concern. For example, Goold and Campbell (1987) distinguish three different 'parenting' styles adopted by large corporate centres, based on differing levels of control:

- The Strategic Planning style based on high levels of influence from the centre in regard to long-term planning and strategic vision, but less stringent monitoring of short-term financial reporting (e.g. Shell).
- The Strategic Control style, which is based on a more decentralized planning approach with responsibilities passed to the businesses or subsidiaries, but with a monitoring role for the centre coupled with equal importance being placed on financial milestones and objectives (e.g. General Electric).

- The Financial Control style, where the subsidiary businesses are seen as strategically autonomous but are subject to stringent and regular financial control and monitoring (e.g. the classic Hanson style).

In addition, such multibusiness companies have to consider the extent to which they need to control closely the behaviour of their employees. For example, one could contrast the levels of individual control required by a global hotel chain and a global information technology consultancy. If the nature of the business requires highly controlled repetitive behaviours, then systems to maintain this control would have to be implemented across the organization from the corporate centre.

Connections

Connections refer to the need for any organization to provide and maintain effective interfaces with the key components of its external environment. Sadler (1998) distinguishes three levels of environmental interaction:

- 'the immediate or "transactional" environment, which relates inputs and outputs – primarily consisting of customers and suppliers
- the intermediate or "constraining" environment which exercises strong and short- to medium-term influences on the organization – pressure groups, trade unions, planning authorities and various governmental agencies
- the general or "contextual" environment, which also powerfully influences the organization's ability to achieve its objectives, but with greater emphasis on the medium to longer term, made up of a wide range of political, social, economic and technological factors.' (Sadler, 1998: 39–40)

While all these levels are relevant to the global organization, the first or transactional level is particularly important for organizational design. Increasingly global organizations are having to build closer links with both their global customers and global suppliers (Hennessy, 2001). These pressures will result in different organizational designs including, for example, a move towards customer-facing business units and integrated operations or alliances with suppliers (Pudney, 2001).

Creativity

The third key choice is the extent to which creativity and innovation are required in the business for organizational success. Of course, all organizations require a certain level of creativity, but the issue here is to what extent internal creativity is crucial for success and thus needs structures that foster this behaviour. As Sadler notes, this 'objective is clearly the prime purpose of organization design in all organizations which have a creative task . . . Creativity is also of primary importance in business organizations which, in order to compete, need to generate a high rate of product innovation or which need to adapt to frequent and substantial changes in market conditions' (1998: 18).

Organizations that require this competence often have decentralized structures with highly autonomous business units and flat internal structures with little hierarchy. They also tend to develop cultures that support innovation. Common features of these cultures would be a tolerance for risk taking, high levels of trust and low levels of control, open communications, a focus on knowledge management and the 'freedom to fail'.

Commitment

Another key choice concerns the level of commitment from organizational members that the organization believes is necessary for successful operation. Of course, all organizations, other than purely coercive ones, need a certain level of commitment from staff and employees. However, organizations have to consider what level of commitment they require and then decide how that level can be achieved via the processes of organizational design.

As Sadler (1998) points out, there are a wide number of things that organizations can do to increase levels of commitment, not all of which are structural. The list would include:

- Careful job design (job rotation, job enlargement, job enrichment and autonomous group working).
- Innovative reward mechanisms (including pay for performance, profit sharing, stock options etc.).
- Single-status cultures and the removal of status hierarchies and 'perks'.
- The creation of a 'sense of mission' (Campbell, Devine and Young, 1993).

Co-ordination

Co-ordination can be seen as the opposite of connections, in that it concerns the internal linkages within the organization rather than the external ones. In all complex organizations there is a need for internal co-ordination and co-operation between departments, divisions and businesses if the overall strategic corporate objectives are to be achieved. For large global organizations the question is one of degree. To what extent are divisions, countries or business units required to co-operate or to what extent can they operate autonomously or even compete directly?

In their study of parental value creation, Goold, Campbell and Alexander (1994) identify, among others, two opposite forms that highlight this key design question. The first is what they term Stand-Alone Influence. Here the corporate parent has a number of businesses that can be run almost totally independently. Thus the role of the parent is limited to the extent that it can add value to the strategy or performance of the individual businesses on a case-by-case basis. As Goold, Campbell and Alexander note, all 'parents exert considerable stand-alone influence on their businesses. [They] will be involved in agreeing and monitoring basic performance targets, in approving major capital expenditures, and in selecting and replacing the business unit managing directors. These activities, in themselves, are powerful influences on the businesses. Many parents, however, go further, exercising influence on a wider range of issues, such as product-market strategies, pricing decisions, and human resource development' (1994: 78).

However, this style creates its own paradox. How can the managers in the corporate parent, in a small percentage of their time and in a sector where they are not continually operating, improve on the decisions made by full-time managers on the ground who are allocating 100 per cent of their time to the task?

The opposite case involves a parent with a number of businesses that are either simply closely linked in terms of business area or inherently linked in terms of an overall supply or value chain. Here the parent would be wise to adopt a 'Linkage' influence. As Goold, Campbell and Alexander point out, many 'parents seek to create value by enhancing the linkages that exist between their different business units. Through corporate decision-making processes and structures, through policies and guidelines, through transfer pricing mechanisms, and through personal pressure, they encourage, or mandate, relationships between their business units that would not occur if the businesses were independent companies. In this way, they aim to create value by making the "whole" worth more than the "sum of the parts" ' (1994: 79–80).

Competence

The final 'C' refers to the level of competence that the organization requires in order to be successful. Obviously there is a clear link here to the overall corporate strategy. Different strategies will require different 'bundles' of competencies and we will consider this in more detail in the next section.

Alignment to Strategic Intent

Given that organizational design is a question of strategic choice and that any particular design has costs and benefits, one of the key drivers to take into account is the strategic intent of your organization. Strategic intent can be explained as a reflection of how the organization intends to respond to challenges in its environment by creating a unique and sustainable competitive advantage (Moncrieff, 1998). To illustrate this, let's explore a simplistic view of the strategic choices facing global organizations.

Figure 2.1 is adapted from Bartlett and Ghoshal (1995). They had been exploring the reasons for organizations deciding to globalize their operations. Their research identified that there were three primary external drivers that led to organizations beginning to operate outside their domestic markets. The first – global integration – was organizations seeking economies of scale, particularly in sourcing, purchasing and manufacturing. Companies moved facilities to cheaper sources of local labour or raw materials, which then provided them with competitive advantage over other domestic producers.

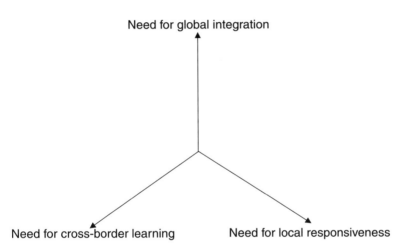

Figure 2.1 Strategic options for global organizations.
Source: Figure from *Managing Across Borders* (2nd edition) by Bartlett & Ghoshal published by Random House Business Books. Used by permission of The Random House Group Limited

The second axis – local responsiveness – is a key driver for organizations where the product or service they are offering is highly dependent on the tastes and preferences of local consumers, or where the supply of the activity needs to be physically close to the customer (in speed or distance). The third axis – cross-boundary learning – has become more important as technology, in particular the Internet, has created knowledge-based industry. Bartlett and Ghoshal identified that companies can gain competitive advantage by leveraging their internal best practice and transferring the learning to other parts of their organizations facing similar competitive challenges.

Depending on which of these strategic axes the organization chooses to focus on, the optimum design for the organization will change.

Global integration

If your primary strategic driver is to deliver a cost-effective or standardized product or service to all your chosen global markets, you need to design your organization to deliver economies of scale, cost efficiency and replicable standards irrespective of location. You will not be overly concerned with creativity or innovation in the local markets, as your aim is to deliver value for money consistently. Organizations that have historically adopted this strategic focus could include PC manufacturers, soft drinks manufacturers, oil and gas companies. Figure 2.2 illustrates some of the key design features of an organization designed for global integration.

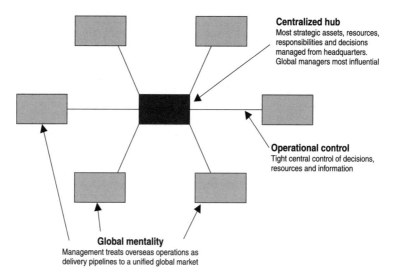

Figure 2.2 Designed for global integration.
Source: Adapted from Bartlett & Ghoshal

In this design, the power in the organization is primarily held at a centralized headquarters. Key functions such as finance, IT and human resources are head office functions, which set strategy and policy centrally and then cascade it to the regional operations for implementation. Strategic intent (including product or brand strategy) is likely to be determined centrally, possibly supported by a corporate strategy function. There are likely to be global brand managers, key account managers and so on who exercise most influence if there is conflict between a global priority and a local customer requirement. The key design principles here are standardization and alignment.

Local responsiveness

If, however, you are operating in an industry where the demands of the customer are heterogeneous, your primary strategic driver may be to tailor and adapt your offering. The food industry, insurance companies and retail banking have traditionally operated with this focus.

You will be encouraging creativity and responsiveness. Authority and power need to be close to the customer to enable flexible and appropriate solutions to be delivered in a timely fashion. Your aim is to deliver what the local market requires and you will not be overly concerned if this leads to duplication. This would clearly require a different global design, as illustrated in Figure 2.3.

In Figure 2.3, given that the key strategic driver in this design is local responsiveness, it is not surprising that power lies closer to the market, customers and suppliers. Country managers or local general managers would have significant autonomy to make appropriate strategic decisions for their local requirements without reference to headquarters or other parts of the organization. Each local operation will be a profit centre, with the key control measures being financial. As long as they are delivering the numbers local managers are given relative strategic freedom to operate. Each local operation is likely to have its own finance, IT and HR functions who set policy and implement practice in line with local business requirements and legislation.

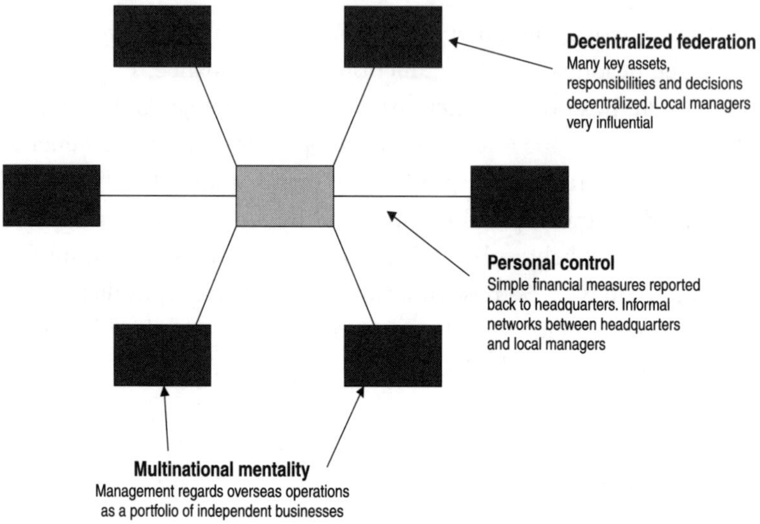

Decentralized federation
Many key assets, responsibilities and decisions decentralized. Local managers very influential

Personal control
Simple financial measures reported back to headquarters. Informal networks between headquarters and local managers

Multinational mentality
Management regards overseas operations as a portfolio of independent businesses

Figure 2.3   Designed for local responsiveness.
Source: Adapted from Bartlett & Ghoshal

Cross-boundary learning

Increasingly organizations are finding that achieving either global integration or local responsiveness is not giving them a significant competitive advantage and they need to leverage their ability to transfer knowledge and learning throughout their organizations. For example, in the advertising industry some creative teams can now offer around-the-clock responsiveness by positioning design teams in each time zone and passing briefs from a designer whose day is ending to another who has just got into the office. Similarly, the learning from a successful product launch in one market may be able to increase market penetration in another market by building on the previous success and avoiding costly mistakes.

The critical design issue for an organization with this strategic priority is to ensure that it can draw on talent and resources and apply them to key opportunities irrespective of location, as illustrated in Figure 2.4.

The organizational design in Figure 2.4 provides maximum flexibility if implemented effectively, allowing the organization to draw on

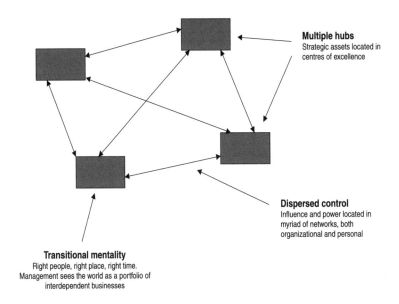

Multiple hubs
Strategic assets located in
centres of excellence

Dispersed control
Influence and power located in
myriad of networks, both
organizational and personal

Transitional mentality
Right people, right place, right time.
Management sees the world as a portfolio of
interdependent businesses

Figure 2.4   Designed for cross-boundary learning.
Source: Adapted from Bartlett & Ghoshal

appropriate expertise and knowhow irrespective of location. For example, some aspects of R&D might be located in India and China to take advantage of high levels of education coupled with low labour costs, whereas other aspects of manufacturing might be located in Poland, Hungary or the Czech Republic to take advantage of lower costs close to major markets in Europe. Employees are connected to the wider organization rather than one piece of it and power is dispersed throughout the organization. Power tends to sit in informal networks rather than in a formal structure, so the organization is likely to have processes that reinforce connection and common values and beliefs.

These different approaches to the design of a global organization are summarized in Figure 2.5. This highlights the key choices that managers must take into consideration when they are attempting to align their organization to deliver its strategic intent. Clearly, if your organization has been historically designed with one set of strategic drivers in mind, e.g. global integration, it is not surprising that you will have difficulty implementing a new strategic direction if you leave the existing design in place.

Organizational characteristics	Local responsiveness	Global integration	Cross-boundary learning
Configuration of assets and capabilities	Decentralized and nationally self-sufficient	Centralized and globally scaled	Dispersed, interdependent and specialized
Role of overseas operations	Sensing and exploiting local opportunities	Implementing parent company strategies	Differentiated contributions by national units to integrated worldwide operations
Development and diffusion of knowledge	Knowledge developed and retained within each unit	Knowledge developed and retained at the centre	Knowledge developed jointly and shared world-wide

Figure 2.5 Organizational characteristics.

This is necessarily a simplified illustration of the dilemmas facing most global organizations, but does serve to illustrate that the first steps for leaders wanting to design optimum organizations are to recognize the interplay between the organization and its environment, to be able to articulate a clear strategic response to those challenges and then to align the design of the organization to deliver this.

The real world is of course not this simplistic and in fact few organizations have one strategic focus for the whole business. As mentioned earlier, different parts of the organization may have legitimate but competing strategic priorities. The critical issues are to be able to articulate which strategic intent and, therefore, which organizational design is appropriate for which part of the business and then to consider how to design the interfaces between the different parts. As already discussed, there are no 'perfect' organizational structures and there will always be choices and tensions in complex designs.

The Tensions of a Multi-focus Design

Discussion in the early part of the chapter mentioned that too many managers shy away from the complexities inherent in running a global organization. The organization needs to invest in the development of conflict-resolution skills, so that it can begin to deal with the inevitable tensions in a constructive manner. Too many organizations have become trapped in a 'blame' culture, where excessive energy is spent looking for the enemy within, rather than focusing on what the competition is doing.

Some managers are uncomfortable dealing with ambiguity and conflicting views, and attempt to design organizations to avoid conflict. In a global context this is a very naïve view of the world and one that potentially means that the organization does not capitalize on some of its most promising business opportunities simply because they conflict with the dominant view in the organization.

To enable legitimate conflict to be resolved constructively, leaders need to focus at two levels: interpersonal and organizational. Many leaders have not taken the opportunity to consider their personal strategies for resolving conflicts and to reflect on the effectiveness of these strategies in a multi-functional and multicultural context. Nevertheless, these leaders are role models for the wider organization and their behaviour shapes the organizational culture and its response to conflict resolution (Schein, 1992: 231).

Ask yourself what your response is to an organizational crisis. How do you react when a member of your staff or a colleague makes a mistake? What happens when different parts of the organization have differing views on how to move forward? Are the differences openly explored and discussed or buried and hidden until they explode? Is there a shared sense of responsibility for solving the issue or a rush to look for the nearest scapegoat to whom to attach blame?

What is your preferred style of conflict resolution?

- Are you competitive or collaborative?
- Do you avoid the situation or confront it head on?

Developing a greater awareness of your own style and preference will enable you to develop better skills at handling a wider range of conflict situations successfully. It will also enable you to build more effective resolution processes into the fabric of your organization.

At an organizational level, to be able to respond effectively to the conflict inherent in a global organization, you need to be able to hold the tension between healthy competition and collaboration. Too much competition and the organization will waste precious time and resources on internal fighting that adds no value to the customer. Too much collaboration and the cosiness of the club develops and the organization becomes complacent and at risk. This involves creating an organization where difference is legitimized and where debate and dialogue are design features. They then become an integral part of the way of doing business.

In many organizations, one function or nationality has traditionally held more power and status than the rest (Canney Davison and Ward, 1999) and this has a strong influence on the organization's ability to resolve competing priorities. In the worst case it leads the organization to reject business opportunities because they do not fit with the dominant assumptions. For example:

In Volkswagen, the global automotive company, German engineers and designers who have worked in production have historically held key positions throughout the globe. Their production-driven perspective can sometimes make it difficult for other functions in the organization to have a strong voice, which may lead the organization to miss early signals that the industry is shifting or to overlook specific marketing opportunities.

In a City of London financial services organization, board members have only ever been actuaries. This has led the organization to develop a strongly risk-averse culture, which has hindered the organization's response to the far-reaching changes within its industry.

In organizations where the difference in power and status between one function or nationality is very wide, leaders need actively to design the organization to enable 'minority' views to have a legitimate voice, if they wish to capitalize on the diverse opportunities in the global marketplace. For example:

In a Swedish consulting organization, the bi-annual strategic conference for the top 100 global managers was always designed and organized by a steering group that included no Swedish managers. This group had the final say on the content and design of the conference as a counterbalance to the Swedish-dominated board.

In an engineering organization, non-engineers (with relevant leadership skills) always lead cross-functional project teams. The budget and resource allocation for the project sit with the team leader, thereby helping to balance the power in the rest of the organization.

A less risky and lower-profile attempt to shift a dominant perspective in a pharmaceutical organization was to introduce non-executive directors into the key senior management forum. These directors were specifically recruited for their outspokenness and their lack of knowledge and experience of the pharma industry.

Lastly, one of the most effective ways to resolve these competing priorities is to look externally and use the market and customer demands as the final arbiter. Some of the most powerful strategic dialogues, which really shift the dominant perspective of an organization, are those where customers are intimately involved in all the discussions. This brings us to our third design principle.

Building a Customer-driven Organization

As the pace of the business environment intensifies and the complexity of the opportunities increases, staying close to your customers, wherever they are in the world, becomes paramount. This is difficult if all the power in the organization is resident in the headquarters or too much of the organization is designed with global efficiency as the key driver (Treacy and Wiersema, 1995: 47). You need to identify which parts of your value chain should be locally responsive to customer needs and push decision-making and budgetary responsibility to the key interfaces. There is nothing more infuriating for a customer than if the person you are dealing with constantly has to refer your queries or complaints to a senior manager or head office to get resolution.

Designing your organization to be customer facing does not mean, however, that you can fudge the decision-making process or avoid allocating accountability for key issues and decisions within the organization. Increasingly, managers are using the design of their organization as an excuse for poor performance and they are getting away with it because no one in the system is sure who is accountable for what.

One method for building accountability into an organizational design is to conduct a RACI review during the design process. This uses a matrix to identify who is Responsible, Accountable, needs Consulting or Informing about a particular task within an organization. It involves identifying all the key activities and decisions undertaken by the business being redesigned and exploring where accountability for each one should reside. For an example, see Figure 2.6.

Examples of tasks that might be carried out in one division of a global company	Global Marketing Director	Regional Sales and Marketing Co-ordinator	Country Manager	Product Manager
Define marketing budget for regional divisions	A	R	C	C
Identify and exploit new business opportunities	I	A	R	R
Recruit and train new staff	I	C	A	R
Define advertising spend on new product launch	I	C	I	A

Figure 2.6   RACI review.

The critical issues when conducting this review are as follows:

■ Involve all the key players in the review. They know the business best and are most likely to be able to identify accurately all the key activities and decisions that are required to run the business. It also enables them to buy into the decisions made.

■ All activities should have one person accountable for their execution, even if the responsibility for carrying out the activity is delegated or shared. The simple rule is that accountability cannot be delegated and responsibility can. If no one is willing to assume accountability, ask whether the activity is necessary.

■ The fundamental difference between being consulted and being informed is the timing in relation to the decision being made. You should be consulted about the issue before a final decision is made and informed of the decision after the event. If you are informed, you do not have the right to attempt to alter the decision retrospectively.

Again, involving customers and suppliers in this process can be a powerful way of identifying potential blind spots that the organization might have.

The final issue to consider is that the needs of customers and the opportunities in the global market are not static. One of the greatest challenges in organizational design is to balance the basic human need for some stability and continuity with an organization's need to adapt to its changing environment. If you reorganize every time the external market requirements shift, you will quickly lose credibility with your staff, as illustrated in Figure 2.7.

However, the opposite extreme is more prevalent. Many global organizations have structures that are so out of alignment with the needs of their customers that employees are unable to deliver high performance because they spend too much time navigating internal barriers.

Designing Organizational Flexibility

The capacity of a system to evolve depends on an ability to move to more complex forms of differentiation and integration, and greater variety in the system, facilitating its ability to deal with challenges and opportunities posed by the environment. (Morgan, 1997: 41)

Figure 2.7 Cartoon taken from *Dogbert's Management Handbook*, Scott Adams, copyright 1995 United Feature Syndicate, Inc. (NYC). Reproduced by permission of United Media. All rights reserved.

One solution is to build flexibility into your organizational design by encouraging experimentation and action learning across the organization. The following example illustrates how an HR function was able to pass on valuable learning about the benefits and disadvantages of a chosen design to the rest of the organization.

Noah's Ark Syndrome

The organization had two predominant national markets: the US and the UK. The HR function decided to set up a number of working parties to explore international HR policy issues. Due to the size of the UK and US HR teams, the working parties were to be headed by an American or British team member. To model teamwork, it was agreed to appoint joint chairpersons, i.e. each working party would be headed by both a US and a UK member of staff. However, after six months of operating with co-chairs, a review of the working parties found that this arrangement was not working. It had led to increased conflict, duplication of resources and blurred accountability, despite the co-chairs being effective leaders.

When the organization proposed establishing global key account teams about a year later with joint leaders from marketing and sales, the experience of the HR global working parties was shared with the relevant senior managers to assist them in thinking through the implications of this decision. It helped them recognize that the proposal for joint leaders was a symptom of an underlying lack of trust between the two functions. This enabled the HR staff to work with sales and marketing on this issue when the global teams were established, thereby preventing difficulties as the teams started to work together.

Often there are parts of the organization that are more skilled at working with ambiguity and can more readily experiment with alternative design options. They can act as role models for the rest of the organization and highlight any potential advantages and disadvantages before a design is implemented more widely.

The best way to illustrate how this can work in practice is using a case study of an HR organization that used experimental design as a learning laboratory. As the organization moved from operating domestically to globally, it adapted the organizational design. As it evolved to the next level of complexity, it reviewed the advantages and disadvantages and passed the learning to the wider organization.

The transition from domestic to global

The organization had operated outside its domestic market for over a century, but had remained organized on a regional basis. The globalization drivers in the industry included the need to have a highly efficient product development process and the need to have the ability to adapt products to accommodate local preferences in a cost-effective manner. These drivers were having the most significant impact on the R&D function and it was therefore decided to create a single global R&D organization, where both the line and the matrix leadership positions were global, forcing a single point of decision making.

HR, like the rest of the organization, was previously organized on a regional basis, as in Figure 2.8.

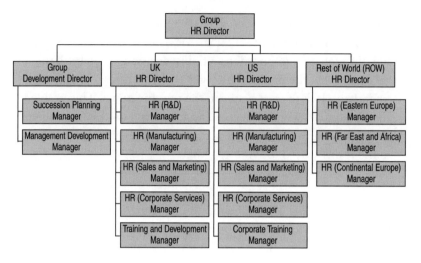

Figure 2.8   Regional organization design.

As the organization chart illustrates, each local HR function provided support to all aspects of the organization: R&D, manufacturing, sales and marketing and corporate services (IT, finance etc.) on a strictly national basis. The only part of the HR organization that had a global remit was a small team that reported to the group HR director and had responsibility for management and career development for a cadre of senior managers globally. Thus the organization operated a conventional HR structure for a global organization.

As it was only one part of the organization (R&D) that decided to organize itself globally, it was not thought to be appropriate for the HR organization to be completely redesigned. However, it became clear very quickly that the existing structure was not sufficiently flexible to meet the changing needs of the business. The HR function and global line managers experimented with several options over a 12–18-month period, as described below.

Phase 1: Retain the existing organizational design and re-skill staff
This phase allowed local HR staff who had supported the R&D organization prior to globalization to continue to work with their clients who had recently been appointed as global managers.

Advantages	Disadvantages
Provided line managers with continuity of support at a time when they were facing many other challenges	Existing staff did not have appropriate skills to operate effectively in a global context
Provided opportunity for personal development for key HR staff	Local HR staff provided seemingly conflicting advice to global managers on policies and practices
Staff knew how to navigate the informal systems to access resources	No dedicated budgets or resources to introduce any 'global' initiatives
Low risk – did not need to confront existing organizational power bases	No authority to resolve 'global' policy queries
Simplicity – did not require additional resource or reallocation of resource	The 'Noah's Ark' syndrome – each global manager had to deal with two or more HR staff for any issue that affected their staff internationally

This option was the organization's initial response, since it represented the least amount of change and was low risk. No one was clear what the impact of the organizational redesign in R&D would be and it seemed premature to be making radical changes to support functions initially. However, within a matter of weeks, there was feedback from the new global managers that this approach was not providing them with the support they required. A different response was developed.

Phase 2: Create global HR teams as pilots

The next experiment was to set up global HR project teams to deal with specific issues and transfer individuals with the appropriate skills to lead these teams on a part-time basis.

Advantages	Disadvantages
Focused resources in areas of greatest need	A few individuals had very high workloads and were travelling extensively, to the detriment of their health and home life
Allowed HR to respond flexibly to changing requirements	Difficult for the project teams to make things happen as budgets and decision making at the senior level were still regionally organized
Low risk – allowed the regional HR structures (and therefore the power bases) to remain untouched	Little opportunity to transfer the learning from these project teams to the wider HR organization
Provided individuals who had appropriate skills with career development opportunities	Temporary nature of the project teams meant that they were not given priority
	Part-time leadership roles led to role ambiguity and role overload

The greatest success of this stage of the experiment was the ability to focus HR resources on the areas of greatest need. It was relatively easy to solve the 'quick wins'. For example, line managers with new global responsibilities simply did not understand the basic terms and conditions and employment law practices in some of the countries where they now had staff. One of the global HR teams developed a handbook and a series of short lunchtime briefings over a very short timescale to overcome these difficulties in a consistent manner.

The greatest downfall of this option was that it left decision-making and budgetary authority residing at regional and local levels. This meant that any of the significant global changes that needed to happen were dependent on the global HR team's ability to influence a range of stakeholders. This was taking too much time and the line managers were demanding that HR provide some more comprehensive solutions to the problems they were experiencing. They were keen to make the new global organization successful and were supportive of HR being given the resources to make things happen. It was also clear that the impact of the globalization of R&D was far reaching and was going to have long-term implications for the wider business. Indeed, if this worked in R&D, manufacturing was keen to follow within the next 18 months.

Phase 3: Embed permanent global teams into the HR structure
The next phase of the experiment was to create a small core team with global roles and appoint staff with appropriate skills into the roles on a full-time basis.

The dedicated global teams were given a clear mandate by the organization and provided with sufficient financial backing to accomplish the goals they were set. They were able to bring in expertise from outside the organization, to enable them to 'fast track' some of the learning. A number of key projects were initiated and completed, encompassing the selection, development and rewarding of international teams. Over 12 months, the organization's capacity to operate effectively across the globe was making good progress.

As the organization became more sophisticated in the way it worked across boundaries, the demand for support from HR grew exponentially, particularly when it came to providing facilitators and

Advantages	Disadvantages
Provided the global organization with a dedicated resource	Created an 'elite', which left some staff feeling excluded from a key strategic initiative
Enabled newly appointed staff to focus on developing interventions specifically for global leaders and their teams	Concentrated the organizational learning in a few people, who quickly became the 'global gurus'
Created new career path for HR staff	Did not provide sufficient flexibility to respond to changes in client demand

coaches for newly created global R&D teams. It became clear that the skills developed by the core HR team members needed to be transferred to a wider population. This wider population needed to extend beyond the HR function if the organization was going to develop a sustainable capability to operate globally effectively.

Phase 4: Create a part-time global network to support the core teams
The final stage of the experiment was to create a network of coaches and facilitators to work alongside the full-time core team on a part-time basis as the needs of the organization changed. Two members of the core team were given responsibility for co-ordinating and developing this network in addition to the other projects on which they were working. The initial members of the network came from HR and from technical training teams in the business, but it soon grew to include global team members from the business who were keen to pass on their learning to others in the organization.

Advantages	Disadvantages
Involved line managers, external experts as well as HR staff	'Messy' – needed some level of co-ordination if organizational benefits were to be realized
Developed a broader base of 'global' capability across the organization	Some people were not comfortable with the level of role ambiguity
Provided the flexibility to meet the changing needs of the business without the need to increase overall headcount	These roles often cut across existing power bases and individuals therefore required effective conflict-resolution skills to make things happen

After the organization had experimented with the options discussed, the solution that proved to work most effectively was to have a full-time core global team who had the budgetary responsibility for delivering solutions to the global organization irrespective of location. This team was staffed with individuals with the most appropriate skills, irrespective of their previous positions in the hierarchies of the regional structures. This team had accountability for working with senior managers to formulate the HR strategy and identify what resources would be required to deliver the agreed strategic priorities. To implement the strategy, this team worked in conjunction with a network of local staff (HR and line) who worked with the R&D organization as coaches and facilitators on an as-needed basis. This provided maximum flexibility at low additional cost, while increasing organizational learning.

This case study is just one illustration of how organizations can build flexibility into their design options and encourage an atmosphere of appropriate experimentation.

CONCLUSIONS

This chapter explored some of the barriers to designing effective global organizations and identified some key principles for leaders to consider:

- Design the organization to make it more effective, not easier to manage.
- Seek out difference and value diversity.
- Dilemmas are inherent in global organizations.
- Global organizations are open systems and interact with their environment.

It then discussed how these design principles might be put into practice and the skills that leaders of global organizations might require when implementing effective designs:

- Ensuring that the design is aligned to the strategic intent of the organization.
- Being comfortable living with the tensions of a multi-focus design.
- Building an organization that simultaneously is customer facing and has clear internal accountabilities.
- Proactively designing in sufficient flexibility to enable the organization to adapt to changes in its environment in a timely fashion.

Finally, if having read this chapter you recognize the need to redesign part of your organization, here are a few thoughts to start you on your way:

1. Organization design is a strategic choice. There is no such thing as a 'perfect' structure. You need to explore the alternatives and assess which design best fits your business.
2. Where the current design broadly meets the needs of the future business strategy and plan, it is better to retain the existing design and look for other means of enhancing performance, e.g. realign reward processes to drive different behaviour, or refocus leadership behaviour to key strategic priorities.

3. Where there is not a good match between current design and future business needs, more redesign work will be required. Design the 'optimal' structure first (on paper), then figure out how you need to modify that design, taking into account constraints or obstacles:

   □ Obstacles may include existing management talent; existing employee skills; organizational culture; regulatory requirements.

   □ When obstacles exist, design a transitional structure that will get you closer to your optimal structure.

   □ Once a transitional structure is in place, create an overall game plan for overcoming these constraints.

   □ Existing HR processes should not be considered obstacles to an optimal structure. These can be realigned later.

4. Design the horizontal structure first.

5. When designing the vertical structure, make sure that each layer adds unique value. Specify what this value is in terms of the general types of decisions for which the layer is accountable.

References

Bartlett, C.A. and Ghoshal, S. (1995) *Transnational Management: Text, Cases and Readings in Cross-Border Management*, Englewood Cliffs, NJ: Irwin.

Binney, G. and Williams, C. (1995) *Leaning into the Future*, London: Nicholas Brealey.

Campbell, A., Devine, M. and Young, D. (1993) *A Sense of Mission*, London: FT/Pitman.

Canney Davison, S. and Ward, K. (1999) *Leading International Teams*, London: McGraw-Hill.

Goold, M. and Campbell, A. (1987) *Strategies and Styles*, Oxford: Basil Blackwell.

Goold, M., Campbell, A. and Alexander, M. (1994) *Corporate Level Strategy: Creating Value in the Multibusiness Company*, Chichester: John Wiley.

Hennessy, H. D. (2001) 'Managing global customers', in Kirkbride, P. S. (ed.), *Globalization: The External Pressures*, Chichester: John Wiley.

Herriot, P. and Pemberton, C. (1995) *Competitive Advantage through Diversity: Organizational Learning from Difference*, Beverly Hills, CA: Sage.

Moncrieff, J. (1998) 'Making a difference', *Directions: The Ashridge Journal*, November 3–9.

Morgan, G. (1997) *Images of Organizations*, Beverly Hills, CA: Sage.

Pudney, R. (2001) 'Managing global partnerships and alliances', in Kirkbride, P. S. (ed.), *Globalization: The External Pressures*, Chichester: John Wiley.

Sadler, P. (1998) *Designing Organizations: The Foundation for Excellence*, 3rd edn, London: Kogan Page.

Schein, E. H. (1992) *Organizational Culture and Leadership*, San Francisco, CA: Jossey Bass.

Treacy, M. and Wiersema, F. (1995) *The Discipline of Market Leaders: Choose Your Customers, Narrow Your Focus, Dominate Your Market*, London: HarperCollins.

MANAGING ACROSS CULTURAL DIVIDES: IS IT REALLY A PROBLEM?

Paul Kirkbride and Robert Westwood

CHAPTER 3

MANAGING ACROSS CULTURAL DIVIDES: IS IT REALLY A PROBLEM?

There's None So Blind . . .

Larry Smith was an American technologist who had decided that he wished to increase his international experience and knowledge by taking a three-year contract at the Hong Kong subsidiary of a US multinational. His area of specialization was R&D management and his role was to develop research in his specialist area. One of Larry's first hires was Daisy Choi, a PhD from Hong Kong University. Larry and Daisy soon found areas of common interest and began several joint research projects.

After two years the new R&D department had grown from just Larry and Daisy to a total of 11 research staff. For the first time in his life, Larry was more of a manager than a scientist. He was quite pleased with this change, as he believed that he would be able to put some of the theoretical approaches learned on his MBA into practice. After a while, he began to notice that a couple of the R&D staff were not performing up to standard. In particular, he was worried about Frank Tam, a young member of staff who had recently joined. Frank seemed much slower in his work than other staff and often made errors of detail. He sometimes missed important project meetings and when he did attend he often had not done the required work.

Larry decided that he needed to take remedial action. Remembering the material on performance objective setting and discipline that he had been taught, he asked Frank to come and see him privately in his office. Larry gave Frank feedback on his performance, asked about any possible barriers to satisfactory performance, outlined the required standards of behaviour and made sure he understood the consequences of non-compliance. Frank seemed to take it well but did not seem very contrite. Larry set him some objectives and deadlines and the meeting ended. Larry was surprised and upset to find that Frank's performance did not really improve over the next three months, so he saw Frank again and repeated the process. Again, he saw no real improvement in performance.

Frustrated and unhappy, Larry decided that he needed to confide in someone. He consulted Daisy, who had now become deputy head of the R&D department. He outlined the problem and was surprised when Daisy simply smiled. 'What's so funny?' demanded Larry, by now dangerously close to losing his temper.

'You,' replied Daisy. 'You have worked in a Chinese culture for over three years and despite studying it in your spare time you appear blind to the cultural foundations of your own behaviour or those of your staff.'

This vignette represents an everyday story of cross-cultural misunderstanding. There's none so blind as those who cannot see. We are all often blinkered by our own cultural lenses and we believe that they are universal. That is, until we come across situations such as that faced by Larry. Larry tries hard to deal with Frank's lack of performance but purely from within his own cultural orbit. As we shall see, Larry comes from a culture characterized by low power distance and individualism, whereas Frank comes from a culture characterized by high power distance and collectivism. While Larry's actions such as private discipline would probably have worked well in his own culture, they failed to solve the problem in this very different culture. Obviously a very different approach is required. The key to understanding this situation is the fact that there are two very different forms of society: guilt cultures and shame cultures (Benedict, 1989).

Western cultures like Larry's are generally 'guilt' cultures while eastern cultures like Frank's are generally 'shame' cultures. Guilt refers to an internalized form of control. We feel guilt inside because we believe that we have done something we know to be wrong. Thus guilt is a process by which we fail to measure up to an internalized standard. In western cultures guilt can be a powerful lever to change human behaviour, a fact not unnoticed by the Catholic church. Shame, in contrast, refers to an externalized form of control. We feel shame when others whom we value let us know that we have done something wrong. This lever was used extensively in the Chinese Cultural Revolution, when senior cadres were humiliated publicly on stage. Of course, in all cultures one has both guilt and shame. Yet Benedict noted that in most cultures one dominates over the other. Larry was using private interviews to try to inculcate guilt feelings in Frank that would lead to improved performance. However, this was not working. What Daisy suggested to Larry was that he should try to use some public shaming mechanisms on Frank, or, alternatively, leave the performance improvement problem to her and the rest of her team. Larry asked Daisy what this would mean and was told that she would use group pressure and shaming to bring Frank into line. From this episode, Larry learned that managing in a global setting was harder than he imagined and that what worked 'at home' did not necessarily work abroad.

WHAT IS CULTURE?

Any attempt to explain the effects of culture on global-scale economic action and managerial behaviour faces two problems. The first is defining and conceptually clarifying the concept of culture. The second is providing a plausible explanation of how culture actually functions as a determining variable that affects action and behaviour. In much cross-cultural management writing, culture is often inadequately theorized and the link to behaviour remains at the level of inference or, worse, assumption and speculation.

Culture is a profoundly problematic and contested concept. It is, of course, a concept of high abstraction, or perhaps better yet, a concept of multiple levels of abstraction. At its most abstract it refers to 'the human ability to use complex linguistic and non-linguistic symbols to transmit shared traditions and patterns of social interaction through time and space' (Evans, 1993: 21). It also refers, more concretely, to the material outcomes of social action. Culture has frequently been conceptualized in terms of layers or levels: from core basic assumptions, through expressible values, to overt behaviours and other material manifestations (e.g. Hofstede, 1991; Schein, 1985; Trompenaars, 1993). The concept also implies difference: that the culture of one social group is unique and distinguishable from another. Thus cultures can be distinguished by the varying patterns they display in their symbolic systems, modes of social interaction and concrete artefacts. While culture differentiates, it would be a mistake to conclude that it homogenizes. Analytically and abstractly to identify and classify the set of shared assumptions, values, interactional patterns and artefacts of a group of people as 'a culture' is not to eradicate individual differences nor to capture the kaleidoscopic possibilities for particular, situated attitudes and actions.

Culture only began to be incorporated into business/management theory as international business became more intensive and extensive in the post-war period. Even then, the earliest cross-national management research paid little attention to culture *per se*, preferring to use 'nation' as the unit of analysis (Harbison and Myers, 1959; Farmer and Richman, 1965). This work was situated, at the time, within the wider debates on development and the chief focus was on the relationship between management and economic development. Culture was defined in terms of nation, and national identity was taken as a single and permanent characteristic of individuals. Culture itself was rarely defined or operationalized *a priori*, and mostly functioned as an independent variable invoked *post hoc* to explain any observed differences between nations studied. This has largely remained the case in cross-cultural management writing and been the subject of a good deal of criticism (Punnett and Shenkar, 1996; Peng, Peterson and Shyi, 1991).

A more specific focus on culture only really emerged in the early 1980s, again stimulated by the widely declared uniqueness of Japanese culture and its impact on a distinctive management style and system (Ouchi, 1981; Pascale and Athos, 1981). Of great significance was Hofstede's (1980) operationalization of cultural value dimensions and explicit theorizing of culture and its impact on management. This enabled the measurement of value differences across cultures and the explicit inclusion of 'culture' in empirical studies. However, even Hofstede has little to say about how culture actually affects behaviour. He defines culture as 'the collective programming of the mind which distinguishes the members of one human group from another' (1984: 21). Presumably, such 'mental programming' shapes how people interpret their environments and social situations, and at least partially determines how they respond to them and construct lines of action. In effect, Hofstede merely says, 'As nearly all our mental programmes are affected by values, nearly all are affected by culture, and this is reflected by our behaviour' (1984: 23). The assumption is therefore that values thus mediate between culture and behaviour.

The measurement of espoused values has been a prominent strategy in cross-cultural management research. Many studies have drawn on Rokeach's (1973) conceptualization of values and provided various operational measures to generate cross-cultural data. However, a noted problem with this approach is that questionnaires for measuring values were often designed in the US and constructed in relation to values of relevance to that culture. Any universal qualities of such values are only assumed and there is no guarantee that the instrument will effectively resonate with the values prevalent in other cultures. This is a problem with any cross-cultural research and is sometimes referred to as the emic-etic dilemma (Berry, 1990; Peng, Peterson and Shyi, 1991). Doubts persist as to whether the responses to values questions provided in surveys do in fact correspond to the operative values of managers and, even if they do, whether the values held are actually converted into behavioural outcomes.

Hofstede's work also pursues a values-measurement approach. While his derived dimensions do appear to reveal important cross-cultural differences, the actual link with organizational/managerial behaviour remains speculative. As Punnett and Shenkar (1996: 168) note:

> Often, the large scale inclusion of national dimensions in cross-cultural comparative research has meant forgoing any fine-grained understanding of how culture impacts individual behaviour. Thus, while we have learned **that** national differences are important, we still do not have a good understanding of **how** cultural differences influence behaviour in and of organisations.

This remains a significant problem. Even when cultural dimensional differences are measured, the actual relationship with specific organizational behaviours is rarely empirically demonstrated.

An additional critical problem is that of unpacking the impact of culture from other potential determining factors. In observing actual differences in organization or management, how can it be shown that those differences are attributable to culture and not to some other variable such as political economy, educational system or other institutional factor? As Kelley, Whatley and Worthley (1987) state, 'Isolating the influence of culture on the development of managerial values is a perplexing problem for comparative international management researchers'. As noted, earlier models of comparative management gave less credence to culture as the prime explanatory variable, giving as much, if not greater, weight to a range of other possible variables (Harbison and Meyers, 1959; Farmer and Richman, 1965).

TEN DIMENSIONS OF CULTURAL DIFFERENCE

Notwithstanding some of the criticisms noted above, it is clear that 'culture', whatever it may be, has some effect on managerial behaviour and management practice. What, then, are the main dimensions of cultural difference that have been identified by existing research work?

A good starting point would be to examine the results of Hofstede's (1980) cultural values survey, since this is one of the few existing attempts to measure cultural differences empirically on a large scale. From his extensive survey data he derives four dimensions describing basic problems of humanity with which every society has to cope; the variation of country scores along these dimensions shows that different societies do cope with these problems in different ways. The four derived dimensions (Power Distance, Uncertainty Avoidance, Individualism–Collectivism, Masculinity–Femininity) represent patterns of response to universal problems that people face. Similarity in dimension patterning among cultures therefore suggests that they have developed similar values in relation to preferred patterns of response to these problems.

There are some other well-known schemas of broad cultural differences to which we can also refer. The root of these schemas is the classic work of Kluckhohn (1951), Kluckhohn and Strodtbeck (1961) and Kroeber and Parsons (1958). Variations on their descriptions of dimensions or patterns of cultural difference can be found in Adler (1991) and Trompenaars (1993). By putting these schemas together with Hofstede's dimensions, we can identify the ten most important aspects of cultural difference worldwide.

Power Distance

Hofstede defines power distance as the extent to which power is distributed unevenly in a society and the degree to which this is accepted (1984: 65–109). People in high power distance cultures accept a hierarchical order in society, in which everyone has their proper place. People in low power distance cultures try to minimize differences in power and expect any actual differences to be justified.

Thus power distance in an organization refers, among other things, to the 'perceptual' gap between 'boss' and 'subordinate'. In high power distance cultures this gap is perceived, by both parties, to be large. Subordinates see themselves as occupying a much lower place in the organizational hierarchy and are reluctant to criticize or openly challenge bosses. Subordinates expect bosses to provide clear and decisive leadership and to manage in a rather autocratic way. Bosses in such cultures expect subordinates to be hard working and compliant and to follow directions and orders. They expect subordinates to know their place and not to 'talk back'. In contrast, in a low power distance culture the gap between boss and subordinate is perceived to be relatively small or negligible. Indeed, in such cultures both parties would be unhappy with the notion of 'boss' and 'subordinate' status. In such cultures, subordinates feel able to speak freely with their boss and offer advice, assistance and challenge where necessary. Bosses expect 'good' subordinates to be forthcoming with their ideas and to challenge the status quo in a creative and innovative manner.

Dangerous Treatment

Dr Duncan White is a senior British surgeon working on assignment at a major hospital in Los Angeles. He becomes concerned when he realizes that a Mexican nurse, Amy Torres, is improperly using a particular machine for patient treatment.

He finds Mrs Torres in a corridor and explains that there is a problem. He outlines the proper procedure to her and asks if she understands. She says that she does.

Two hours later, Dr White checks on the patient, only to find that the patient is still doing poorly as Nurse Torres has continued to administer the treatment improperly. Again, Dr White queries her and again she affirms her understanding of the procedure.

The scenario above could, of course, potentially have many causes and explanations. It could be that the nurse is deliberately applying the incorrect treatment for some reasons unknown to us. It could be a simple case of miscommunication. But if we scratch the surface we can see that power distance is playing a part in this potentially lethal problem. The nurse comes from a high power distance culture (Mexico) and thus is reluctant to admit to the doctor that she does not fully understand his instructions. Such a query may be seen as an implied challenge to authority in her culture and could make the authority figure lose face. The doctor comes from a low power distance culture where subordinates would feel free to raise their lack of understanding and thus he would expect the nurse to apply the correct treatment, as she has not raised any queries. How can this problem be resolved? There are two clear options. First, the doctor can finesse the power distance gap by getting the nurse to demonstrate the correct procedure in his presence so that he can coach and correct. Second, he could seek to lower the power distance gap by having a senior nurse instruct Mrs Torres in the correct procedure. In this lower power distance situation she would be more likely to voice her lack of understanding.

While this is only a small example, it does raise some important issues for organizations attempting to be global. What is the culture of the parent or head office? Often for western multinationals (MNCs) this will be a low power distance culture such as the UK, Germany, Scandinavia, Australia or the US. Managers from these cultures will have to learn to manage in rather different ways in the high power distance parts of their global empires.

Uncertainty Avoidance

Every society is faced with the fact that the environment and the future are uncertain. However, the ways in which different cultures react to this uncertainty vary. Uncertainty avoidance has been defined as the degree to which people experience uneasiness in ambiguous situations and their degree of tolerance for deviant or innovative ideas or behaviours (Hofstede, 1984: 110–47). Strong 'uncertainty avoidance' cultures feel threatened by uncertainty and try to control it. They do this by attempting to remove the uncertainty through certainty-creating mechanisms. These would include bureaucratic rules, planning systems, control systems and the use of experts. Such cultures are characterized by fear of failure, lower levels of risk taking, a preference for clear instruction, the upholding of corporate rules and the suppression of conflict. Examples of such cultures cited by Hofstede are Greece, Japan and France (1984: 122).

Weak uncertainty avoidance cultures, on the other hand, feel happy with ambiguity and uncertainty and are happy to 'roll with the punches'. They tend to be more pragmatic and flexible. Such cultures are characterized by a high propensity to change, greater optimism, higher levels of risk taking, the bypassing of corporate rules and a greater tolerance of conflict. Examples of such cultures as cited by Hofstede are the UK, Ireland, the US and Canada (1984: 122).

Are there any particular implications for MNCs in relation to this dimension? It can be suggested that this dimension is of particular importance for the ways in which managers operate and could potentially cause problems within a global organization or between global partners from different cultures. Good examples would be in the creation of international joint ventures (IJVs) or mergers. It has been noted that the British and the Dutch have historically had a number of successes in both major mergers (Royal Dutch/Shell) and IJVs. This can partially be attributed to the fact that they are both relatively low in uncertainty avoidance (as well as both being low in power distance and highly individualist). On the other hand, the record of Franco-British mergers is not so good (e.g. GEC Alsthom). This is probably to do with the fact that the French have a strong uncertainty avoidance culture with a preference for hierarchy and rules, which irritates the more flexible and weak uncertainty avoidance British. On the other hand, the French have often accused the British of being without principles, which the British defend as being pragmatic or flexible.

Individualism and Collectivism

Hofstede's third dimension contrasts individualist and collectivist societies. Individualism is defined as a preference for a loosely knit social framework in society in which individuals are supposed to take care of themselves and their immediate families. Children in such societies are raised to become autonomous and to express their individuality. In organizational terms individualism is manifested in a simple calculative involvement with the employer, emotional independence from the company, desire for work autonomy, a focus on creativity and innovation and a drive towards leadership roles. In Hofstede's data the five most individualist countries were the US, Australia, UK, Canada and the Netherlands.

Collectivism, on the other hand, is a preference for a tightly knit social framework in which individuals can expect their relatives, clan or other in-group to look after them, in exchange for unquestioning loyalty. Children in such societies are raised to understand the importance of networks and relationships and to suppress individual viewpoints to preserve group harmony. In organizational terms collectivism is manifested in a more moral involvement with the employer, emotional dependence on the company or work group, a focus on security and harmony, an acceptance of one's place in the hierarchy and aspirations for conformity. Collectivist countries include clusters in both Asia (Philippines, China, Singapore, Taiwan and Thailand) and South America (Chile, Peru, Colombia and Venezuela).

Masculinity and Femininity

Hofstede's final dimension was perhaps the most fiercely debated of the four. A factor was identified that Hofstede labelled Masculinity–Femininity. He was immediately attacked by feminists and others for gender stereotyping. He later tried to retract and relabel the dimension as tough minded–tender minded. Masculinity (tough minded) can be simply defined as the extent to which aggressiveness, assertiveness and materialism are present as a shared value set within the culture. Masculine cultures tend to be ones where there is a high level of work centrality, where companies intrude on the private lives of their employees, where there is an achievement ideal, where performance and growth are valued and where people live to work.

Femininity (tender minded), on the other hand, can be defined as a preference for relationships, modesty, caring for the weak and the quality of life. Feminine cultures tend to be those where work is only part of people's lives, where company interference in private life is resisted, where there is a service ideal, where quality of life and environment are important and where people work to live.

The case of the Japanese–Swedish joint venture

J. 'Ben' Shaw leaned back in his leather executive chair and began to reflect. When he had first been approached to become the CEO of Hi-Qual in India he had been both surprised and delighted.

For most of his career since graduating from Stanford with an MBA, Ben had worked in the semiconductor industry in California's 'silicon valley'. He had always wanted to work abroad but had never really had the opportunity, apart from the usual short business trips. In this sense he had been delighted when he was asked to become the CEO of a new international joint venture company (Hi-Qual) to be established in India to service the growing Asian chip market. On the other hand, he had been surprised. Hi-Qual was a joint venture between two unlikely partners. Toku was a growing Japanese electronics company that had recently entered the semiconductor industry. SRD was a Swedish conglomerate with both a high-technology research and development division and extensive sales and marketing operations in Asia. Both companies had agreed that the new joint venture (JV) should be headed by someone from a 'neutral' country.

In his mind Ben reviewed the three-year history of Hi-Qual. In many ways there had been few problems. Setting up business in India had been easier than expected and the Indian workforce in the production plant was highly skilled and very efficient.

The real problems appeared in the managerial and technical ranks, which were jointly staffed by roughly equal numbers of Japanese and Swedish executives. There had been a series of different problems, including the following:

1. Initially there had been some difficulty in getting Swedish staff to come to India for short contracts (up to 18 months)

without families. No such problems had occurred with Japanese staff. Since company housing had become available for expatriates that allowed dependants to accompany staff during contracts, the difficulties seemed to have eased.

2. There was a comparatively high labour turnover among the Swedes and the expatriation failure rate was higher than for the Japanese (where it was virtually zero).

3. The Swedish staff had complained to Ben that the Japanese were overly zealous in their work and worked excessive hours in the evening and at weekends. They felt that the workload at Hi-Qual did not justify such work patterns. They also felt that the Japanese tended to make decisions among themselves in private before issues were discussed in committees or task forces.

4. On the other hand, Ben had heard from a trusted colleague that the Japanese executives felt that the Swedish staff were lazy as they all left work at around 6 pm and did not work weekends. The Japanese felt that the Swedes were not 'pulling their weight' on projects. They also felt that there had been occasions where senior Japanese executives had been challenged and insulted in meetings.

Ben reflected that things seemed to be heading from bad to worse. Now there were signs that task forces and project teams were *either* Japanese *or* Swedish in composition. Extra layers of bureaucracy seemed to be increasing as reporting relationships, committees and task forces were parallelled. And to make matters worse, there was evidence of both senior Japanese and Swedish executives bypassing Ben and reporting directly to their home country managements!

'Heck,' exclaimed Ben. 'What's the matter with these people? Why can't they work together?'

The answer to Ben's question is that the key problem is the large differences between Swedish and Japanese culture. Japan is strong on uncertainty avoidance and is the most 'masculine' of the original 39 countries in Hofstede's data set. Sweden is weak on uncertainty avoidance and the most 'feminine' of the countries in Hofstede's database. The Japanese 'masculinity' can be seen in their willingness to be expatriated to India without their families, their lower level of turnover and their 'workaholic' lifestyle. The Swedish 'femininity' can be seen in their reluctance to expatriate without families, their higher turnover rate and their insistence on balancing work time with leisure time. This case shows the difficulties involved in working together across cultural boundaries when the cultures involved are clearly divided in terms of some important facet of culture.

Long- and Short-term Orientations

Hofstede's original four dimensions have been complemented by a fifth, Long-term Orientation (initially labelled 'Confucian Dynamism'). This followed Bond's development of the Chinese Value Survey (CVS) as an attempt to construct a values survey from a purely indigenous Chinese perspective (Chinese Culture Connection, 1987). Bond asked a number of Chinese social scientists to identify the core values of Chinese culture. The process eventually led the construction of a simple questionnaire that was translated and administered to 100 students in each of 22 countries (a sample from the People's Republic of China (PRC) was added later). Analysis revealed four dimensions, three of which correlated significantly with three of the Hofstede dimensions (not with uncertainty avoidance). However, the fourth CVS factor had no correspondence (Hofstede and Bond, 1988). It was this factor that Bond labelled 'Confucian Dynamism', since he felt that the items composing it reflected central values of Confucianism. Hofstede (1994: 164) argues, 'In practical terms, it refers to a long-term versus a short-term orientation in life'. At the 'long-term' end of the dimension are located the values of persistence, thrift, having a sense of shame and ordering relationships by status and observing this order. At the other end are personal steadiness and stability, protecting your 'face', respect for tradition and reciprocation (of greetings, favours and gifts).

At a macro level this dimension has implications for how people relate to time. One example is the perspective taken with respect to saving. Long-term orientation cultures tend to be more concerned with saving for the future (even for future generations). This has implications for the perceived function of capital accumulation, for rates and levels of savings and ultimately for the structure of capital within the society. These issues have organizational effects, but the dimension has numerous more direct implications for management and organization. For example, it has likely implications for planning activity and for decision making. The time horizons for plans and decisions will vary according to where cultures lie on this dimension. US culture tends to be very present and/or future oriented, but its future orientation tends to have a short time horizon. The short-term perspective of US business has been frequently commented on, characterized by the tyranny of the quarterly report. Japanese culture, along with others in Asia, tends to have a longer time horizon. Investment planning for Japanese organizations in the PRC indicates that they plan for returns on investment over periods in excess of ten years. Early investments by US companies tended to work on typical three- to five-year return cycles.

Universalism and Particularism

In universalistic cultures, general, abstract and universal principles are developed that both guide behaviour and are the prime means of its evaluation. A person confronting a dilemma will ask, 'What is the general principle here and if I act inappropriately what universal principle will I have breached?' Because of the high level of abstraction, the universal principle is made to cover a wide variety of particular cases and should be adhered to and applied despite the specifics of the particular situation. In particularistic cultures the guidance and evaluation of behaviour and action are considered much more with reference to the particular concrete circumstances. When confronted by a dilemma or breach of behavioural norms, people will not refer to some internalized, universal principle, but to the practical exigencies and implications within that particular situation.

Trompenaars (1993) sees the practical contrast between the two as one of a different perspective on rules versus relationships. That is because in particularistic cultures it is the overriding importance of specific and concrete relationships that demands attention in determining lines of action or in judging behaviour. People will ask themselves, 'What does my intended line of action mean for those with whom I am in a relationship, how will they judge my actions and how will they respond to my actions?' These calculations have far more impact than any superordinate abstract universal principle.

Hire My Daughter

Jaswal Singh had trained as an engineer in India prior to moving to Germany in the late 1960s. After working in a succession of engineering jobs, Jaswal joined Hannover Motor Bus in the late 1970s and has now risen to his present position as superintendent of the coachwork repair shop.

Jaswal's youngest daughter, Sonia, has recently graduated from Heidelberg University with an engineering degree and a business diploma. Jaswal feels that it is his duty to help her find employment, as he has done for all his other offspring.

Recently Jaswal noticed that a junior engineering position has been advertised in the depot where he works. It is in a different section to his own but is also under his immediate boss, the depot manager. Jaswal goes to see Rolf Gutmann, the depot manager, and asks him to hire Sonia. Rolf is appalled and enraged. Although he noted that Sonia was extremely well qualified for the vacancy, he refuses to have a father and daughter working in the same depot. Indeed, the very suggestion of hiring family members is repugnant to him. He flatly rejects Jaswal's request. Jaswal is very upset and believes that Rolf is acting unfairly. He sees no problem in working in the same depot as Sonia. He is so upset that he lets it be known that he is thinking of leaving.

Rolf is reluctant to lose such a skilled and experienced superintendent and asks you for your advice. In particular, he wants to know why Jaswal is behaving in such an odd way and what he should do to solve the problem.

This case demonstrates the practical difficulties that often emerge from a clash between universalistic and particularistic cultures. Rolf comes from a universalistic culture that is also moderate in terms of uncertainty avoidance and is individualistic. Jaswal comes from a particularistic culture that is weak on uncertainty avoidance and is moderately collectivist. Jaswal feels that it is his job as a patriarchal father to help his daughter find suitable employment and has thus approached Rolf. While Jaswal is aware of company rules designed to prevent 'nepotism', he believes that his long service and exemplary record mean that an exception can be made in his case. He also believes that by hiring his daughter the company can be sure that they are not making a selection mistake, because he can guarantee her good behaviour and work performance. On the other hand, Rolf supports the company position because he believes in a meritocracy and the universal application of rules. Rolf believes that people should get jobs strictly on merit and not through family connections, however well qualified they might be. He is also against family members working together as he believes this could result in favouritism and the formation of cliques. This cultural clash seems to be heading for an unhappy ending. However, we shall see later that if the parties are aware of the cultural drivers of their own positions, a 'win–win' solution is possible.

Specificity and Diffuseness

This dimension deals with the extensiveness of our relationships with others and the extent to which people in different cultures compartmentalize and privatize different life spheres and the relationships that go with them. Diffuse cultures tend to view things holistically and in a deeply contextualized manner. It does not make sense to parcel things up and to separate thing out analytically into discrete components. An extreme version of this is embodied in Taoism and in the Chinese notions of ying and yang. What most often appear to a westerner as bipolar opposites are to most Asians two sides of a coin, inextricably interwoven. Western thought is characterized by analytical strategies that abstract things into categories and build them into linear processes. Asian thinking tends to try to retain elements in their relationship complexity. Things remain elementally interrelated and embedded in a context.

This notion of diffuseness and specificity relates to things in the environment and in cognitions, but it also relates to a difference in sense of self and identity. People from specific cultures are able, as it were, to divide themselves. A person has little trouble behaving and thinking in one mode for one specific context, but turning to another in a different situation. Thus in a business negotiation, a US manager functions as a negotiator. He only wants to engage with that aspect of himself and does not conceive that it is his whole self that is engaged in the negotiation situation. On the golf course between negotiation sessions, the US manager is happy to be 'Brad', a different type of social identity. He does not feel that the negotiation identity has continued fully formed on to the golf course. This way of looking at things and behaving will seem odd to most Asians, Latin Americans and others from diffuse cultures. The person and their identity are not divisible in this manner. The person is a totality and that totality is present in all situations, however diverse. Thus on the golf course the business negotiator is still present, and things that happen or are said may have a bearing on how the negotiation is viewed.

Achievement and Ascription

This dimension refers to the mechanisms by which people in a society attain status, power and position. In achievement-oriented cultures there is more emphasis on what people do, their competencies and accomplishments. This contrasts with ascriptive cultures where the focus is on who you are, where you come from and what your connections are. Most western cultures are towards the achievement end of the continuum, with their focus on a 'meritocracy' and the extolling of individual success stories. Eastern cultures are towards the ascriptive end of the continuum, but there is significant movement in the direction of achievement, particularly in the business world. In Malaysia, for example, there is a vestigial traditional status hierarchy based on notions of nobility, family and clan. This is reflected in the nomenclature that is still important within indigenous Malay society. Even in contemporary overseas Chinese business, nepotistic practices are very common and it is difficult for non-family members to get into key positions. This cultural inclination has implications for, among other things, leadership in Asian contexts (Westwood, 1997).

Internal and External Control

Kluckhohn and Strodtbeck (1961) discussed variable values and orientations of cultures to their environments. It is possible to contrast three different perspectives: harmony with nature; subjugation to nature; and dominance over nature. Trompenaars (1993) reconfigures this into an internal versus an external orientation, linking it to the psychological concept of the locus of control. US culture is perhaps the pre-eminent internally oriented culture, where there is an exceedingly strong belief in the capacity, indeed the right, of humans to intervene and manipulate the environment in the pursuit of the well-being and interests of people. A strong internal orientation is associated with firm values of personal self-efficacy and the capacity of people to intervene and determine outcomes. It also relates to the emergence of applied science and all that has entailed for control and manipulation of the environment. In cultures with an external orientation, there is more of a belief that nature is the dominant force and that humans are a component in a holistic cosmology; integral not dominant. This is reflected, for example, in Chinese medicine, which is holistic in nature and focuses as much on retuning the person to natural rhythms and proper connections as it does on treating a specific symptom. Core religions in East Asia such as Buddhism and Taoism also place great emphasis on a harmonious cosmology. Externals will tend to give greater emphasis to the determining impact of external forces rather than internal efficacies. Such an orientation has implications for planning, decision making and motivation.

Time Orientations

Following Hall (1976), there are presumed cultural differences in terms of how time is conceived. Western conceptions of time are linear, sequential, discrete and monochronic. There is also a strong orientation towards the future, at least in the US. Linear time is the view that time flows like a river and that once a moment of time has elapsed it is gone for good. Thus people in these types of cultures tend to plan sequentially and at the extreme use detailed time planning and management systems. A monochronic approach means that people tend to do one thing at a time. The implications of such an approach are that people:

- tend to concentrate on the job at hand;
- regard keeping to project and time schedules as essential;
- emphasize promptness as a virtue;
- have a strong preference for adherence to plans.

Eastern conceptions of time are non-linear, non-sequential, episodic and polychronic. They are also somewhat more oriented towards the past or the present and tend to be circular or even spiral in nature. People in such cultures tend to be more fatalist in orientation and to plan holistically rather than sequentially. A polychronic approach means that people are happy to do several things at the same time. The implications of such an approach are that people:

- are more willing to move from task to task before full task completion;
- consider time commitments as desirable rather than essential;
- place more emphasis on completing human transactions rather than objective tasks;
- base promptness on the nature of the particular relationship;
- are more willing to change previously specified plans.

DEVELOPING CULTURAL SENSITIVITY

As organizations increasingly globalize, they tend to deal with more cultures both as customers/consumers and as employees. To use Bartlett and Ghoshal's (1992) terms, as organizations move from being international to being more global or multinational and towards being transnational, they have to face increasing cultural complexity (see Kirkbride, Pinnington and Ward, 2001 for a more detailed exposition). Of course, in the process there is a difference between the more global firms whose key issue is global penetration and multinational firms whose key issue is national responsiveness. One might expect cultural sensitivity to be more relevant to the latter strategy than to the former. Nevertheless, cultural sensitivity and understanding remains a key success criterion for transnational organizations.

Cultural diversity is thus a fact of life for such organizations. It can bring a number of benefits. These include:

- Increased creativity
  - better problem definition
  - wider range of perspectives
  - greater volume and quality of ideas
  - less 'group think'
- Better decision making
  - greater number of solutions generated and considered
  - more holistic evaluation processes
  - technically better decisions
- More effective and productive team work
- Better communication
  - enhanced concentration required for communication
  - leads to better understanding
- Improved marketing responsiveness
  - better knowledge of consumer behaviour patterns

It is well known in the psychological literature that heterogeneous ('diverse') groups tend to do better than homogenous ('similar') groups in a number of areas. On one level global, multinational and transnational organizations are simply an example of a very large heterogeneous group. However, a number of caveats are in order. Most of the research shows that many of the benefits only emerge in the long term. Thus diverse groups tend to struggle initially and often require strong support and facilitation if they are to reach this superior level of productivity. The implication for organizations seeking to globalize is clear. To reap the benefits of cultural diversity requires a high level of cultural sensitivity and a deliberate policy of support for global teams and global networks (for further discussion see Chapter 7). If the increasing levels of cultural diversity are not handled correctly, these supposed benefits could easily and quickly turn into a litany of problems. These would include:

- Increased mistrust
- A lack of desire to work together in teams
- Increased stereotyping
- More within-culture conversations
- Increased fragmentation within groups – polarization and exclusionary practices
- Increased miscommunication due to non-native speakers, slower speech, translation issues etc.
- Increased stress
- Inability to gain agreement
- Less efficient and productive teams

How can some of these problems be avoided? In the next section we will consider what organizations have done, and can do, to alleviate these problems. However, we also believe that on one level it is up to individual managers to handle cultural differences in a more productive way by creating cultural synergy. When faced with possible cross-cultural problems such as some of those outlined in this chapter, we believe that managers have to follow a simple three-point process to create cultural synergy.

Step 1: Situation description

- Stand back from the situation and reflect.
- Try to describe the situation objectively from your own position.

- Try to put yourself in the other person's shoes and see the situation from their perspective.

Step 2: Cultural interpretation

- Try to assess the underlying cultural assumptions that each party might be holding.
- What are the cultural values that can help explain your own behaviour?
- What are the possible cultural values that could explain the other culture's behaviour?

Step 3: Cultural creativity

- Try to generate culturally synergistic alternative solutions.
- Brainstorm new solutions based on, but not limited to, the cultures involved in the problem.
- Subject any solution to the following tests:
  - Does the potential solution fit your cultural values?
  - Does it fit the other culture's values?
  - Is it new?
- Implement the solution and observe the effects.
- Refine the solution for future use based on multicultural feedback.

Using this methodology we can find solutions to many cultural impasses. Take the 'Hire my daughter' case earlier. Here Rolf and Jaswal appear to be locked in a zero-sum game with mutually exclusive objectives. Rolf wants to uphold the hiring rules, while Jaswal wants him to make an exception in his case. Yet there is a synergistic win–win solution available. The issue turns on what is really Jaswal's motivation in this situation. If we define it as the need to get his daughter a job in the depot, then it appears to be zero sum. However, if we define it as to get his daughter a good job with a good firm as a start on her career ladder, then we have the possibility of a positive sum solution. Rolf needs to probe Jaswal's motivation more closely as well as considering the basis of his own resistance to hiring Sonia. If Rolf can use his network of contacts in other companies to obtain interviews for Sonia, and as a result she gets a job, then Jaswal is likely to be happy, both that he has succeeded in placing his daughter in a good job and that his boss has valued their relationship enough to do him a 'favour'.

GLOBALIZING THE LEADERSHIP CADRE

What can companies do to develop a cadre of managers capable of operating in this international and culturally diverse environment? Research work pioneered by Ashridge at the start of the 1990s identified some competencies that appeared to be shared by such individuals (Barham and Oates, 1991; Barham and Wills, 1992; Barham and Berthoin Antal, 1994). Unlike others such as Bartlett and Ghoshal (1992) who focused on the most senior decision makers only, Barham and his colleagues focused on the competencies required by both senior and middle managers. Indeed, they found the role of the latter to be particularly crucial in creating a 'global' culture. From detailed research in a number of 'international' companies such as ABB, Airbus, Cathay Pacific, Nokia and SKF, Barham and Wills identified two distinct sets of competencies. The first, which they termed 'doing' competencies, represented a set of roles and role behaviours that seemed to be shared by successful international managers. These were summed up under the following four headings:

- Championing international strategy
- Operating as a cross-border coach and co-ordinator
- Acting as an intercultural mediator and change agent
- Managing one's own personal effectiveness for international business

In addition, they identified a set of personal or 'being' competencies that appeared to distinguish the more successful from the less successful international managers. As Barham and Berthoin Antal note, 'This second side to international competence underpins the active side of the job and concerns the way that the manager thinks and reasons, the way they feel, and the beliefs and values that motivate them' (1994: 235). These competencies are grouped under the following three headings:

- Cognitive complexity
- Emotional energy
- Psychological maturity

These competencies are discussed in more detail by Wills (Chapter 8) later in this volume.

What can large international organizations do to try to develop these cultural competencies and skills in their managers? Many organizations are now explicitly trying to address these issues through various forms of management development. For example, Volkswagen has specifically targeted the issue of cultural capability in its Group Junior Executive Programme (Mollet, 2000).

The Volkswagen Group Junior Executive Programme (GJEP)

This programme has been running for eight years and is organized by Volkswagen Group Management Development in conjunction with Ashridge. The target group is high potentials from around the world who are in junior management positions and aged around 30–40. These individuals are seen as future senior executives and are nominated and supported by a major business unit (brand or region). One of the major selection criteria is an openness to cross-cultural experiences and a willingness to travel (Mollet, 2000: 156). The programme has three main sets of learning objectives: individual self-awareness; managerial skills; and global and intercultural awareness. The latter contains the following detailed objectives:

- 'To understand and manage globalization issues affecting our business,
- To gain first hand experience of intercultural perspectives,

- To broaden business and managerial competence in an international climate,
- To offer interfunctional, intercompany and intercultural development opportunities,
- To develop the ability to transfer successful ideas from one culture to another.'

The programme consists of three modules spread over nine months. However, its core consists of strategic projects on which the participants work throughout the programme prior to presenting their recommendations to senior managers, including board members, in the final module. Each year 30 participants are selected for the programme and six project sponsors present projects to them. Participants are then allocated to project groups that are multicultural, multi-functional and multi-company. Recent projects have included:

- How to identify sources of local supply for a potential new factory in India
- How to improve delivery times to customers in North America
- How to change the image of Skoda
- Alternative channels for second-hand cars

Participants attend the three modules and work in project teams between the modules. Each participant is expected to spend up to 40 days above and beyond the modules on project group work. Given that a typical group will contain managers from Germany, the US, South America, Spain and possibly Japan, one can easily see that the group has to deal with large cultural differences, both when together as a group and when working apart.

While the participants report a wide variety of learning from the GJEP experience, the cultural learning always comes at the top of most participants' lists. Many remark that although they had worked with people from other cultures before, they had never worked so intensively and in such stressful situations in multicultural groups. Many report that when things got tough in their group due to task-related problems, the cultural differences surfaced and had to be addressed. This is invaluable learning for future senior managers in a company that seeks to be a global manufacturer.

IS CULTURE REAL OR IS IT AN EXCUSE?

Of course, not all behaviour is influenced by national culture and even those behaviours that are influenced by it are not necessarily determined by it. Thus culture is one, and only one, of the influences on managerial behaviour. One could therefore argue that cultural differences can be overplayed and that other factors such as personality, corporate culture or economics are more important influences. National cultural differences can easily be used as an excuse for lack of commercial progress. However, our position is that cultural differences are real and that culture plays an important, and often unacknowledged, part in organizational processes and managerial behaviour. Consider the following true, but disguised, vignette.

The Cross-Cultural Team

Harry Ford received the researchers' report in silence. When they finished he thanked them for their efforts and suggested a couple of minutes' 'thinking time' to review their findings.

He reflected on the events of the last two months. It had begun with a request from the project's joint managers for an informal meeting to 'talk through some difficulties'. The two joint managers of the project worked well together and had cooperated to produce a joint statement of the difficulties. Their list of problems seemed substantial:

- We are behind schedule and it seems to be getting worse.
- The Germans are not really committed to the project. They consistently refuse to work after 5 pm while the Americans are still slogging away.

- The Americans are undisciplined, they just won't follow the procedures.
- The appraisal system with its mutually agreed goal setting is bound to produce unfairness. Team members who set their own goals are bound to opt for easy targets.
- It's not right to ignore seniority in calculating merit payments.
- Turnover of the German staff is higher than we expected and the constant influx of new members causes continual problems.

The joint venture to develop a new generation of diagnostic systems had involved teams of researchers working collaboratively in laboratories in the US and Germany. The suggestion to bring a number of German researchers to the US to form a large joint US–German research team had seemed a natural development.

Ford had been aware at the time of the possible difficulties arising from differences in national culture, but had felt reassured by the knowledge that the joint venture was going well. He knew that he had also believed that those who opted to work on the joint project would be among the more adaptable and flexible members of both teams and that they would be able to resolve any difficulties that arose.

The joint managers of the project had been convinced that national differences were at the root of the current problems. Ford was inclined to agree with them, but was worried about jumping to conclusions. Consequently he had insisted on commissioning some research to see whether there were any real differences.

The researchers' data suggested that there were real and significant differences. They had begun by quoting some early research on cultural differences by Hofstede. His research indicated the values given in Table 3.1 for the two countries in this case and over the 40 countries included in his survey.

Table 3.1 Cultural differences

	Power distance	Uncertainty avoidance	Individualism	Masculinity
Germany (FR)	35	65	67	66
USA	40	46	91	62
Mean	52	64	50	50
Standard deviation	20	24	25	20
Range (high–low)	(94–11)	(112–8)	(91–12)	(95–5)

In addition, the researchers conducted some interviews with members of the joint research teams, with the results shown in Table 3.2.

Table 3.2 Percentages of American and German project team members who agree with statements

	US (N = 93)	GER (N = 89)	P* less than
1. In an organization everyone should know clearly who has authority over whom	35	54	0.01
2. In order to maintain authority, it is important for a manager to keep a certain distance from subordinates	20	45	0.01
3. In order to have efficient work relationships, it is often necessary to bypass the hierarchical line	28	38	n.s.
4. It is important for a manager to have precise answers to questions	16	38	0.01
5. An organizational structure where you have two bosses should be avoided	36	56	0.01
6. It is desirable to question managerial authority	87	68	0.01
7. Merit should be the primary determinant of a person's pay rise	78	49	0.01

8. Decisions in projects are best made in groups	46	38	n.s.
9. Project members should be encouraged to take risks	78	54	0.01

Note: P★ estimated on the basis of Z scores.

The researchers concluded their presentation by drawing attention to the similarities between American and German societies, which were greater than between many other pairs of countries, and to the tensions, which are greater in project teams than in other forms of organizations.

Ford drew himself up. 'There are three questions,' he concluded. 'What is the root cause of the problems? What can we do to improve the current situation? What could we do in the future to minimize such difficulties?'

We would argue that the root cause of the problems was cultural and that the solution required a greater level of cultural understanding and cultural competence from both sets of managers.

CONCLUSION: CONVERGENCE OR DIVERGENCE?

It is our belief that culture is an important, but certainly not the only, variable determining managerial behaviour. It has to be acknowledged that much empirical work demonstrating the link between cultural values and specific organization/management practices is weak or absent. However, detailed, careful and cautious analysis of cultural value systems does allow for reasonable and plausible inferences to be drawn that give important insights into differences in organization, management and organizational behaviour. Nevertheless, there is a need to move beyond crass generalizations about the relationship between extremely broad cultural depictions and management practice and behaviour. Where possible, detailed empirical work is required, of an indigenized nature, that carefully examines the actual practice of organization and management in the region and explicitly links that to cultural values, while taking account of the possible determining effects of other factors.

This leaves open the question of the dynamics of change and the specific issue of whether, under the forces of internationalization, globalization and cultural homogenization, the differences currently apparent in organizing and managing throughout the world will be eroded and some sort of convergence take place, or whether there are factors at play that will sustain difference and divergence. This is an exceedingly complex issue and unfortunately a thorough examination is precluded by the space limits of this chapter. In broad terms we tend to agree with an earlier analysis suggesting that trends in both directions can be discerned (Webber, 1969). Interdependence and interpenetration are obviously increasing in the business world as levels of international trade and foreign investment levels continue to escalate. This fosters a trend towards convergence as accommodation and familiarization take place. Then there is the presence of forces of cultural homogenization such as global mass consumerism, standardization of products, global mass media and telecommunications, and the commodification of culture itself. A particularly pertinent force for convergence with respect to business and management is the management education and training 'industry'. It needs to be acknowledged that the US occupies a dominant position in terms of management theory, research and pedagogy. It has also been eminently successful in the promotion and promulgation of its perspective on a worldwide basis. The US has an approach to business/management that is perceived to be successful and is an object of desire and emulation for many in the rest of the world. These are highly significant forces for the convergence of management practice and there is some suggestion that the business world actually constitutes its own subculture, which may override national cultural differences and generate a shared managerial ethos that is international and pan-cultural in nature.

On the other hand, culture itself is a source of sustained difference. Despite the impact of the forces described above, cultures are robust and do not change easily. Core aspects of culture are entrenched in socialization processes within societies and in this way culture penetrates deep into a person's psyche, forming a taken-for-granted bedrock of assumptions and values that are not altered easily by surface changes. Furthermore, culture has become a component of political and ideological discourse. For example, there has been a resurgence of cultural pride in East Asia and elites are responsible for promoting that and generating notions of distinctiveness, identity and nationalism. It is these rhetorics and sentiments that have partly contributed to the search for, and declaration of, Asian, Chinese or Confucian management. There is some sense of resistance to the cultural hegemony of the West and a desire to see the promotion of distinctive Asian ways, including in the business and management area. Finally, beyond the cultural level, the institutional frameworks for business and management in many parts of the world remain different – both from one another and with respect to the West. These variable and distinctive institutional frameworks are alone sufficient to sustain some important differences in business and management practice.

These forces are all in dynamic motion and will continue to play out in the future; it is extremely difficult to predict where they will lead. For the moment, however, there *are* substantial and important differences in culture, management and organization around the world. These pose certain difficulties for international business transactions and cross-cultural management. It is very important that these differences are properly apprehended so as to facilitate such exchanges and interchanges.

Note

A number of the vignettes included in this chapter were originally developed from research papers and written up as class exercises. Over time they have been rewritten by the lead author to improve their use as teaching aids to such an extent that the true authorship remains unclear.

References

Adler, N. J. (1984) 'Understanding the ways of understanding: cross-cultural management methodology reviewed', in Farmer, R. N. (ed.), *Advances in International Comparative Management*, Greenwich, CT: JAI.

Adler, N. J. (1991) *International Dimensions of Organizational Behaviour*, Boston, MA: PWS Kent.

Barham, K. and Oates, D. (1991) *The International Manager*, London: Business Books.

Barham, K. and Wills, S. (1992) *Management Across Frontiers*, Berkhamsted: Ashridge Management Research Group and Foundation for Management Education.

Barham, K. and Berthoin Antal, A. (1994) 'Competencies for the pan-European manager', in Kirkbride, P. S. (ed.), *Human Resource Management in Europe: Perspectives for the 1990s*, London: Routledge, pp. 222–41.

Bartlett, C. A. and Ghoshal, S. (1989) *Managing Across Borders: The Transnational Solution*, London: Hutchinson Business Books.

Bartlett, C. A. and Ghoshal, S. (1992) 'What is a global manager?', *Harvard Business Review*, Sept–Oct: 124–32.

Benedict, R. (1989) *The Chrysanthemum and the Sword: Patterns of Japanese Culture*, London: Mariner Books.

Berry, J. W. (1990) 'Imposed etics, emics, and derived etics: their conceptual and operational status in cross-cultural psychology', in Headland, T. N., Pike M. and Harris, M. (eds), *Emics and Etics: The Insider/Outsider Debate*, London: Sage.

Chinese Culture Connection, The (1987) 'Chinese values and the search for culture-free dimensions of culture', *Journal of Cross-Cultural Psychology*, 15: 417–33.

Evans, G. (1993) 'Introduction: Asia and the anthropological imagination', in Evans, G. (ed.), *Asia's Cultural Mosaic: An Anthropological Introduction*, New York: Prentice-Hall, pp. 1–29.

Farmer, R. N. and Richman, B. M. (1965) *Comparative Management and Economic Progress*, Homewood, IL: Irwin.

Hall, E. T. (1976) *Beyond Culture*, New York: Anchor Press.

Harbison, F. and Myers, C. A. (1959) *Management in the Industrial World*, New York: McGraw-Hill.

Hofstede, G. (1980) *Culture's Consequences: International Differences in Work Related Values*, London: Sage.

Hofstede, G. (1984) *Culture's Consequences: International Differences in Work Related Values*, abridged edn, London: Sage.

Hofstede, G. (1991) *Cultures and Organisations: Intercultural Cooperation and its Importance for Survival*, London: McGraw-Hill.

Hofstede, G. (1994) *Cultures and Organisations: Intercultural Cooperation and its Importance for Survival*, 2nd edn, London: HarperCollins.

Hofstede, G. and Bond, M. H. (1988) 'The Confucius connection: from cultural roots to economic growth', *Organisational Dynamics*, 17: 4–21.

Kelley, L., Whatley, A. and Worthley, R. (1987) 'Assessing the effects of culture on managerial attitudes: a three-culture test', *Journal of International Business Studies*, 19(2): 17–31.

Kirkbride, P. S., Pinnington, P. and Ward, K. (2001) 'The state of globalization today', in Kirkbride, P. S. (ed.), *Globalization: The External Pressures*, Chichester: John Wiley.

Kluckhohn, C. (1951) *Toward a General Theory of Action*, Cambridge, MA: Harvard University Press.

Kluckhohn, F. and Strodtbeck, F. L. (1961) *Variations in Value Orientations*, Evanston, IL: Row, Peterson & Co.

Kroeber, A. L. and Parsons, T. (1958) 'The concept of culture and social systems', *American Sociological Review*, 23: 583–94.

Mollet, G. (2000) 'Volkswagen: action learning and the development of high potentials', in Boshyk, Y. (ed.), *Business Driven Action Learning: Global Best Practices*, London: Macmillan.

Ouchi, W. (1981) *Theory Z: How American Business Can Meet the Japanese Challenge*, Reading, MA: Addison-Wesley.

Pascale, R. T. and Athos, A. G. (1981) *The Art of Japanese Management*, New York: Simon and Schuster.

Peng, T. K., Peterson, M. F. and Shyi, Y. P. (1991) 'Quantitative methods in cross-national management research: trends and equivalence issues', *Journal of Organisational Behaviour*, 12: 87–107.

Punnett, B. J. and Shenkar, O. (1996) *Handbook for International Management Research*, Cambridge, MA: Blackwell.

Rokeach, M. R. (1973) *The Nature of Human Values*, New York: Free Press.

Schein, E. H. (1985) *Organizational Culture and Leadership*, San Francisco, CA: Jossey Bass.

Trompenaars, F. (1993) *Riding the Waves of Culture: Understanding Cultural Diversity in Business*, London: Nicholas Brealey.

Webber, R. A. (1969) 'Convergence of divergence?', *Columbia Journal of World Business*, 4(3): 75–83.

Westwood, R. I. (1997) 'Harmony and patriarchy: the cultural basis for "headship" in East Asia', *Organisation Studies*, 18(3): 445–80.

ORGANIZATIONAL CHANGE IN THE GLOBAL COMPANY: IS IT ANY DIFFERENT?

Paul Kirkbride

CHAPTER 4

ORGANIZATIONAL CHANGE IN THE GLOBAL COMPANY: IS IT ANY DIFFERENT?

*B*ob Dylan's song the 'Times they are a'changing' is often regarded as an icon of the revolutionary 1960s and probably sums up the *Zeitgeist* of the times. And certainly the decades since that song was written have witnessed an explosion of books and articles on organizational and managerial change. Change has replaced stability as the new managerial orthodoxy. Books with titles such as *Managing at the Speed of Change* (Conner, 1993), *The Change Masters* (Kanter, 1984), *The Challenge of Organizational Change* (Kanter, Stein and Jick, 1992), *Liberation Management* (Peters, 1992), *The Dance of Change* (Senge *et al.*, 1999) and *Leaning into the Future* (Williams and Binney, 1997) are now legion. Together they have established what may be termed the 'authorized version' of change. This is a commonly accepted set of precepts that are encapsulated in most of the managerial change literature and are now widely articulated by managers worldwide.

What are the central precepts of this canon? It is generally argued that organizations exist in environments that are becoming increasingly turbulent over time and that sector after sector is facing faster change and greater environmental discontinuities. As a result organizations have to manage at, or just faster than, the rate of change of their external environment or they will not survive. However, change is often difficult due to the various resistance forces that are present within most organizations. Nevertheless, if change is managed well and skilfully, organizations can, and do, change successfully. And where this occurs change is most often the result of the presence of 'change leaders' within the organization, often at a very senior level.

Yet very little has been written explicitly about the issues of change in global organizations or about the possible effects of globalization itself on the process of organizational change. This chapter will seek to remedy that deficiency. I will seek to argue that being global raises some *a priori* problems for the change process in large organizations that have often been neglected in the rush to globalize. In what follows we will focus explicitly on the global aspects of change as opposed to the local aspects. In other words, what is in question is the extent to which large organizations can change on a global scale, rather than whether a global organization can change in one part of its global operations or simply in a locality (i.e. country). The issues involved can perhaps be best explained by reference to Figure 4.1.

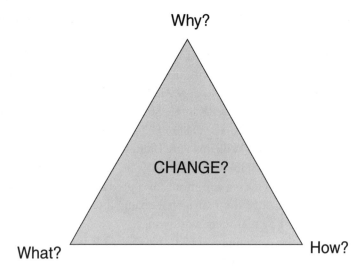

Figure 4.1 A model of global organizational change.

In any organizational change there are three core elements that need to be considered and these can be expressed as the 'why', 'what' and 'how' of change.

- *Why is/was the change necessary?* Why is the change happening? And why should people within the organization change? Here we are obviously referring to issues such as the rationale for change and the forces causing the change to be necessary.
- *What is the nature of the change itself?* Changes are always solutions to problems, but to what extent are solutions culturally transferable around the globe to all parts of a multinational organization?
- *How is the change (solution) to be implemented and achieved?* Any change process involves both task and process elements. The task is the change itself and the process is the method by which it is to be achieved. For example, we recently worked with a multinational that was seeking to implement a 'Six Sigma' quality programme (task − what) by means of a training programme designed in the US, which was to be rolled out worldwide (process − how). The question here is to what extent the change tools and methods generated in one part of the world are applicable and effective in other parts of the world.

Finally, there is the issue of change itself; that is, change as a concept. While change is regarded very positively in the western managerial literature (if not always in organizational populations undergoing change), other parts of the world may see it in a rather different light. Is change a uniform concept or is it culturally dependent?

Another way to look at the potential issues of changing a global organization is to consider the key ways in which such organizations differ from purely domestic or even international organizations. While there are a number of such differences, we would argue that two are particularly salient for organizational change. These are:

- *The problems of size and scale.* Global organizations, or organizations that are trying to be global, are usually distinguished by their relative size. Thus DaimlerChrysler has 416 000 employees worldwide, Siemens has 446 000, Hitachi has 338 000, General

Motors has 313 000, General Electric has 340 000 and Volkswagen has 306 000. While this size and scale of operations offer
many advantages, we would argue that it has its downside in
terms of change efficiency and effectiveness.

■ *The problem of cultural differences.* Global organizations, almost by
definition, operate in a large number of countries around the world
and often employ a heterogeneous mix of different nationalities
within their employee and managerial ranks. As a result, global
organizations need to be particularly cognizant of differences in
cultures, both in terms of the countries in which they operate and
in terms of the cultural mix of their workforces (see Chapter 3).

In this chapter we will seek to discuss and debate some of these issues
and provide answers to some of the questions posed.

THE PROBLEM OF SCALE

Global organizations are, almost by definition, large organizations in,
or rapidly entering, the maturity phase of the organizational lifecycle.
This fact, in and of itself, leads to a question mark as to whether the
global corporation can effectively change on a major scale. However,
such reservations are rarely expressed; on the contrary, the managerial
literature is replete with exhortations to change and advice from consultants on how to do so.

The 'Authorized View' of Change

In the last 25 years there has been a massive explosion in pundits and
consultants arguing that mature global organizations can 'transform'
themselves. Organizational change has become big business and most
of the major consulting firms have established change practices. Books
and articles on change are now prominent and ubiquitous on the
airport bookstall. For the purposes of the argument I wish to develop
here, I propose to take two of the major gurus in this field as exemplars
of what I term the 'authorized view' of change.

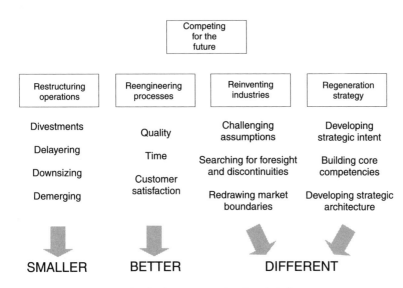

Figure 4.2 Competing for the future (Hamel and Prahalad).

The first is Gary Hamel, who is particularly well known for his book *Competing for the Future* (1994), co-authored with C. K. Prahalad. In this book Hamel and Prahalad argue that in order to 'compete for the future' and survive in the long term, organizations need to do a number of things. First, they need to 'restructure their operations', which often involves downsizing and delayering as well as divesting non-core businesses and demerging if appropriate. However, these actions are not enough in themselves. Indeed, Hamel argues that they often lead to nothing more than 'corporate anorexia', leaving the organization with insufficient resources and capabilities to compete successfully. Second, organizations need to 'reengineer their processes' to make them more efficient, despite the fact that at best this simply means improving up to the industry standard benchmark.

However, these two steps alone are not sufficient. Hamel and Prahalad argue that in order to compete for the future, organizations have to go further and attempt to reinvent both their industries and themselves. Instead of simply becoming 'leaner and meaner' or more efficient, they have to 'transform' themselves and become different in some way. It is the ability of large mature corporations to do precisely this that I want to challenge in this chapter.

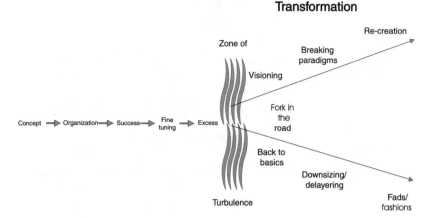

Figure 4.3 Pascale's model of transformation.

In 1994, Richard Pascale produced a series of training videos for the BBC entitled *Transformation*. He argues that large mature corporations over time become more and more in 'fit' with their external environments and thus more and more successful. He sees this process of 'over-adaptation' to a particular environment as one of a drift into what he terms 'excess'. However, Pascale points out that such organizations are often suddenly faced with discontinuities in their environments and thus enter what he terms a 'zone of turbulence'. He suggests that at this point organizations have a choice between two paths forward. They can take the path of 'incremental change', which often comprises a back-to-basics theme coupled with cost cutting and reengineering. Alternatively they can take the path of 'transformation', which involves challenging and breaking organizational paradigms and recreating of a new organization. As Hamel does, Pascale urges organizations to move beyond the merely incremental and to boldly take the transformational route.

The Evidence For and Against Transformation

However, what evidence exists to support these claims that mature and/or large organizations can transform themselves? I have recently challenged groups of managers to quote examples of mature organizations that have successfully completed such a transformation. The lists they produce are quite interesting. On the one hand they cite firms such as Dyson, Virgin Atlantic or Microsoft, which, while they are certainly examples of firms that have revolutionized industries or products, are not really examples of mature organizations transforming themselves. On the other hand, they cite examples such as Bass, which has gradually moved out of its original core business of brewing into hotels and retailing. However, these examples are more illustrative of a 'portfolio' approach to business than examples of transformation of particular business sectors.

The examples cited by both Hamel and Pascale are also interesting and less than convincing. Hamel cites JVS as an example of revolution in a product area (VHS format videotapes), but there is no evidence of transformation in JVS as an organization. He cites Swatch as the leading player in the transformation of the Swiss watch industry, but this change was led more at the national industry level through the Manufacturer's Association than it was at a single organizational level. Finally, he cites EDS as an example of an organization deliberately trying to transform itself before it is forced to by the market, but little evidence is produced to demonstrate the long-term success of this transformation attempt. Pascale cites British Airways in the period from the 1970s to the late 1980s under Lord King and Sir Colin Marshall, although it can be persuasively argued that this was more an example of Hamel's restructuring operations and reengineering processes than true transformation. It succeeded in moving BA up to industry standard benchmarks in terms of winning the Airline of the Year Award, but the later failure of the Bob Ayling years point to the absence of true 'transformation'. Pascale also cites Thomas Cook as an example of an organization that knows it has to transform itself in the face of the decline of a core product (traveller's cheques) as a result of increased use of ATMs and the possibility of a common European currency. However, as with EDS, little evidence of the transformation is presented and the subsequent performance of the business would not tend to support the transformation thesis. Finally, he cites Häagen-Dazs's penetration of the European ice-cream market, which he sees as the transformation of the way European customers perceived and bought ice cream, but which can equally be argued as simply the extension of a new product-positioning recipe to a new marketplace.

If the evidence for 'transformation' is rather patchy, is there any evidence supporting the assertion that mature organizations cannot change? Many studies have shown that market share leaders or the most successful organizations in one time period are replaced by newer competitors in a later time period. For example, Weiss and Pascoe (1983) found that the market share leaders in 1950 were the same in 1975 for only 39 per cent of industry segments studied; a finding shared by Mueller (1986), who found market leadership stability in only 44 per cent of industries during the 1950 to 1975 time period. These findings are commonplace and, indeed, the danger of citing successful exemplars is that they seem to fail so quickly. Many commentators noticed that several years after Peters and Waterman's *In Search of Excellence* (1982) many, if not most, of their so-called excellent companies had fallen from grace. It seems very difficult for mature organizations to survive increasing environmental turbulence in their markets. As Clayton Christensen at Harvard has noted:

> Very few of the mainframe makers succeeded in mini-computers, hardly any mini-computer makers moved successfully into PCs and almost none made it from PCs to laptops. The record of transition is dismal . . . The sources of competitive advantage become handicaps . . . (Abrahams and Heavens, 2000)

Structural Inertia Theory

This evidence should not surprise us, as it was predicted over 20 years ago by population ecology theorists and in particular by structural inertia theory (Hannan and Freeman, 1984). This theory makes a number of key and pertinent assertions.

Fortune favours the rigid

Hannan and Freeman argue that the processes of natural selection within industry niches favour organizations with higher levels of performance (profit, sales, market share, new product development etc.) and higher levels of accountability in terms of providing stakeholder return. In order to achieve such levels of reliability of performance, these organizations have to have highly reproducible structures. In other words, success needs to be more than a one-off and instead needs to be driven by a clear and consistent business recipe. However, this very reproducibility of structure generates strong inertial pressures and resistance to change. Thus success seems to be correlated with inertia. Of course, these propositions merely describe, at one level, the move up the life cycle from birth to growth and then maturity.

The elderly slow down with age

Research has shown that older, mature and larger organizations have more reproducible structures and greater degrees of structural inertia. Thus older organizations find change more difficult.

Old oak trees do not die quickly

Paradoxically, research has also shown that older, mature and larger organizations have lower death rates than newer organizations. Everyone is familiar with the huge failure rates of start-up organizations and among small businesses; a trend we are seeing proven once again in the e-business sector. However, the corollary of that is that when organizations survive into maturity, the chance of their dying reduces markedly. This is particularly true if they are large, global corporations with vast scale and resources.

Be careful in the gym if you are old and fat!

It is well known that organizational change often causes a dip in organizational performance. Indeed, Rosabeth Moss Kanter at Harvard has remarked, 'All changes are failures in the middle'. But this risk is greater for older and larger organizations than it is for smaller, newer ones. Just as older people (among whom I count myself!) are correctly warned against moving from indolence to radical exercise regimes, so older organizations should be careful of radical transformation. Evidence exists suggesting that attempts at reorganization by mature organizations increases death rates (Singh, House and Tucker, 1986) because it produces what Hannan and Freeman have termed the 'liability of newness' (1984: 160).

If you are going to overtake – put your foot down!

Similarly, it is suggested that the death rates of organizations attempting structural change rise with the duration of the transformation. This is because mature organizations require reproducibility of structure and processes to survive and compete and these are reduced by organizational transformations.

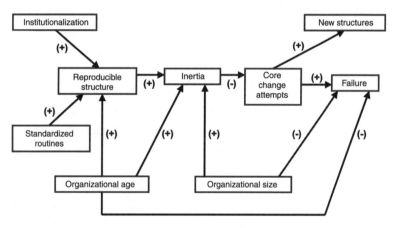

Figure 4.4 Structural inertia theory.
Source: Kelly and Ambugey, 1991: 593

We can sum up the argument propounded by structural inertia theory by reference to Figure 4.4. Standardization of routines and institutionalization of processes produce a reproducible structure, which leads to increased inertia. The rigidity of structure and inertia both increase with age and size. Increased inertia leads to a reduced likelihood of radical organizational transformation and organizations that do attempt such changes are likely to fail. However, if instead such organizations avoided the exhortations and the lure of transformation, they would probably continue to mature and decline slowly over a long period because of the effects of their size and inherent resources.

A final question remains unanswered: what counts as a core organizational change or transformation? Hannan and Freeman are very clear on this point. For them a core organizational change would include one of the following, with the list ranging from most to least core:

- Radical change in the organization's stated goals and purposes.
- Radical change in the organization's forms of authority (such as, for example, a move from coercive to normative control).
- Radical change in the core technology of the organization, including the organizational core competencies required.
- Radical change to the client or customer base of the organization (such as switching from targeting intermediaries to a focus on individual end users).
- Radical changes in how the organization attracts resources from the environment (i.e. marketing strategy).

Thus the argument would be that mature global organizations are both less likely to attempt such transformations and less likely to be successful when trying to implement such transformations. Research evidence exists supporting these propositions. Ferrier, Smith and Grimm (1999) studied market share leaders and found that they 'were more likely to experience market share erosion and/or dethronement when – relative to industry challengers – they are less competitively aggressive, carry out simpler repertoires of action, and carry out competitive actions more slowly'. However, there is little research that focuses on global organizations directly.

Assuming that I have managed to convince you of my argument, what would be the implications of taking structural inertia theory seriously? It could be argued that there are serious implications for global organizations. The essential implication can be understood by contrasting some of the philosophical and political strategies of Mao

Tse-tung. Organizations need to reject the exhortations to adopt a 'Great Leap Forward' by attempting to transform the mature corporation. Attempts at a 'Cultural Revolution', where the existing culture of a mature society or organization is totally changed in a radical fracture with the past, are equally likely to fail. Instead, organizations should adopt Mao Tse-tung's slogan, 'Let 100 flowers bloom, let 100 schools of thought contend'. However, unlike Mao who used this movement inauthentically to flush out dissident intellectuals, organizations should use it as an authentic strategy to prevent the onset of maturity and structural inertia. Thus organizations should seek to break up mature units, or even the organization itself into smaller units, perhaps within a federal structure. Examples might include ABB and 3M. Large, mature organizations should continually question the 'break-up' potential of the whole and the extent to which the 'centre' adds value or causes increased structural inertia. Here there is a link to the 'parenting' role of the centre, which is described in more detail by Alexander (2001).

THE PROBLEM OF CULTURE

In this section we will focus on the effects of national culture on change processes. In doing so we will evaluate the transferability of change approaches; actual changes themselves; change tools and techniques; and the concept of change itself. In order to illustrate these issues I will refer to a number of research projects that I have conducted focusing on the transferability of western approaches to eastern cultures in general, and Chinese cultures in particular.

Can a Single Change Approach Work Across Cultural Boundaries?

Unfortunately, despite the obvious existence of national and other cultural differences, management researchers have tended historically to ignore such differences. This is particularly true of those management researchers who, in the last 25 years, have focused on the creation and dissemination of organizational cultures within large multinationals (Frost *et al.*, 1985; Kilmann, *et al.*, 1985; Schein, 1985). It has been argued that this neglect is not accidental but occurs because 'implicit in the organizational cultural notion as it is widely used is a fundamental set of assumptions, which . . . coincides with American cultural assumptions . . . this coincidence makes the assumptions difficult for Americans to see, if not outright invisible' (Adler and Jelinek, 1986). These assumptions include free will and the ability to create, maintain and change the culture of a large organization. The result of this kind of 'blind spot' is that organizations and their members are often seen in splendid isolation from the culture around them.

To illustrate some of the potential cultural barriers to the transfer of a single change approach, we can take as a case some research I did a number of years ago on the transfer of corporate cultures, and particularly corporate mission statements, across cultures by multinational or global organizations (Kirkbride and Shae, 1987; Westwood and Kirkbride, 1998, 2000). The example involves the transfer of Hewlett-Packard's corporate culture from the US parent to the Hong Kong subsidiary.

Hewlett-Packard (Hong Kong)

Hewlett-Packard (Hong Kong) was, at the time of the research study, a small subsidiary of the large US-based computer multinational. Two engineers, Bill Hewlett and Dave Packard, who produced an audio oscillator in their garage, founded Hewlett-Packard (HP) in 1938 in Palo Alto, California. The company grew steadily for 20 years before growth accelerated and a corporate philosophy emerged. Hewlett-Packard (Hong Kong) was first established in 1979 and was part of the Far East Region of Hewlett Packard. It was purely a sales, marketing and service operation at the time of the research and did not carry out any manufacturing. It grew rapidly from around 46 staff in 1981 to around 200 at the end of the decade. At the time of the research study, HP (Hong Kong) was totally staffed by local Hong Kong

Chinese staff, with the sole exception of one English expatriate who was the CEO. The US parent multinational is well known in the management literature for its distinctive, admired and well-developed corporate culture (Ouchi, 1981; Peters and Waterman, 1982; Peters and Austin, 1985; and Collins and Porras, 1996). The culture is frequently revised and at any time is formally contained in two documents that are widely disseminated throughout the organization and are issued to all employees during orientation programmes.

The first document is a small pamphlet entitled 'Statement of Corporate Objectives', in which the following seven key objectives are distinguished:

- PROFIT – To achieve sufficient profit to finance our company growth and to provide the resources we need to achieve our other corporate objectives.
- CUSTOMERS – To provide products and services of the highest quality and the greatest possible value to our customers, thereby gaining and holding their respect and loyalty.
- FIELDS OF INTEREST – To build on our strengths in the company's traditional fields of interest, and to enter new fields only when it is consistent with the basic purpose of our business and when we can assure ourselves of making a needed and profitable contribution to the field.
- GROWTH – To let our growth be limited only by our profits and our ability to develop and produce innovative products that satisfy real customer needs.
- OUR PEOPLE – To help HP people share in the company's success which they make possible; to provide jobs security based on their performance; to insure them a safe and pleasant work environment; to recognize their individual achievements; and to help them gain a sense of satisfaction and accomplishment from their work.
- MANAGEMENT – To foster initiative and creativity by allowing the individual great freedom of action in attaining well-defined objectives.

- CITIZENSHIP – To honor our obligations to society by being an economic, intellectual and social asset to each nation and each community in which we operate.

The second document is 'The HP Way', which focuses on both business and people-related aspects of the company, and outlines HP's policy on 'Management by Wandering About' (MBWA) and its open door policy. (For a detailed discussion of HP's corporate philosophy, see Ouchi, 1981.)

The question in this case is to what extent this culture, created and developed in the US, was successfully transferred and absorbed by the Hong Kong subsidiary, operating as it does in a very different social and cultural milieu. Hewlett-Packard is not unique among multinationals in seeking to codify its distinctive human resource management style, and then to transfer and operate this culture worldwide. For example, as Angle, Manz and Van De Van (1985) have observed in the case of 3M:

> Even though 3M has dispersed its facilities across most of the world, the culture of 3M has been quite homogeneous throughout the organization. Somehow, the coherence of this culture has been sustained through a practice of frequent moves of key personnel, and, in particular, by establishing a critical mass of cultural role models at new sites during the time that local norms are being established. There is a deep-seated belief among nearly all the 3M executives we interviewed that this culture is robust and fully 'transportable'.

A very similar perspective and strategies appear to be employed by HP. Indeed, the idea is seductive and, if possible, has much merit. As Laurent (1986) has conjectured: 'What if our corporate culture could act as a "supra-culture" and be expected to supersede some of the annoying specificities of the different national cultures in which we operate?'

It is to these annoying cultural specificities that we now turn our attention. In order to examine the potential cultural pitfalls involved in transferring a US organizational culture into Hong Kong, we need a mechanism to compare and contrast the two national cultures. Perhaps the simplest way to do this is to use the fairly standard work of Hofstede

(1980, 1984) on international cultural dimensions (see Chapter 3). Hofstede identified four key cultural dimensions at the national level that have significant effects on organizational life and, by extension, on managerial behaviour. The four dimensions are by now well known, but is may still be useful to restate them here:

- *Power distance*: The extent to which power is distributed unevenly, and/or the degree to which people accept that power should be distributed unequally.
- *Uncertainty avoidance*: The degree to which people experience uneasiness in ambiguous situations, or their degree of toleration for deviant/innovative ideas and behaviours.
- *Individualism*: The extent to which individuals prefer loosely knit frameworks of social relationships in which individuals take care of themselves and their immediate families only. The opposite, 'collectivism', is a preference for a tightly knit social framework in which individuals look after their relatives, clan or other group.
- *Masculinity*: The extent to which aggressiveness, assertiveness and materialism are prevalent in social and organizational life. The opposite, 'femininity', refers to the extent to which preferences for relationships, modesty, caring for the weak and quality of life are prevalent.

Both countries are characterized by a fairly high degree of masculinity and a relatively low degree of uncertainty avoidance, although Hong Kong is significantly lower than the US (see Table 4.1). The main areas of difference are on individualism and power distance. The US has the highest individualism score of all 39 countries in Hofstede's study, while Hong Kong is markedly collectivist. Similarly, Hong Kong is high in terms of power distance while the US is low to moderate on this dimension. Given the origins of 'The HP Way' in American culture, to what extent is it transferable to the rather different cultural characteristics of Hong Kong?

HP advocates consultative and participative management as opposed to more autocratic and centralized styles. HP believes in delegation and decentralization wherever possible. Informality and open-

Table 4.1 Hong Kong and US scores on Hofstede's four cultural dimensions

Dimension	Actual range		Hong Kong	United States
	Low	High		
Power distance	11	94	68	40
Uncertainty avoidance	8	112	29	46
Individualism	12	91	25	91
Masculinity	5	95	57	62

Source: Data from Hofstede, 1984

door communication are praised and encouraged. These values are explicitly stated in 'The HP Way':

- Confidence in, and respect for, our people as opposed to depending upon extensive rules, procedures, etc.
- Depend upon people to do their job right (individual freedom) without constant directives.
- Opportunity for meaningful participation (job dignity).
- Informality – open, honest communications; no artificial distinctions between employees (first name basis); management by wandering around; and open door communications policy.
- Relationships within the company depend upon a spirit of cooperation among individuals and groups, and an attitude of trust and understanding on the part of managers towards their people.

It can easily be seen, *a priori*, that these values are based on low power distance and would potentially face difficulty in a high power distance culture such as Hong Kong.

The HP culture contains aspects of both individualism and collectivism. It can be said to be collectivist to the extent that it attempts to cultivate a sense of belonging and loyalty among their employees. In this sense HP seems to stress a family-oriented style of management. However, at the same time there is also great stress on individualism in terms of behaviour. Themes stressing the importance of team spirit and corporate identity exist side by side with emphasis on individual merit and autonomy at work. Juxtaposing these dual orientations can bring this inherent tension to light more clearly:

Individualism

- To recognize individual achievements.
- The company has been built around the individual, the personal dignity of each and the recognition of personal achievements.
- To allow the individual great freedom of action in attaining well-defined objectives.

Collectivism

- Relationships within the company depend on a spirit of co-operation among individuals and groups.
- Emphasis on working together and sharing rewards (team work and partnership).
- Share responsibilities; help each other; learn from each other.

By highlighting this dual vision and contradiction in the HP culture statements, we are far from suggesting that it is irreconcilable either in theory or in practice. But it does appear to present certain difficulties, not least of which is the problem of reconciling these value orientations with the local 'collectivist' culture.

Table 4.2 HP culture and Hong Kong culture compared

Dimension	Hong Kong	Hewlett-Packard
Power distance	High	Low
Uncertainty avoidance	Low	Low
Individualism	Low	High/low
Masculinity	Medium–high	Medium–high

Thus our analysis suggests, *a priori*, that HP and other American multinationals might face some steep cultural barriers to the transfer of their cultures from the US to countries such as Hong Kong. But what was the reality of the situation on the ground? To investigate this we conducted extensive qualitative research in Hewlett-Packard (Hong Kong). Together with a Chinese co-investigator, we conducted formal and informal interviews with staff at all levels of the organization as well as engaging in informal observation. Our research showed some interesting patterns of behaviour. When interviewed by the western interviewer, most staff demonstrated that they were well aware of the HP culture, even down to being able to quote parts of 'The HP Way'. Most stated that they followed the precepts of the culture and were committed to it.

However, when interviewed in Cantonese by a local Chinese researcher, the staff were more open. Most admitted that they had 'learned' the HP way on orientation and on various HP training courses, including visits to the US. They also spoke about the fact that they had 'officially' to follow certain HR practices that were standardized and laid down in an HP HR manual. These practices, they suggested, were particularly American in orientation. When questioned on whether they actually followed the practices to the letter, most staff admitted that they did not, having adapted them slightly to fit the local culture. We explicitly focused on certain HR practices such as performance appraisal that we knew were done rather differently in the local culture and found that, while staff could articulate the 'formal' procedures, these were not exactly followed in practice. When we questioned staff on why this was the case, we were told one had to understand that elements of the local culture meant that such policies and practices were not workable in Hong Kong. When we asked if this issue had been raised with HR staff in the US, we were given the clear signal that staff felt that this course of action would not be in their own interests.

Thus our clear conclusion was that the transferability of the HP culture was clearly affected by aspects of the local Chinese culture. This is only one illustrative example. Nevertheless, we strongly believe that on many occasions global organizations seek to impose changes on a total and worldwide basis, only for there to be covert resistance and divergence of practice at local levels.

Can Particular Changes Be Equally Applied in All Cultures?

In the last section we looked at attempts by large multinational or global organizations to create overall organizational change by use of organizational culture mechanisms. We saw that such initiatives often flounder on the rocks of local culture values. But surely there are other types of change, which are not cultural in nature, which might have a greater chance of succeeding across the cultural divides of the global organization. The last 25 years have seen a plethora of so-called technical change initiatives, ranging from quality circles, total quality management (TQM) and Six Sigma, to business process reengineering (BPR) and Enterprise Resource Planning (SAP, Oracle, J. D. Edwards). Surely these more technical, and often IT-driven, processes are more culture neutral and therefore have a greater chance of success?

Our answer would be a qualified no, for two reasons. First, because any change involves task factors, organizational factors and people factors as well as technology. And second, because we would argue that all these supposedly neutral processes clearly carry within them 'cultural genes'. That is, they clearly show signs of having been generated in a particular culture and are informed by a particular set of cultural norms and values. This means that they are very likely to be successful in that culture, but as a corollary of that, are less likely to be successful in different cultures. To illustrate this argument I will again refer to some of my previous research work in Hong Kong. This case involves the transfer of quality circles from Japan to Hong Kong.

Quality Circle Transference to Hong Kong

The concept of quality circles (QCs) was first formally and institutionally introduced to Hong Kong in 1981 when the Hong Kong Productivity Council (HKPC) organized a study mission to attend the International Convention on Quality Circles in Tokyo (Hsia, 1987). Delegates from the HKPC mission returned converted to QC philosophy and began a programme of publicity and dissemination, including seminars, training courses and case presentations. At the same time a prominent local personnel manager attended a similar conference in Kuala Lumpur and on his return attempted to promote the concept via articles in the local managerial press and a training course run for the Hong Kong Management Association. As an indirect result of both these initiatives, the Hong Kong Industrial Relations Association organized a Quality Circles Conference in late 1981 that attracted participants from over 60 organizations in Hong Kong.

In 1983 the Hong Kong Quality Circle Association (HK-QCA) was formed and by 1985 began to hold QC conventions. By 1986 a HKPC survey revealed that at least 20 companies had set up QC programmes. The publication of case studies on the use of QCs in Hong Kong (HKPC, 1985) also revealed an interesting phenomenon, with 'early adopters' being either the larger local companies such as HongKong Bank, The Mass Transit Railway Corporation and Shui On Construction or subsidiaries of MNCs such as IBM (HK). By 1987 Hsia, the Chair of the HKQCA, was able to report that 30 companies had implemented QCs and that there were a total of over 400 circles in operation (Hsia, 1987). By 1988 QCs had apparently spread to a total of 50 companies (Hsia, 1989). These included some of the largest and best-known local and foreign companies, such as the Kowloon and Canton Railway Corporation, Hong Kong Soya Bean products, Outboard Marine Asia and Motorola Semiconductor. A major survey of human resource management (HRM) at the end of the decade (Kirkbride and Tang, 1989) noted that 25 per cent of the responding companies reported that they had introduced, or attempted to introduce, QCs during the preceding five years.

Yet despite the increasing incidence of companies trying to implement QCs evidence was emerging by the end of the decade of extremely high failure rates in QC implementation, and rates which were very high by Japanese standards. The HRM survey (Kirkbride and Tang, 1989) noted over 40 per cent failure rates and also that even in companies where QCs had been successfully introduced, they still only applied to the minority of workers. Hsia (1987) also noted the high failure rates and based on extensive research offered the following list of factors that she argued contributed to QC failure in HK:

> - Chinese organizational and managerial styles
> - Short-term Hong Kong business orientations
> - A lack of top management support
> - Low levels of commitment from middle managers and supervisors
> - Employee apathy
> - Low levels of worker education
>
> While most of these are standard factors that could apply to QC failure anywhere in the world, it is interesting to note the key position in the list accorded to factors that could be said to be cultural in nature.

How can we analyse both the quick adoption and relative failure of QCs in Hong Kong? On the one hand the quick adoption can easily be explained. During the 1980s, with the handover of Hong Kong to China scheduled for 1997, there was a swing against copying managerially from the West and a tendency to look to China or Japan for inspiration. To many observers Japan shared a common cultural heritage and therefore it was thought particularly appropriate to adopt practices and processes that originated there. But is Japan culturally similar to Hong Kong? Are Japanese and Chinese cultures similar? Using the work of Hofstede (1984) mentioned earlier, we could compare the two societies on his four cultural dimensions (Table 4.3).

Table 4.3 The contrasting positions of Hong Kong and Japan on Hofstede's dimensions

Value dimension	Hong Kong	Japan	Mean
Power distance	68 (high)	54 (medium)	51
Uncertainty avoidance	29 (low)	92 (high)	64
Individualism	25 (low)	46 (medium)	51
Masculinity	57 (medium)	95 (high)	51

As we can see, there are marked differences between the cultural profiles of Hong Kong and Japan. Hong Kong is higher in terms of power distance, much lower in terms of uncertainty avoidance, more collectivist and lower in masculinity. Let us look at each of these differences in turn and consider the implications for the successful transference of quality circles.

Hong Kong scores very highly on power distance. Hofstede has suggested that power distance cultures share a list of common characteristics that are a result of the high power distance norm (1984: 92, 107). From this list we have abstracted those significant characteristics that would seem to have implications for the operation and successful implementation of QCs. These include:

- Greater centralization of decision making
- Taller organizational pyramids
- Larger proportions of supervisory personnel
- More autocratic managerial styles
- Employees reluctant to trust each other
- Employees afraid to disagree with their boss

These characteristics very accurately describe organizational realities in Hong Kong. They mirror similar lists of characteristics produced by authorities on Hong Kong, including Redding (1984), Lau (1982) and Kirkbride and Westwood (1993).

We can suggest that in high power distance cultures, senior management will be naturally reluctant to dilute their perceived authority and managerial prerogative by the adoption of participative methods such as QCs. The highly autocratic and paternalistic styles found in many of the medium to small Hong Kong companies would not easily assimilate the degree of participation and openness required to operate QCs successfully. As a result, we would expect to find greater QC penetration among foreign-owned firms and less among the smaller indigenous Chinese family firms, where top management support would not be generally forthcoming. Similarly, in high power distance contexts, employees are less likely to want to be in a position that may be seen (especially in oriental cultures) as one of implied criticism of company management. Equally, the existence of a 'low trust' Chinese culture (in relation to others outside the family) would tend to make the operation of QCs difficult. Finally, the more hierarchical nature of organizations raises the issue of the role of supervisory management, who may feel threatened by the introduction of participatory mechanisms such as QCs.

Hong Kong and Japan are at opposite ends of the uncertainty avoidance continuum, with Hong Kong having the fourth lowest score and Japan the fourth highest. Again, it is possible to abstract from Hofstede characteristics of low uncertainty avoidance cultures that might affect the operation of QCs (1984: 132–3, 140–43). These are:

- Low employee loyalty to employers
- High labour turnover
- Lower job satisfaction

These characteristics are confirmed by empirical research in Hong Kong that has pointed to high turnover rates (HKIPM, 1990) and lower levels of job satisfaction (Bond and Hwang, 1986). Here the implications for QCs are fairly clear. QCs are less likely to operate successfully in situations of high labour turnover and revolving membership, and the combination of lower intrinsic satisfaction, higher extrinsic motivation and low employee loyalty mitigates against the enthusiastic acceptance of QCs, especially in the smaller Chinese family firm.

Hong Kong and Japan are both commonly regarded as 'collectivist' countries, although it is possible to argue that the collectivism takes a rather different form in each country. In Japan, the key collectivity is usually work based, with high levels of organizational allegiance. In contrast, Hong Kong collectivism is usually family based. Indeed, one expert commentator has summed up the cultural ethos of Hong Kong by the term 'utilitarian familism' (Lau, 1982). The central facets of this orientation are:

- A family-based collectivism where family interests are placed above those of society and other groups within it
- A materialist orientation whereby material interests take precedence over non-material ones

It has been argued that this cultural orientation is a major determinant of high levels of political apathy in Hong Kong (Lau, 1982) and we can equally suggest that such norms will contribute to a workplace-based apathy and antipathy to participative mechanisms such as QCs, especially if no pecuniary advantage is involved.

Finally, Japan is more masculine than Hong Kong and is actually the most masculine country in Hofstede's study. Key characteristics of masculinity (1984: 200–1, 205–6) include:

- A focus on recognition and challenge as motivators
- High work centrality
- The acceptance of company interference in private life
- A preference for larger organizations
- A 'live to work' attitude

Given this list of orientations, it is perhaps not difficult to see how and why the Japanese were able to take simple statistical quality control ideas from the US and develop them into a distinctive total quality control philosophy and the associated methodology of QCs. Hong Kong, in contrast, would tend to have more people who preferred smaller organizations and were less likely to accept company inter-ference in their private lives and non-essential demands on their time. It has already been noted that Hong Kong has a greater extrinsic orientation than intrinsic and a higher family centrality than work centrality. The implication of these materialist and familial orientations is that Hong Kong people generally work to live and do not live to work.

These differences in culture go some way to explaining the rela-tive lack of success of QCs in Hong Kong. As such, it is a good illustration of a more general problem. It points clearly to the fact that even supposedly 'technical' changes have cultural components to them. It also points to the fact that such changes are not neutral but, instead, are often rooted in some specific cultural context. As we have seen, the whole TQM and QC movement grew from a specific set of Japanese cultural norms. It suggests that some cultures may be naturally unre-ceptive to certain changes. Thus although many leading practitioners wished for QC success in Hong Kong and wanted desperately to improve quality levels in both the manufacturing and service sectors, they faced a distinctive cultural barrier to implementation.

So what are the implications of this analysis for global organizations? We would argue that there are four clear implications:

- The change agents should examine the 'change' (e.g. QCs) in detail and try to ascertain the key cultural 'drivers' that have informed or produced the particular managerial process or practice. In doing so, particular attention should be paid to the culture of the country where the practice originated ('sender culture').

- The change agents should then analyse the country or countries where it is intended that the 'change' be implemented. In particular, attention should be paid to the cultural make-up of the 'target culture'.

- The 'sender' and 'target' cultures should be examined and potential cultural resistance points identified. The change agents should try, if possible, to modify the 'change' in the light of these potential barriers to see if the 'change' could be made to work in the 'target culture'.

- Finally, if this is not possible, the change agents should try to work out, *a priori*, how the particular 'problem' to which the change is a 'solution' could be resolved in a manner that would be culturally compatible as opposed to culturally inappropriate. For example, it was important during the 1980s and 1990s for Hong Kong to try to resolve the 'problem' of low quality. However, it soon became apparent that the selected 'solution', QCs, had some cultural limitations. The challenge for practitioners in Hong Kong was then to invent a better solution to the quality problem. Interestingly, some organizations managed to do just that. The Mass Transit Railway Corporation, despite being largely led by western expatriates at that stage, cleverly used an understanding of local cultural norms to introduce successfully a form of QCs (Work Improvement Teams) (Kirkbride and Tang, 1993). What was interesting about this example was that significant changes were made to both the technique and its presentation and implementation to take account of local cultural values. Another good example was in the service sector, where Giordano, a local clothing retailer, massively improved its

service levels in stores using a quality improvement process designed and implemented by local Chinese consultants who were
cognizant of and sympathetic to local cultural norms.

Are Change Tools and Techniques Transferable Across the World?

So far in this chapter we have seen that it may be easier said than done for
global companies to attempt to create global cultures. We have also seen
that certain 'changes' such as QCs may be culturally rooted and therefore
difficult to transfer to other cultures. But is all change culture specific?
Do cultural barriers limit the whole change process? Are the change tools
and techniques commonly used by western global corporations equally
effective around the world? To answer these questions we can return to
Hofstede's cultural dimensions and analyse how cultures at the poles of
each dimension would tend to handle change (see Table 4.4). In doing
so we are producing a stereotypical view of each dimension, but, nevertheless, one that contains useful hints for potential problem areas.

Table 4.4   The effects of Hofstede's cultural dimensions on change

High power distance	**Low power distance**
■ Top down	■ Bottom-up
■ Autocratic	■ Participative
High uncertainty avoidance	**Low uncertainty avoidance**
■ Change resistant	■ Experimental
■ Incremental	■ Flexible
■ Structured	■ Unstructured
Individualist	**Collectivist**
■ Individual accountability	■ Team accountability
■ The cult of the leader	■ Decisions by consensus
■ Radical	■ Incremental
■ 'Winners and losers'	■ Harmonious
Masculinity (tough minded)	**Feminine (tender minded)**
■ Task focused	■ Process focused
■ Goal focused	■ Social outcome focused
■ Efficiency focused	■ Consideration for casualties

In high power distance cultures, change would tend to be the prerogative of top management and to be managed in a very top-down and autocratic manner. In low power distance cultures, a range of views will often be taken into account through participative mechanisms. High uncertainty avoidance cultures do not like risk and would therefore tend to shy away from change and be relatively change resistant. When change becomes inevitable they would approach it in an incremental way to minimize risk and their uncertainty avoidance needs would lead to change being very structured. In contrast, low uncertainty avoidance cultures would be less fearful of change and, as a result, would tend to be more willing to experiment and to try different options in a relatively unstructured manner. Individualist cultures, with their ego-driven personal focus, would tend to stress the individual accountabilities for change and would revere 'macho' change leaders. As a result, change would tend to be more radical and characterized by winners and losers. In contrast, collectivist cultures would stress team accountabilities and focus on establishing a consensus around the change. As a result of the compromises necessary for consensus, the changes implemented may well be less radical and more incremental than under an individualistic culture. Finally, masculine (tough-minded) cultures would tend to be more task, goal and efficiency focused, whereas feminine (tender-minded) cultures would tend to be more process oriented and to have a greater consideration for the casualties of any change process and for social outcomes.

Of course, in the real world cultures are not simple positions on the extremes of these scales, but are the complex interactions of positions on all four (and other) dimensions. If we look at 'western' and particularly American culture, we can see from Hofstede's data (see Chapter 3) that it is characterized by extreme individualism, relatively low power distance and a tendency towards the masculine. Thus it is no surprise that organizational change in the West has in recent years been characterized by the cult of the 'change leader' and a focus on radical transformations, as noted earlier in this chapter. Yet multinationals are often trying to effect the change in subsidiaries located in cultures that may be high in power distance and collectivist. These cultures would naturally tend to handle change in a completely opposite manner. They would tend to launch the change fairly auto-cratically, but then involve all staff in an attempt to build consensus and roll out any change in a relatively incremental and harmonious manner. Or consider the American multinational trying to manage change in Scandinavia, with its much higher femininity score. The US parent, with its more macho inclinations, would tend to provoke some resist-ance from the Scandinavians, with their much more involving styles and greater attention to both people and social outcomes.

IS 'CHANGE' A UNIVERSAL TRUTH?

Finally, we can question whether the concept of 'change' itself is regarded in the same way around the world. Given that many of the world's global corporations are rooted in Anglo-Saxon (American, Australian, British, Canadian) or European (Dutch, French, German) culture, it is not surprising that many of these large organizations share a common perception of 'change' and the change process. Change, for most global organizations, is a taken-for-granted concept that can only be made explicit by surfacing sets of deeply hidden assumptions. However, many of these organizations make the natural, but often fatal, mistake of assuming that their subsidiary organizations and local managers around the world share these views. But do they?

Part of the difficulty in answering this question lies in the deeply seated nature of some of these assumptions. Ask managers around the world about organizational change and you tend to get regurgitated rhet-oric from popular managerial textbooks such as those mentioned at the start of this chapter. And most of these books are of Anglo-Saxon, par-ticularly American, origin. Thus managers around the world are slowly and gradually inculcated into a largely Anglo-Saxon view of change, which they then verbalize when the topic is raised. However, under the surface often lurks a rather different, though often unarticulated view.

For the last ten years I have been attempting to research this phenomenon and get to grips with some of the deeper views of the change process. In order to do so, I have made use of the methodology of drawing pictures. Managers on training programmes are asked to draw a picture, diagram or symbol to illustrate what 'change' means to them. To date my associates and I have collected over 1000 pictures from managers originating in countries such as China, Germany, Hong Kong, Netherlands, the UK and the US. We have analysed the various types of picture or diagram that tend to be drawn by managers from different cultures. Although this research is still not complete, the early results show some interesting differences across cultures.

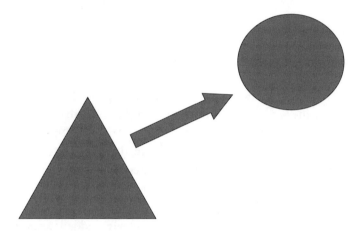

Figure 4.5   A 'state' model of change.

By far the most common picture drawn by managers around the world is what may be termed the 'state' model of change (see Figure 4.5). This is drawn by around 70 per cent of all western managers. Change is seen as a move from one 'state' to another. This is quite a static model of change, as it sees it as a move from one situation of stasis to another via a period of change that is unusual in some regard. Thus stasis is normal and change 'punctuates' the normal equilibrium. This is what has been termed 'punctuated equilibrium' theory (Tushman and Romanelli, 1985; Tushman, Newman and Romanelli, 1986). The pictures are also interesting in that they usually draw the move from one state to another as a move from a 'lower' (bottom left) state to a 'higher' or 'better' state (upper right). Thus 'progress' and positive transformations are obviously implicit in these state models.

The origins of the model are quite interesting. The pictures that managers draw are obviously related to Lewin's (1951) model of change. This has been widely used in managerial texts and is probably the most commonly understood model of change with managers. Lewin suggested that in order to make a change you first need to 'unfreeze' the organization, after which you can make the 'change', and then you need to 'refreeze' the organization again into the new equilibrium position. Most commentators would argue that this is a rather outdated view of organizational change in an increasingly turbulent environment. Yet the model is actually much older than Lewin's exposition. In drawing on systems theory for his underlying framework, Lewin simply reflected an existing view of change that can be traced back to Newtonian classical mechanics. Newton talked of billiard balls at rest and that in order to make them move a 'force' had to be applied that could overcome the natural inertia and resistance (through friction) of the inertial or equilibrium position. After the force was removed, the object would come to rest and revert to an inertial position. That this metaphor is still informing managers' internal views of change after 300 years is quite remarkable and yet disappointing, in that it is increasingly an inappropriate metaphor for organizational change in the modern world. What is interesting is that this relatively static view exists deeply within managers despite the continuous change rhetoric of both organizational pronouncements and managerial texts.

Have managers internalized these notions of continuous change at all? In western cultures we have found very little evidence of this. Yet when we look at the pictures drawn by our Chinese and Japanese subjects, we find a much greater incidence of examples of continuous change (see Figures 4.6–4.8).

Indeed, it is possible to argue that western and eastern conceptions of change are radically different. Change in the West tends to be seen as:

- Linear
- Progressive
- Destination oriented
- Based on the creation of disequilibrium to reach a later equilibrium

- Planned and managed by people outside the system being changed
- Unusual

In contrast, change in eastern cultures tends to be seen as:

- Cyclical
- Processual
- Journey oriented
- Based on the maintenance or restoration of harmony and equilibrium
- Observed and followed by people who are within the system experiencing change
- Natural

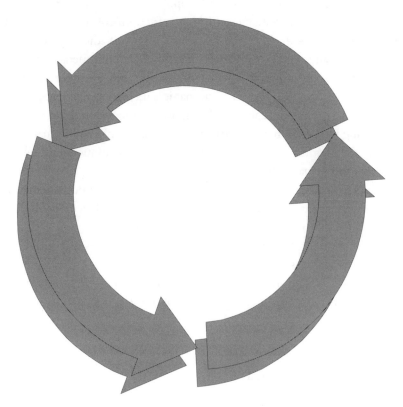

Figure 4.6 A circular model of change.

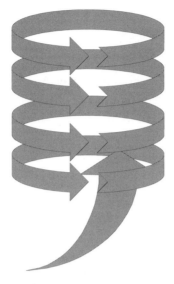

Figure 4.7   A spiral model of change.

Figure 4.8   A yin and yang model of change.

These views of the circular and dynamic nature of change are deeply rooted in Chinese culture. For example, Chou Tun-I, the Sung philosopher, argues:

> Great Ultimate through movement generates yang. When its activity reaches its limits, it becomes tranquil. Through tranquillity the Great Ultimate generates

yin. When tranquillity reaches its limits, activity begins again. So movement and tranquillity alternate and become the root of each other, giving rise to the distinction of yin and yang.

Thus, while our research does not cover Africa or Arab countries, we are clear that people's conceptions of change are not uniform around the world, but are instead influenced by culture, religion, philosophy and history. The implication for western multinationals is clear. Do not expect everyone in your organization worldwide to accept or agree with your view of change as a positive and beneficial 'transformational' leap to a brighter future vision.

CONCLUSION

Our analysis has hopefully raised some of the *a priori* problems that organizational change poses for organizations that seek to be multi-national, global or transnational. One of the biggest problems must be that of scale. Such organizations have to co-ordinate changes on a global scale across time zones, national boundaries and company divisions. In doing so, they are hampered by a myriad of communication and co-ordination problems. In addition to these simple barriers, such organizations face the additional problem that their own maturity may ensure that they are unable to transform themselves and thus unable to avoid inevitable decline.

The other major problem, as we have seen in Chapter 3, is that of cultural difference. This places severe limits on the extent to which such organizations can manage change in a uniform way around the world. Cultural differences also affect the 'what' and 'how' of change. That is, they affect the extent to which 'changes' are transferable around the world and they affect the extent to which change tools and methodologies are universally applicable.

So what should large multinationals or global companies do when faced with the need to change? On the basis of our argument here, they should seek to avoid radical transformations, restricting themselves to more incremental processes. They should also critically examine each potential organizational change prior to implementation and ask a number of key questions:

- Is this particular change (e.g. BPR, Six Sigma, customer focus etc.) a culturally appropriate solution for all the cultures where it might be applied?
- Are the methods we are planning to use to implement the change acceptable and transferable to all the cultures where they will be used?
- Is 'change' seen in the same way in all the parts of your 'global' organization?

With greater care paid to the cultural ramifications, such organizations should be able to improve their overall success rate for organizational change.

References

Abrahams, P. and Heavens, A. (2000) 'Speeding to halt', *Financial Times*, 1st December, 22.

Adler, N. J. and Jelinek, M. (1986) 'Is "organizational culture" culture bound?', *Human Resource Management*, 25(1): 73–90.

Alexander, M. (2001) 'Global parenting', in Kirkbride, P. S. (ed.), *Globalization: The External Pressures*, Chichester: John Wiley.

Angle, H. L., Manz, C. C. and Van De Ven, A. H. (1985) 'Integrating human resource management and corporate strategy: a preview of the 3M story', *Human Resource Management*, 24(1): 51–68.

Bond, M. H. and Hwang, K. K. (1986) 'The social psychology of Chinese people', in Bond, M. H. (ed.), *The Psychology of Chinese People*, Hong Kong: Oxford University Press.

Collins, J. C. and Porras, J. I. (1996) *Built to Last: Successful Habits of Visionary Companies*, London: Century.

Conner, D. (1993) *Managing at the Speed of Change: How Resilient Managers Succeed and Prosper Where Others Fail*, New York: Villard Books.

Ferrier, W. J., Smith, K. G. and Grimm, C. M. (1999) 'The role of competitive action in market share erosion and industry dethronement: a study of industry leaders and challengers', *Academy of Management Journal*, 42(4): 372–88.

Frost, P. J., Moore, L. F., Louis, M. R., Lundberg, C. C. and Martin, J. (1985) *Organizational Culture*, Beverly Hills, CA: Sage.

Hamel, G. and Prahalad, C. K. (1994) *Competing for the Future*, Boston, MA: Harvard Business School Press (and associated video).

Hannan, M. T. and Freeman, J. (1984) 'Structural inertia and organizational change', *American Sociological Review*, 49:149–64.

Hofstede, G. (1980) 'Do American theories apply abroad?', *Organizational Dynamics*, Summer: 63–7.

Hofstede, G. (1984) *Culture's Consequences*, Beverly Hills, CA: Sage.

Hong Kong Productivity Council (1985) 'Q.C. circles: in search of excellence', *Hong Kong Productivity News*, 19(4): 4–7.

HKIPM (Hong Kong Institute of Personnel Management) (1990) *HKIPM Pay Trend Survey*, Hong Kong: HKIPM.

Hsia, S. M. (1987) 'Quality circles development in Hong Kong', paper presented to the *Conference on the Changing Environment of Management in Hong Kong*, Baptist College, Hong Kong.

Hsia, S. M. (1989) 'Quality circles: the way to attain quality through people', in Welsh, A. N. and Coleman, S. Y. (eds), *The Hong Kong Management Development Handbook: – Part One*, Hong Kong: Vocational Training Council, Government Printer.

Kanter, R. M. (1984) *The Change Masters: Corporate Entrepreneurs at Work*, London: Routledge.

Kanter, R. M., Stein, B. and Jick, T. D. (1992) *The Challenge of Organizational Change: How Companies Experience it and Leaders Guide it*, New York: Free Press.

Kelly, D. and Amburgey, T. L. (1991) 'Organizational inertia and momentum: a dynamic model of strategic change', *Academy of Management Review*, 34(3): 591–612.

Kilmann, R. H., Saxton, M. J., Serpa, R. and Associates (1985) *Gaining Control of the Corporate Culture*, San Francisco, CA: Jossey Bass.

Kirkbride, P. S. and Shae, W. C. (1987) 'The cross-cultural transfer of organizational cultures: two case studies of corporate mission statements', *Asia Pacific Journal of Management*, 5(1): 55–66.

Kirkbride, P. S. and Tang, S. F. Y. (1989) 'Personnel management in Hong Kong', *Asia Pacific Human Resource Management*, 27(2): 43–57.

Kirkbride, P. S. and Tang, S. F. Y. (1993) 'From Kyoto to Kowloon: cultural barriers to the transference of quality circles from Japan to Hong Kong', *Asia Pacific Journal of Human Resources*, 32(2): 100–11.

Kirkbride, P. S. and Westwood, R. I. (1993) 'Hong Kong', in Peterson, R. B. (ed.), *Managers and National Culture: A Global Perspective*, London: Quorum.

Lau, S. K. (1982) *Society and Politics in Hong Kong*, Hong Kong: Chinese University Press.

Laurent, A. (1986) 'The cross-cultural puzzle of international human resource management', *Human Resource Management*, 25(1): 91–102.

Lewin, K. (1951) *Field Theory in Social Science*, New York: Harper and Row.

Mueller, D. (1986) *Profits in the Long Run*, Cambridge: Cambridge University Press.

Ouchi, W. G. (1981) *Theory Z*, New York: Avon.

Pascale, R. (1994) *Transformation*, London: BBC Video.

Peters, T. (1992) *Liberation Management: Necessary Disorganization for the Nanosecond Nineties*, New York: Knopf.

Peters, T. and Austin, N. (1985) *A Passion for Excellence*, London: Collins.

Peters, T. and Waterman, R. (1982) *In Search of Excellence*, New York: Harper and Row.

Redding, S. G. (1984) 'Varieties of the iron rice bowl', *The Hong Kong Manager*, 20(5): 11–15.

Schein, E. H. (1985) *Organization Culture and Leadership*, San Francisco, CA: Jossey Bass.

Senge, P., Kleiner, A., Roberts, C., Ross, R., Roth, G. and Smith, B. (1999) *The Dance of Change*, London: Nicholas Brealey.

Singh, J. V., House, R. J. and Tucker, D. J. (1986) 'Organizational change and organizational mortality', *Administrative Science Quarterly*, 31: 587–611.

Tushman, M. L. and Romanelli, E. (1985) 'Organization evolution: a metamorphosis model of convergence and reorientation', in Staw, B. and Cummings, L. (eds), *Research in Organizational Behavior, Volume 7*, Greenwich, CN: JAI Press.

Tushman, M. L., Newman, W. and Romanelli, E. (1986) 'Convergence and upheaval: managing the unsteady pace of organization evolution', *California Management Review*, 29(1): 29–44.

Weiss, L. and Pascoe, G. (1983) 'The extent and permanence of market dominance', paper presented at the Annual Meeting of the European Association for Research in Industrial Economics, August.

Westwood, R. I. and Kirkbride, P. S. (1998) 'International strategies of corporate culture change: emulation, consumption and hybridity', *Journal of Organizational Change Management*, 11(6): 554–77.

Westwood, R. I. and Kirkbride, P. S. (2000) 'Asian corporate symbols in rapidly changing times', in Haley, U. C. V. (ed.) *Strategic Management in the Asia Pacific*, Oxford: Butterworth Heinemann.

Williams, C. and Binney, G. (1997) *Leaning into the Future: Changing the Way People Change Organizations*, London: Nicholas Brealey.

INTERNATIONAL CLIMATE

LET ME LEARN!
A CHALLENGE TO
THE GLOBAL
ORGANIZATION

Samreen N. Khan

CHAPTER 5

LET ME LEARN!
A CHALLENGE TO THE GLOBAL
ORGANIZATION

Years after I moved to Britain, I joined some English friends on a visit to Manchester. We went out for drinks to a country pub, ordered a round of drinks and then I faced the dreaded question. 'Ready for a game of pool?' asked Stevie. No explicit agreement seemed necessary, they had already made their way to the table. I cringed and apprehensively followed them there.

When asked whose team I wanted to be on I said, 'Oh, I'll just watch.' Luckily there were five of us. 'Phew!' I thought and it was a good thing, because to me, it seemed like everyone of them was very skilled at playing. I felt embarrassed that I didn't know how to play. I knew then that if I tried I wouldn't be able to hit the balls, let alone get them in the holes.

Three years later, I was in Spain with my partner. He gave me a hard time for immediately turning down the option of playing a game of pool. When asked why not, I thought about it and grew increasingly frustrated. I thought to myself, 'Why can't I just know how to play, why didn't I learn 14 years ago like he did?'

I felt stuck. Then he intuitively asked me, 'What is so wrong and so bad about learning? If you don't know how to play, you could learn. I had to learn once, you know? So what is so wrong or bad about learning?' His question was a fair challenge.

I reflected on this event and realized that my background and environment hugely influence my passion, courage and ability to learn. The incident encouraged me to think about my learning history, a history that transcends a timeline of learning, growth and development, four continents and six cultures. I then made a connection from my own experience to how often passion, courage and ability are not reflected in learning within organizations.

This chapter is about how a global organization can increasingly learn. Implicit in this statement is that a global organization has a desire to learn. To fulfil this desire, it is necessary that two requirements be equally met. Success and survival require the organization rigorously to ensure that the business needs are met. In order to achieve this, the global organization must define the learning needs, tools, vehicles and media that ensure learning for each of its individuals. At the same time, the organization needs to understand how its individuals learn across diverse cultures and backgrounds. Using this understanding effectively requires the global organization to allow individuals to use their identities, achieve their personal ambitions and use their creativity and passion to guide their learning for their own as well as for the organization's growth and development. This chapter proposes that these two requirements are necessary conditions for a global organization to achieve its ambition to learn increasingly.

Little or none of this may come across as a revelation. In fact, a great deal has been written in this area by leading academics such as Argyris (1995) and Hirschorn (1999). The difference that this chapter proposes is that the means to achieving these two conditions are in direct conflict with each other (see Figure 5.1). Defining individuals' needs and allowing individuals their own freedom is where the conflict

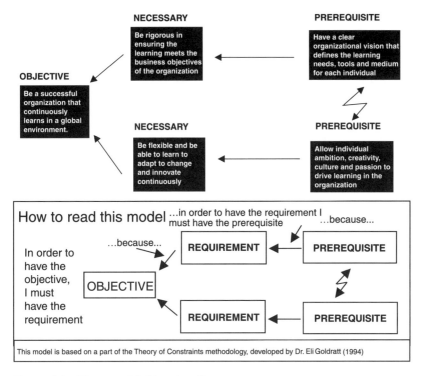

Figure 5.1 The core global learning dilemma.

lies, and it is this conflict that gets in the way of creating a true learning organization, let alone a global one!

The chapter demonstrates how to break this conflict by respecting the requirements of ensuring that a global organization's business needs are met as well as understanding how a global organization's individuals learn, but *preventing* the means by which these requirements are achieved continuing to be in conflict with each other. In order to break the dilemma, we must understand some of the assumptions that underpin each of its sides. The chapter will present both sides by first exploring the question of how a global organization can be rigorous in ensuring that learning meets its objectives.

It will then present the perspective of the individuals who are accountable for the organization's overall economic health and success, on the premise that if the individuals learn, the organization will learn. In *The Fifth Discipline*, Peter Senge articulates the learning organization as a place 'where people continually expand their capacity to create the results they truly desire, where new and expansive patterns of thinking are nurtured, where collective aspiration is set free, and where people are continually learning how to learn together' (Senge, 1993: 3).

By starting from the perspective of the global organization and then looking at the individuals story, we will be in a position to start to address the dilemma and respond to the key question that this chapter poses:

> How can an organization learn in a global environment given the complexity, diversity, uncertainty and unpredictability that it faces in our continuously evolving economy?

Returning to the story that introduced this chapter will shed some light on what the chapter sets out to achieve.

That night I realized something that I had not come to terms with before. All those times I avoided playing pool, or games such as charades and backgammon, was because, quite genuinely, I feared exposing that I did not know what I was doing. My assumption was that I had failed because I didn't know how to play a game of pool like they did. The easy way out was to withdraw.

Things clicked for me that day, I was just different, my past experience was not shared by my friends in the UK because I was born in one continent, educated in another and worked in yet another. So far, I have not come across another Venezuelan-born woman with a father from India, who was educated in the American and British systems and has lived in five countries. That does not mean that any other person with a different experience is inferior! So why do I make the assumption that I am inferior?

I realized that I do have something to contribute and share regardless of the fact that I was not brought up playing pool or charades. Acknowledging that makes me feel a little different when I attempt to learn something new. I am not starting from not knowing something, I am starting from being different and therefore able to share something of my own and learn something new.

WHAT IS THE KEY CHALLENGE FOR THE GLOBAL LEARNING ORGANIZATION?

Why Do We Want to Learn as a Global Organization?

In today's globalized economy, competitive edge is crucial. Organizations must learn to remain alert, become responsive and be imaginative to face external competition. On the other hand, they also need to capitalize on the rich potential of their self-evolving nature. This is a complex and fertile ground with infinite possibilities. The dynamic between their external and internal qualities and strengths is a tremendous incentive to propagate learning. The organizational learning curve has become steeper in the last 20 years and this millennium sees the momentum picking up even more.

Why Do We Need to Consider Our Business Needs Carefully?

Fierce global competition amplifies the need to be distinguished and to have a unique personality, brand and competitive edge. This applies even more strongly to younger sectors such as the high-tech industry. The global perspective in particular introduces the very important need to be able to operate in an environment where national differentiation, ranging from political paradigm, to legislation, to varying economies, throws a spanner in the works of any organization's business activity. Generally, unpredictability and cyclical economic gyrations require organizations to be on the ball and be clear about their strengths as well as their position in their respective industries.

Learning in organizations has its own cost. The classical view of running a profit-making business is based on the maximization of profit. Shareholder value is described by Milton Friedman as the key social responsibility of business, where it is to use its resources and engage in activities designed to increase its profits, as long as it stays within the rules of the game (1970). For not-for-profit public-sector bodies, the objective may be to provide good service and care. The UK

National Health Service is an example where the currency is, meta-phorically speaking, patients. In both cases, the organizations must find a way to ensure that their future is secure by guaranteeing demon-strated performance or delivery of their services. Organizations are continually threatened by immense competition. If they devote re-sources to activities that do not add value to the business, they are easily overtaken by competitors. To add to these demands, organizations are under tremendous pressure from their shareholders to achieve better and better economic results.

For all these reasons, to ensure success it is essential that a global organization carefully monitor the 'bottom line' to guarantee the res-ults and the credibility of the company. This applies both to the organ-ization's short-term as well as long-term growth and survival. Organizations cannot afford for employees to waste valuable time learning things that are not instrumental to the business or in line with its immediate as well as its long-term needs. Focused learning then becomes imperative. One example is an affiliate of the publicly owned oil corporation in Venezuela, which implemented a programme called the 'Accelerated Learning Programme' in 1987 for middle manage-ment. Its main purpose was to focus exclusively on growth and pos-itioning issues that the corporation faced in view of declining oil prices.

How Can We Ensure We Meet Our Business Needs?

Business awareness is manifestly crucial to organizational learning. The only way to be rigorous in making sure that our business awareness in-forms our learning is by agreeing on a clear vision that defines the learning needs for each individual and how they can best be satisfied. Organiza-tions, particularly traditional ones that have been around for a long time, have significant experience and a wealth of intuition. Substantial resources are dedicated to research and development activities in numerous indus-tries. The experience of some of the more traditional and well-established organizations serves as a valuable insight into what individuals need in order to be prepared for operating in the evolving marketplace.

The growing consciousness of organizational learning has encour-aged many organizations to create departments and appoint specific individuals for knowledge management and organizational learning and development posts. These departments are invaluable in that they commission extensive market analysis to gain a better understanding of what the organization's learning needs are and what will best help to meet these needs. Many organizations form partnerships that help them develop insight and explore what other equally successful leading companies, organizations and academic institutions are doing to fulfil the same kind of needs.

Is Focusing on Our Business Needs Sufficient to Guarantee that We Are a Successful Global Learning Organization?

The need to be agile and innovative becomes more apparent as we recognize the extreme complexity and unpredictable nature of an organization's internal and external environment and accept that these uncertainties will not go away, but continue to increase. This unpredictability is matched by the fact that organizations are inherently complex human systems. The uncertainty that emerges is therefore large and growing. To add even more complexity and uncertainty, global environments breed diversity and difference of multiple cultures and traditions. Understanding and interpreting between cultures prove more difficult, causing unknown or indeterminate outcomes. Peter Senge talks about this in *The Fifth Discipline* in reference to organizations' learning capabilities, and argues that as a complex system, an organization 'has a life of its own and that the system can produce unpredictable outcomes not in the foresight of management' (1990: 71). He seems to suggest that managers will be unlikely to cope with today's reality unless they reframe their thinking around constant and unexpected change.

Why Do We Need to Be Flexible and Responsive to Change?

An organization must therefore be flexible and capable of learning to adapt quickly to change, particularly if it wants to operate globally.

What enables an organization to be flexible, nimble and adaptable? A global organization desperately needs a reliable change gauge and, since its individuals are its heart and blood, the most accurate barometer it can make use of is its people. Low morale, for example, can often be a reflection of how the organization is responding to wider environmental realities. Being a human system, an organization is made up of individuals. Organizations therefore learn at a rate in line with that of its individuals.

An Anglo-American company, that I will refer to as Plastiseal Ltd, provides exceptional quality packaging for Waitrose, Sainsbury's, Asda as well as smaller local food markets in the UK. The current focus of the major retail multiples on low price, at the expense of quality – sometimes referred to as the 'Wal-Mart syndrome' – is, however, driving many of their suppliers such as Plastiseal to lose market share. This is a good example of how the consolidation of the industry into giant companies is putting huge pressure on small to medium enterprises. Plastiseal is finding itself losing numerous relationships with its key customers because it is reluctant to compromise the quality of its product in order to maintain cost competitiveness. This has significantly affected the morale of Plastiseal's employees. However, the company has redirected this negative energy to innovate in order to convert these threats into new business opportunities, such as penetrating a new market like logistics.

How Can We Be Flexible and Able to Learn to Adapt to Change?

It is crucial that organizations are able to recognize the uniqueness of its individuals, otherwise they would be ignoring a vital part of the whole. Flexibility requires the ability to work with difference and to nurture innovation so that something new and better develops. To be able to do this, we have to want something different to what we currently have. At the root of wanting is passion. An individual is born with passion, and passion only manifests itself through choice. In order for an organization to exercise flexibility, adaptability and the capacity to innovate, it must therefore allow individuals to make choices in order to best contribute their innate capabilities, to be creative and to use their personal ambition to drive learning in the organization.

Progressive organizations strongly agree with the need for a focus on creating environments where individuals are given space to be themselves and are strongly empowered. These environments strive towards providing individuals with safety and freedom while simultaneously offering sufficient challenge to nurture learning. In the past, organizations traditionally operated in environments that were once characterized by stability and continuity. During the 1960s and 1970s, organizations believed that the implementation of rigid control measures and pyramidal structures were the only ways to ensure that people could successfully deliver the organization's business needs (Sloan, 1964). The 1980s and 1990s were a transition period, with increasing uncertainties in business environments. We now see a growing number of organizations becoming increasingly aware of this transition, but still faced with having to deliver business results.

Apple's Steve Jobs is the classic example of an entrepreneur who in the early 1980s understood the value of talent and innovation. This was clear in the way that the products Apple sold and currently sells reflect personal creativity, welcoming and boldly illustrating the notion of difference. The oil industry is an example of how innovation was used to respond to environmental need, to reduce the sulphur emissions from the burning of fossil fuels, the cause of acid rain worldwide. It is apparent that such achievements resulted from tremendous innovation ranging from scientific advancements to corporate management and government policies, where individual talent and contribution played a key role.

Is Focusing on Our Ability to Be Flexible and Responsive Through Our Individuals Sufficient to Guarantee that We Are a Successful Global Learning Organization?

The success of organizations depends greatly on their ability to match the skills of their people with company needs. If the types of skills required are not carefully considered, they may result in the employment of overqualified people who can end up being superfluous. Organizations also need their individuals to learn on an ongoing basis in order to give management information to run the business. In the example of the oil company's 'Accelerated Learning Programme' described earlier, the programme was designed to address the immediate needs of the company under a crisis situation, which resulted in the trade-off of further generic learning by focusing on the crisis. Without an appropriate focus for learning and consideration of the current reality of the business, the learning would not have been as effective or as transferable.

In global environments, organizations are also faced with having to answer ethical questions and assume greater social responsibility. They are finding that they have to be increasingly sensitive to and ultimately responsible for social and environmental implications in host countries. Some argue that this behaviour rather instinctively finds its roots in the hearts of individuals. David Korten says in his book *When Corporations Rule the World*:

> We inherit through our birth a responsibility far beyond ensuring our own survival . . . [this idea] calls on us to accept responsibility for the impact of our actions on the course of evolution and to assume a conscious and responsible role in creating conditions that advance the continuing evolutionary process of the planet. (1995: 261–76)

To supplement this, anti-capitalist movements against the increasing power of corporations are accelerating the general awareness of individuals of the need to assume more social responsibility.

For instance, the fast-moving consumer goods industry has taken initiatives to eliminate the harmful chemicals that cause the depletion of the ozone layer, primarily through the elimination of chemicals such as those from all products that use aerosols as a propellant. The household appliance industry has made similar efforts by eliminating CFCs (chloro-fluoro-carbons) from refrigerators and other appliances. Although some of these changes were made in response to international treaties and local laws, there has also been a growth in voluntary sentiment for social responsibility.

These efforts require a tremendous shift in culture and attitude, involving massive levels of learning and relearning for individuals who work for such corporations, especially by the older generations. This task has been made more difficult as companies and their shareholders have to absorb the loss of profits by a squeeze on margins. For these reasons alone, purely focusing on developing organizational flexibility and adaptability by appreciating the diversity of thought, creativity and intuition offered by individuals is not enough to satisfy the desire to be a successful learning global organization.

Where Does This Leave the Organization?

What this is telling us is that both the organization's business needs and individual needs are equally important and must be fulfilled. Focusing on one or the other in isolation is not enough.

To be a successful organization today and in the future, it is necessary to continuously develop the capability of individuals. An equally important requirement is to respond to the immediate business needs. Developing individuals' capabilities requires the organization to invest time and money for the future; responding to the immediate business needs requires the organization to focus on today's bottom-line results. The dilemma is a generic yet incredibly difficult one for many if not most organizations today.

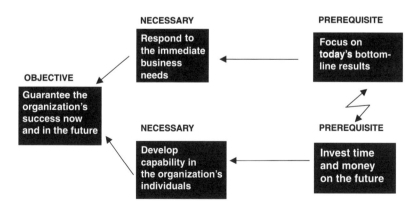

Figure 5.2   The organization's dilemma.

Organizations have struggled with this dilemma for decades. When faced with the choice, management instinct will tend to focus on the immediate needs of the business. Naturally, investment of time and money for the future requires economic feasibility today. The only way to guarantee this feasibility is by maintaining a firm grip of the immediate business needs.

Unsurprisingly, this instinct has commonly manifested itself in a halfway house between focusing on the bottom line and investing in the future. What many organizations have done is to go through the motions of developing future capability but implicitly responding to immediate needs as means of providing a solution. The following case study illustrates this behaviour demonstrated by a well-known global management consultancy trying to achieve the best of both worlds.

An example of an organization that lived out this dilemma was a major global consulting firm. From 1994–97, at the height of the knowledge management craze, tremendous efforts were made by this particular company to develop and grow a number of centres of excellence. These centres were developed globally with a view to inform organizational learning and knowledge management and, more importantly, to provide a basis for their client offerings.

The centres of excellence were fuelled by country representatives worldwide. In one instance, a project was carried out in partnership with a large IT consultancy, holding meetings once every six weeks in varying locations around the world. The learning initiative perpetuated a world of political activity and networking that served as a framework to develop, test and take the resulting offers to market.

There was vast opportunity for international team work, where consultants could share networks and leads to new client projects and develop good working friendships across cultures, making the project highly desirable. There were exceptional levels of learning on a local and global scale.

The downside was described by a highly respected consultant to be that the very necessary senior sponsorship was more focused on the revenue that the project would generate than on dedicating time to the growth and sustainability of the project. As a result, arguments were provoked between country representatives on issues such as how to classify knowledge. Learning was implicitly shoved to a back burner where limited degrees of learning were allowed to take place, 'single- rather than double-loop learning was understood where little or no feedback was fed into the learning process'. This particular consultant, who served as a leader/facilitator between country representatives, described himself as a political football. The result was increasingly low morale, a general feeling that the organization stifled creativity and blocked innovation and a growing number of highly pressurized, depressed individuals who found no choice but to leave.

This example provides a useful insight into the effects that the organization experienced. The short-term effects were positive, but lack of true senior-level sponsorship reflected a duplicitous message about commitment to the initiative. On the other hand, management's implicit focus on revenue was perceived as a block to creativity and innovation, defeating the purpose of the organization's original ambition to propagate learning.

An interesting angle is one that Argyris and Schon have articulated in their book *Organizational Learning II*:

> We believe that Organizational Learning occurs within the context of dialectical processes which stem from two conditions of organizational life. First, organizations are necessarily involved in continual transaction with their internal and external environments which are continually changing in response to both external forces and organizational actions. Secondly, organizational objectives, purposes and norms are always multiple and potentially conflicting. (1996: 9)

Seeing the development of future capability as a means to maximize immediate business needs is therefore a likely opportunity for undesirable effects.

The case study exposes a fundamental issue common to countless efforts by organizations desperate to solve their business dilemma. Again, a choice lying in between both sides is not an option. For any organization, the way out of this conflict is not to settle for either side or to find a compromise between the two, but to find different means to achieving responsiveness to the business's immediate needs and the development of the organization's individuals, so that success now and in the future is guaranteed.

WHERE DOES THE INDIVIDUAL FIT IN?

Is Learning an Individual Process?

What drives the need for learning in individuals? The learning process is personal. We normally have a reason to go to work where we have roles and responsibilities in our jobs. Generally speaking, our personal objective is to be successful in our roles at the organization in which we work. How well we perform depends not only on the competency and skills that we have developed in the past, but also on how effective we are at responding to new, everyday changing situations. How we build these responses into our working practices generates a feedback loop, which is what enables us to learn. We then generate assumptions based on our experience and learning that inform the way we work and react to future challenges.

To be successful at our roles within our organizations, we must fulfil our utmost potential. Competition introduces a dilemma to achieving this. Ideally an organization could take the learning that each individual experiences as a contribution to its overall organizational response to ongoing challenges. This, however, might lessen our own enhancement in comparison to other individuals. Do we learn for ourselves? Sharing what we learn in service of the organization takes away our personal competitive edge, so learning tends to be a personal activity and ultimately our own asset.

Another element that influences our ability to achieve our full potential is the concept of image. Image adds an element of sensitivity to how we learn and use our learning. Stereotypes, superiority complexes and basic social constructs inform the way we see others and ourselves. Across cultures, this becomes highly sensitive to varying identities. In response to these factors, the perception of our own image is highly versatile. In organizations, our performance regardless of position, seniority or culture is appraised and evaluated continuously, introducing yet more complexity in terms of personal assertion and inhibition.

Can an Individual Own Their Learning?

In order to achieve full potential and really make a difference, individuals must learn what they want to learn. But individuals surely cannot totally own their learning process? The organization for which they work has accumulated rich experience, tradition and wisdom that offer its individuals a tremendous learning playing field. For this reason, the organization feels confident and qualified to dictate the learning for each individual. Argyris and Schon also wrote:

> Organizations have been conceived as behavioral settings for human interaction, fields for the exercise of power, systems of institutionalized incentives that govern individual behavior, or socio-cultural contexts in which individuals engage in symbolic interaction. (1996: 16)

Organizations have an inherent power that projects a tremendous element of control.

Legacy provides a powerful learning tool and an opportunity to integrate 'old' experience with 'new' aspirations. This lesson became a painful one to learn for dot-com start-ups. Extremely creative and technically savvy individuals and groups of ambitious entrepreneurs became carried away with the 'new' and forgot about what the 'old' had to offer. What they forgot was that all they possessed was 'new' tools for 'old' rules. While a dot-com might want to pioneer the new economy, it must never ignore the classical laws of economics and fail to realize the transitions it must make to accommodate the new rules.

Mike Lynch, chief executive of the Internet software company Autonomy, said with reference to the demise of global e-tailer Boo.com, 'It's a sad example of what we'll see more of, because so many Internet retailers have gone out and just thrown cash at the problem' (Sabbagh, 2000: 3). This never solved a problem in the old economy, so why should it in the new? Why should the organization relinquish control of what its individuals should be learning? Is the learning not in service of its well-being? Does experience not prove that senior management knows best?

To be successful at our roles at work, there is an equally necessary condition for fulfilling our outmost potential. To be successful we must also avoid making mistakes. Our belief of how others perceive us can strongly influence our attitude to how and what we learn and often act as a barrier to our learning. Education systems reinforce this relationship. Traditionally, subject areas that were more highly regarded in the American system, for example, were those in the more analytical schools of thought, where development of hard skills was encouraged. The assessment process for entrance to secondary school and university was – and still is to a great extent – based on the strength of these hard skills. What has recently emerged is a consciousness that creativity, intuition and emotion have not been considered as important as the more dominant aptitudes such as analysis and theoretical skills. This awareness has revealed that children whose inclination was less theoretical and more intuitive have been considered to be failures and perceived to be at a disadvantage compared to those whose capabilities were more in line with the mainstream educational culture. There is talk in the California state education system about joining colleges such as Bowdoin College in Maine in abolishing or making optional the requirement to take the university entrance examinations, School Admission Tests (SATs), primarily because the tests were designed for an exclusive student profile. The SAT is believed to weed out minorities and international applicants whose cultural inclination is different to the typical American student.

This pattern extends itself to our working lives, where it can shape our attitude towards different professions. In Venezuela, for example, engineering, law and medicine are seen as the most prestigious professions. In the UK, law and medicine compete for prestige, and professions in the areas of public relations and marketing are often considered to be less important, thereby carrying a stereotype of being less challenging. In Japan, science and technology dominate the scene, so it is highly desirable to work in these areas.

The images that shadow our professions can be detrimental to us. First of all, they can dissuade us from doing something we may have strength in or from living an unexplored passion, forcing us instead into pursuing an area not close to our hearts. The consequences are that we misuse our real potential, leaving our hearts at home when we go to work. Ultimately, the individual may work for the organization, but do they want to? If not, are they going to be motivated to learn and to develop themselves to their full potential? Will the learning be in service of the organization for which they work, let alone make a contribution or foster a sense of shared learning?

Is the Organization Responsible for Facilitating Learning?

Organizations make tremendous efforts to empower their individuals. This movement began with the introduction of the flat and horizontal structures that contrasted with the more hierarchical and top-down approaches that historically dominated most industries. In the Tayloristic approach, traditionally employed by most organizations, power was centralized at the top, leaving little room for individuals to have a say unless they were higher up or well connected. With the transition towards a flatter model for leading organizations, individuals have a far better opportunity to use their own initiative to influence their careers. In this model, individuals are allowed to contribute to the organization's direction, which encourages them to use and share their learning across the organization.

Organizations generally hire people with the expectation that they will do their best to contribute. Recruitment standards are very high; visible talents, outstanding academic records and superior intellectual capabilities are always key criteria for leading companies. Companies value individuals who are self-directed, motivated and driven to contribute high-quality performance. Companies also expect individuals to bring with them different perspectives, diverse thinking and cultural traits so that they can strengthen their global competitive edge.

With these expectations, organizations design work environments where learning is promoted and shared. Large amounts of investment go into creating infrastructures that support the learning needs of individuals. Human resources and development departments are very creative in finding new ways that encourage people to learn. Many organizations are focused on implementing new ways to embed learning into their corporate cultures. In order to capitalize on the diversity of individuals within the organization, cross-cultural workshops and other similar initiatives have proved very effective. To further the global parameters within which they operate, organizations look for innovative ways to extend learning remotely.

With the exponential growth of technological innovations, organizations invest heavily in the use of intranets, databases such as Lotus Notes and warehouses, document management and artificial intelligence to capture, hold and use huge amounts of explicit knowledge. These tools, combined with organizational expectations, offer self-driven and capable individuals ample opportunities to learn and produce concurrently. This increases the opportunities to learn across geographic boundaries within organizations across the globe and externally with global client bases.

Under these environments, individuals could learn at their own prerogative. Investment in such resources is essential because there may be some useful pay-offs, but how valuable are these pay-offs in reality? The following case study provides a story about a well-respected global financial services and investment house that has reaped some of these benefits, but realized that a technical infrastructure alone is far from delivering the desired output of a global learning organization.

A global financial management investments group, branded in the UK and managing assets globally, launched an intranet-based learning environment in 1999 aiming to create a stronger link between training and its business needs. The system is globally accessible to all its employees on the Internet but is used primarily by its UK population. High-quality, updated and live information is available at every individual's fingertips in what the company describes as 'just-in-time learning'. The system is highly interactive and dynamic and was designed with individuals' needs in mind.

The company underwent a significant change in strategic focus and subsequently acquired another company, causing undesirable consequences for the intranet's implementation and roll-out. The organization's response to the learning tool was interesting. Use of the system varied, from younger people making most use of the intranet as a means of support for gaining professional qualifications or completing academic courses to other people not finding the intranet site a tool they could relate to in either medium or content.

The loudest voices described learning within this organization as taking place primarily through conversations, dialogue and experience. The common preference was to 'find and establish relationships with people and pursue ongoing face-to-face support or remote relationships over the phone'. When referring to international exposure on the job, one individual described 'being with, living in and relating to other cultures [as] the richest source of learning'. It was commented by many that 'because of the rapid and fast pace of their work, it is effective to learn while doing and any support to aid that process is valuable'. Many agreed that the most useful support was 'help and guidance [given to them] by colleagues and superiors'. When describing experiences of the use of technology as an enabler for learning, many expressed the view that 'although its use is a valuable resource and can provide a lot of useful knowledge, there is insufficient time to exploit the resource for the purpose of learning'. The use of technology at present is more a tool that 'facilitates day-to-day work and can be an effective medium to disseminate information'.

Organizations also encourage their employees to share tacit experience and knowledge to enrich their corporate knowledge base. In this case study we notice that the employees themselves find the learning to be tremendous. In practice however, it is a great challenge to capitalize on this type of knowledge base because it is typically generated through informal structures. Individuals often find it burdensome to their everyday responsibilities since it requires extra initiative, time and effort and can deliver limited tangible results, particularly on a grander scale across the organization.

The organization's role in the learning of its individuals is clearly an important one. It makes huge efforts to acknowledge the high levels of individual diversity, qualification, skill and motivation that individuals bring. At the same time, organizations can have lofty expectations about what qualities they want their individuals to possess and contribute. Since they have these expectations, they do appreciate the potential that individuals bring and offer infrastructures that can support the cross-fertilization and growth of qualities and contributions to enrich their learning environments. The paradox is that with the exceptional level of awareness and demonstrated commitment to learning, organizations feel that none of this is enough to achieve the right level of organization-wide learning as well as a shared and commensurately motivated response by their people.

What Is 'Unsayable' about the Organization's Role in Developing Learning in a Global Environment?

Desperate to understand and solve the above paradox, organizations often focus on trying to answer the following question: Can we ensure that our development systems and processes acknowledge the individual diversity of backgrounds, aims and personal learning processes and at the same time accelerate learning to ensure that we meet our business needs? This question is a difficult one to answer, and in my opinion has been avoided by most organizations out of lack of a clear understanding of what it actually means.

The good news, however, is that this chapter is about learning in a global environment, where diversity of culture, identity, age, sex or whatever exists and exists in wild and complex ways! The mere existence of the complexity of diversity is what most welcomes organization-wide learning.

To unleash organization-wide learning, we must first understand a third dilemma. So far, we have explored the global organization's learning dilemma and the organization's business dilemma. The third and final level is the individual's dilemma. To do this, we will briefly go back to the story at the beginning of this chapter and explore some of the assumptions that it surfaces.

> *All those times I avoided playing pool, or games such as charades and backgammon, it was because, quite genuinely, I feared exposing that I did not know what I was doing. My assumption was that they were better than I was because they knew how to play a game of pool. The easy way out was to withdraw.*

There is a fundamental flaw with the concept of defining an individual's learning needs in order to match their learning with the organization's business objectives. The 'unsayable' is that the very act of defining an individual's learning needs by another party (i.e. the organization) prevents the individual from taking the vital first step in any learning process. That is to make the personal decision to admit to one of two things: 'I just don't know' *or* 'What I currently assume might be invalid'.

Robbing the individual of the freedom to make this commitment robs them of learning itself. In the story, no one may have overtly robbed the individual of making this choice. She came up against a natural fear of being inadequate at the pool table because the game was unfamiliar territory to her and commonplace for her friends, a type of fear that is not uncommon to many individuals regardless of stature, position, level, culture or role who are in an environment, culture or situation foreign to them. It is therefore essential that the organization ensures that this freedom is granted, nurtured and protected. Doing so will unleash the learning potential that lies beneath the surface in any organization.

In a global environment, an individual's learning is considerably sensitive to their interactions with different cultures, languages, traditions and heritages. This dynamic is heightened for an individual who is a minority in a majority environment, a likely possibility for many individuals working with or for a global organization. The fear described above becomes more potent in such an environment and can prevent individuals from admitting their lack of understanding or knowledge. This is the biggest hurdle to learning for an individual in a global environment. Even worse, it can also prevent individuals from making useful contributions. We will return to the story and try to discover why.

When translating this incident to my work environment, I thought about what it was that made me feel satisfied. To be successful I know that I definitely need to feel that I make a real difference for the organization I work for, for my clients and for myself. Equally, to be happy and successful I avoid making a mistake or failing.

So to ensure my happiness at work, I realized that I have to make a difference in everything I do and to do that I need to take risks (such as having a go at a game of pool!). Equally, to be happy and enjoy success, I feel I must avoid making mistakes or failing. This requires me to shy away from risky situations where mistakes are merely arrows on the learning path.

In the story, the individual believes that in order to be satisfied and fulfilled, she must make a significant difference. Her assumption is that she will be more valued, respected and credible to her colleagues and clients. This makes her proud of her work. In order to make a difference, it is important that she takes risks and lives on the edge of learning. Paradoxically, risky situations are challenges and breed uncertainty, exciting high levels of emotion, uncovering passion and thereby triggering creativity.

On the other hand, wanting to avoid failure is hardly surprising given the undesirable consequences associated with it. For example, traditional schooling has demonstrated through its emphasis on measurement and assessment that gaining low grades evokes humiliation and feelings of not being good enough. This translates to working life in that failure to deliver can hurt professional image and be very embarrassing. Even worse, however, a critical failure might endanger future standing with the organization. To prevent any of this from taking place, she avoids learning in an environment where she is likely to fail because simple fear of failure causes her to freeze. This disables her from performing in the first place. Ironically, she fails without having even tried.

This individual experienced a combination of these effects on both nights at the pool table, but succumbed to the topside of the dilemma both times (see Figure 5.3). Making a difference to her meant being able to play a game that was unfamiliar to her but known to the community in which she has chosen to live. Both times she did not want to demonstrate her inability to play and therefore avoided putting herself in that situation in the first place. She made an assumption.

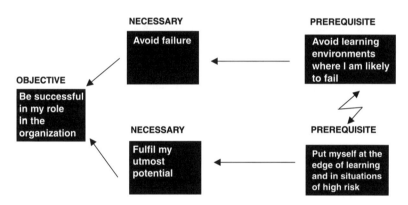

Figure 5.3 The individual's dilemma.

> *My assumption was that I had failed because I didn't know how to play a game of pool like they did.*

Her own assumption clouded her ability to admit that she did not know how to play, thereby inhibiting her desire to learn how to play the game altogether. She simply felt that not knowing was a way of admitting failure. It is this inhibition that can stifle the desire to learn, particularly in global environments. Working in a global environment means working across cultures, political paradigms and societal pressures. In his book *The World of the International Manager*, John Hutton wrote:

> Managers operating in global markets are aware that individual countries, so-
> cieties and cultures are shaped by a blend of emotions about their past inheri-
> tance, and about their current role in the world, with the need to apply reason to
> present circumstances in the pursuance of a variety of national purposes as
> expressed through political will. (1988: 46)

For individuals to use this awareness best, they need to exercise sensitivity about what assumptions are implicit to a dominant culture that
might come across as fact to a minority culture or vice versa.

The dynamic that these assumptions present is not a healthy one.
It can prevent individuals from fulfilling their utmost potential, as it did
in this story, or it can be detrimental to the individuals involved as well
as the whole organization's learning. Amin Maalouf wrote in his book
On Identity a useful passage about immigrants crossing cultures:

> One's feelings towards one's country of adoption are ambiguous. If you have
> come here it's because you hope for a better life for yourself and your family. But
> this expectation is tinged with apprehension about the unknown – the more so
> because you are at a disadvantage in various ways, afraid of being rejected or
> humiliated, and on the look-out for signs of contempt, sarcasm or pity.
>
> One's first reflex is to not flaunt one's difference but to try to pass un-
> noticed. The secret dream of most migrants is to be taken for 'natives'. Their first
> temptation is to imitate their hosts, and sometimes they succeed in doing so. But
> more often they fail. They haven't got the right accent, the right shade of skin,
> the right first name, the right family name or the proper papers, so they are soon
> found out. A lot of them know it's no use even trying, and out of pride or
> bravado make themselves out to be more different than they really are. And
> needless to say some go even further, and their frustration turns into violent
> contestation. (2000: 33)

This passage is powerful and very true for many individuals today, particularly in their working lives. Globalization cultivates places where multiple cultures co-exist, but rarely are they a fully multicultural environments
where assumptions cease to exist and understanding is paramount. Instead,
the global organizations that exist today, with the exception of bodies such
as the United Nations or the European Commission, possess dominant
cultures whose assumptions are often the ones that count.

The 'unsayable' articulated above is a blessing in disguise for an
organization aiming to be global and aspiring to learn increasingly. The
paradox is that a multicultural environment is ideal for overcoming the
challenge with which many organizations have battled in their attempts
to propagate learning.

The highly desirable secret is that the concept of failure does not exist in a true multicultural environment. No one culture is more correct than another. If in one culture a person uses chopsticks to eat and in another a person uses a fork and knife, it does not mean that one of the cultures is better than the other. What it does mean is that the two cultures are different and therefore each can learn from the other. Multicultural environments are inherently those where the notion of failure is substituted by difference and diversity.

This does not suggest that history be ignored. Survival of the fittest, war and past achievements within civilizations or nations are not to be overlooked. Respect and appreciate the past, but encourage openness. Maalouf articulates this sentiment eloquently:

> While the future should be constructed in a certain spirit of continuity it should also incorporate profound changes, together with significant contributions from elsewhere, as was the case in all the great eras of the past. (2000: 34)

Diversity thereby nullifies the concept of hierarchy because diversity is not about superiority, it is about difference. This is a crucial point for organizations attempting to learn. The mere appreciation of and willingness to learn from difference from the key to enabling learning. The truly global organization will welcome this reality.

HOW DOES AN ORGANIZATION SUCCESSFULLY LEARN IN A GLOBAL ENVIRONMENT?

There are a number of learning approaches and methodologies that are already used extensively and have proved to be effective in organizational learning. Learning is difficult to measure. For this reason, many approaches may not demonstrate tangible results and can be dismissed for more measurable approaches. We will look at a few approaches and methodologies that in our experience are well founded on extensive research and development. The learning tools presented in this chapter aim to overcome challenges associated with global environments. The chapter does not offer expertise on each of the methodologies it promotes. Instead, it offers a boutique of possibilities to facilitate global learning, with an invitation for the reader to make their own choices on what is most appropriate for their own environment, and offers suggestions on further reading to support these choices.

The Individual Owns Their Learning

We still need to ensure that individual learning meets business objectives. For this to happen, individuals must own their learning. Owning requires being accountable. Being accountable means that individuals are not only aware of their learning, but also of how their learning will affect the organization as a whole. True accountability requires that each individual understands the business, but, most importantly, where they fit into the whole business. For this, an individual needs empowerment.

In his book *Stewardship*, Peter Block discusses the prospect of accountability:

> To state it bluntly, strong leadership does not have within itself the capability to create the fundamental changes our organizations require . . . the strength in the concept of leadership is that it has connotations of initiative and responsibility . . . It carries the baggage, however, of being inevitably associated with behaviors of control, direction, and knowing what is best for others. The act of leading cultural or organizational change by determining the desired future, defining the past to get there and knowing what is best for others, is incompatible with widely distributing ownership and responsibility in an organization. (1993: 13)

It is the distribution of this ownership that defines true empowerment. Individuals must be accountable to the organization for which they work. This means that they must understand that they are responsible for the well-being and success of the organization; this can only be achieved if the individual is genuinely interested in the business. Young graduates, for instance are often seduced by monetary gains, corporate image and international prospects, but their interest stops there. The trick is to encourage individual ownership of learning by fundamentally shifting the focus of an individual's existence within their organization. This requires three things from the individual:

- A genuine interest in and care for the organization in which they are being hired to work.

- A desire to be responsible for the organization's success and livelihood.
- Total ownership of their contribution to the organization's success.

The task presented here begins with the individual, a unique contributor to the overall livelihood of the organization, who must understand the following:

- Of what is their individual role in service?
- How can the organization help them understand their impact on the organization's success?
- What does the individual uniquely bring to the organization?
- How can the organization support them to make their contribution ?

For individuals to answer these questions, they require support and guidance. A genuine understanding of these questions and their implications will certainly help individuals to prepare themselves for true ownership and accountability. Such individuals will lay the foundation of a nucleus to disseminate the learning further out into the organization.

Responsibility of the Organization to Engender Individual Accountability

The organization therefore plays an essential role in learning. Once an individual is fully accountable for the organization as a whole, they will not only be the owner of their own learning, they will ensure that each person in the organization contributes and learns. The organization's job is therefore to enable each individual to become accountable. The most effective way of facilitating this process is by dedicating significant time to each individual. Two vehicles can help achieve this objective.

Mentoring

Mentoring is not new – it has been used in organizations for years, although perhaps not formally until the past 15 years. Mentoring is a relationship built between two people, the mentor and the learner, who come to a mutual agreement to work together on a conceptual basis for a specific purpose, whether it be a work focus, a problem or an opportunity. Although traditionally mentoring was a skill that managers would develop or be encouraged to develop, the skill is gradually being used by younger and less experienced people. In organizations the process is often set up for career development and personal relationships, but the most important form is a relationship that focuses on real work situations (Honey and Mumford, 1989).

The key to good mentoring is to ensure that the conversations are driven by an agreed objective and that there is sufficient rigour in the challenges that they present to the learner and enough support to help the learner work on them. A mentoring session should be hard work for the learner. Some of the thought processes with which they are faced will be new to them. Such a relationship is an opportunity for the individual or learner to surface some of the voices that often get buried deep down, perhaps subconsciously, and allow these voices to shape their learning process and help them grow aware of their individual learning styles. It is these voices that within a trusting and safe conversation can give rise to a tide of potential opportunities for the individual. It is here that the individual can feel safe to admit, for example, 'I don't know what an alcohol spill might mean for the refinery that I work in' or 'I think that the job I've been doing is not contributing to the bottom line'. Situations such as this drive the development of new opportunities in service of the whole organization's success.

Coaching

Coaching is another useful process that enables learning. Based on similar premises to mentoring, it is a skill that is used frequently in a range of work and personal situations. Coaching is more focused on helping the learner solve problems on a practical and operational level. The conversations that evolve during a coaching session are most effective when there is a realistic objective, a clear understanding of the current reality in which the learner is operating, a broad awareness of what options the learner has to achieve the objective and, most importantly, a decision about the level of willingness and commitment that the learner possesses to do what it takes to achieve the objective.

In using this process with a learner, a skilful coach will encourage the learner to do all the work by asking effective questions and acting as a sounding board. Again, the process can be extremely valuable and, if done with sensitivity and responsiveness, can be instrumental in setting up a very safe yet challenging learning environment for the learner. The beauty of coaching is that anyone can do it, as long as sufficient rigour is exercised in the initial development of the skill and there is an explicit understanding of what it is used for and why. Coaching skills will then grow through experience.

Skill Set to Foster Individual Accountability and Ownership of Learning

Many organizations try to instil coaching and mentoring in order to lessen some of the more directive and authoritative interpersonal approaches that historically dominated their communities. Their main focus, however, is on developing company-wide skills rather than invoking the more subtle yet important aspects of learning, ownership and personal accountability. Coaching and monitoring are extremely beneficial skills, but in isolation their full potential will not be achieved.

Peter Block says, 'We cannot be stewards of an institution and expect someone else to take care of us.' Stewardship to Block means 'accountability without control or compliance' (1993: 6). A mentor needs a high level of skill to ask the right questions, but the individual develops their own accountability and desire to work and learn in service of the organization. Likewise, a coach must be wise in their facilitation to ensure that the learner does their own problem solving.

Both mentoring and coaching are also useful in facilitating cross-cultural activity and can be excellent tools for communication and integration, which in turn facilitate intercultural learning. This chapter suggests that an appreciative approach is used with these tools and a particular emphasis is placed on appreciating difference. A mentor can be instrumental in surfacing the individual's awareness of challenges they are facing in a new and unstable environment, and identifying development needs such as learning a language. A coach could help devise ways in which a person could, for example, learn to deal with specific situations that emerge from radical changes the organization is undergoing, such as an international merger or a takeover. Mentoring and coaching are both means to learning and can provide an infrastructure for individuals to seek support and guidance in their development. An organization should invest significant time in identifying individuals who already demonstrate accountability to the organization. These individuals will constitute a critical group that can initiate a dissemination process of learning by developing and using these skills.

Action Learning

A powerful approach used extensively is action learning. The founder of action learning, Reg Revans, described the approach as follows, 'The central idea is . . . that of a set, or small group of comrades in adversity, striving to learn with and from each other as they confess failures and expand on victories' (1980: 10). The life span is decided by the group and can range anywhere from six times a year to once a quarter. A facilitator leads the group, who ensures that each member is responsible for behaving selflessly in support of colleagues and 'selfishly' in support of themselves in service of learning leads. A skilful facilitator is thorough in their observations of what the group discusses. Each individual is invited to converse about specific situations and asked for reflections, empathy and challenges.

Action learning offers an opportunity for individuals to exercise ruthless challenge and considered support, based on careful analysis, experience and personal intuition. The individual is left with a systematic inquiry into the situation, into themselves and from a variety of external perspectives. The rest of the group has not only developed their own coaching, analytical and intuitive skills; they have also gained useful insight into the individual's issue and learning process.

Action learning encourages respect and appreciation between group members and can be instrumental to enabling learning about difference and diversity. David Casey, another respected pioneer of action learning, wrote, 'the ambience of an action learning set must be an accepting, supporting cradle of love' (1987: 31). An important premise on which action learning is based is that the individual is central to group learning. The group is founded on the critical definition of the relationship between each member and the rest of the group. The quality of this relationship is crucial to the effectiveness of the learning process. Ideally, this is a learning community that supports and challenges individual perceptions and ensures that each individual is able to reveal personal challenges and start their learning processes on the right foot. The group is driven by an agreed purpose and there are therefore ample possibilities for group constellations, from a group of chief executives from different organizations to a more diverse group of individuals of all levels within an organization.

The Learning Community

Learning will take place in any organization if the environment is conducive. Today's working environment shows a trend towards 'hot-desking' or 'open-plan offices'. Traditional office layouts offer environments where individual offices are partitioned. The mid-1980s introduced cubicles that provided some personal space and quiet for most employees and enclosed offices with glass walls for senior people. A new trend initiated by the need to cut costs and optimize space offers desks with docking stations for connecting laptops and individual offices are exclusive to more senior management. The newest extreme is the completely open-plan office with no enclosed offices, except for a few designated meeting rooms. This environment is noisy, chaotic and dynamic and eliminates personal space, privacy and silence.

A parallel can be drawn between the evolution from compartmentalized work environments to more open ones and the progression from Tayloristic styles of management to the more humanistic styles that influence management today. Open environments promote communication and the development of relationships and increase many-fold the possibilities for interconnectivity between individuals in the organization as well as a sense of community. The potential for conversations is huge and offers infinite opportunities for an organization's learning as a community.

Organizations can optimize such informal systems by designing and implementing infrastructures that support community learning. This involves creating opportunities where individuals are invited to contribute their own perspectives and this is shared among a 'community' that then disperses these contributions to the whole of the organization. The combination between demonstrated individual accountability and organizational commitment to growing a safe and inviting environment offers space for individuals to share their unique learning and allows others to learn from this, enabling the organization to learn as a whole.

The Global Learning Community

A true global learning organization requires more than merely formal mechanisms supported by an informal culture. Organizations must take a strategic initiative on global learning. To start with, learning must lead from the global level and then feed into national levels to ensure that diversity is inherent. Global and complex teams should be held accountable for the most difficult tasks so that working cross-culturally is experienced and learned. For this to happen, recruitment should focus on creating diversity within each local entity or nation as well as across countries or offices. Diversity should not just be based on nationality; it must consider many more dimensions of age, sex, race, language and culture. The organization will in this way develop its organic complexity in order to learn to deal with the external complexity it faces.

For an organization to take these bold steps, taking risks such as promoting individuals too soon and hiring people who would normally not fit the corporate mould must be common practice. This will also require organizations to think differently about how the individuals within them relate to each other. Methods will have to be designed and implemented to help them work together. Because of the likely abundance of different languages, backgrounds and experiences, communication and standard practices will be not be as organizations might expect. This will require educating individuals and organizations alike about differences rather than similarities between them. Such a scenario will force individuals to value and respect childhood and early moments of learning, cultural heritage and linguistic differences. Learning will have to be based less on facts and more on metaphors to allow unfamiliar perspectives to be communicated between cultures. To complement this, illustrative tools such as story telling will overtake best practice, enabling individual voices to disseminate learning. This is a future where today's mainstream or status quo will cease to exist. Diversity and difference will be the drivers for learning and not the barriers.

CONCLUSION

This chapter is about organizational learning in a global environment. It presents the growing importance of learning in a modern organization to ensure that:

- the organization achieves its business objectives, and
- the organization improves responsiveness to the complexity and uncertainty that globalization continually introduces.

Organizations are aware that they need to achieve these objectives, but in doing so they face a major dilemma. In order to match the organization's learning to its business objectives, the organization must define individual learning needs, on the other hand, in order to be responsive it must use its individuals as a gauge of change and therefore must let them drive the learning for the organization. Defining their learning and allowing them to drive their own learning are in direct conflict.

By identifying this generic learning dilemma, organizations are able to surface some of the implicit assumptions that inform the approaches that are currently in place to ensure organizational learning. This chapter provides the reader with an opportunity to challenge some of these assumptions and encourages them to surface and examine their own.

During this process, one assumption was fundamentally challenged: that defining an individual's learning needs and the tools required to meet them is the only way to ensure that business objectives can be delivered. The challenge to this was that the act of defining an individual's learning needs violates the crucial first step in any learning process, to admit not knowing something and/or to admit that an assumption might be invalid. Robbing an individual of the choice of admitting this is robbing them of learning altogether. The lack of conditions for true learning in today's global environment where dominant cultures exist can perpetuate inhibitions that stifle shared learning. This dynamic eradicates the possibility of global organizational learning.

This third dilemma exposed the conflict between an individual's desire to take risks for the sake of learning in order to make meaningful contributions and their tendency to shy away from situations where they are likely to make a mistake out of fear of failure. To avoid failure, individuals often cover up what they do not know and on which they are expected to have an opinion. The downfall occurs when the assumptions that underlie the opinion are fundamentally flawed and remain unsurfaced. There is no room for learning. The opportunity that this chapter offers is that globalization and hence multicultural environments are ideal for learning, because the concept of failure between cultures does not exist. Diversity also nullifies hierarchy, enabling empowerment of individuals at any level.

This chapter then presents a few approaches that are used extensively, but invites the reader to enrich these enablers with their experience of learning in their own organization. Together with a solid understanding and appreciation of accountability, one can use the fundamental challenges and suggested approaches proposed in this chapter as a catalyst for learning in any environment. Finally, the chapter is based on the belief that whichever constellations of approaches are called on, the informal and natural diversity that global organizations breed will complement the journey to becoming a rich and powerful global learning community.

You may be asking, did the person in the story finally learn to play pool? She did, in exchange for a few lessons of salsa dancing!

References

Argyris, C. and Schon, D. (1996) *Organizational Learning II: Theory, Method and Practice*, Addison-Wesley.

Block, P. (1993) *Stewardship: Choosing Service over Self-Interest*, San Francisco, CA: Berrett-Koehler.

Casey, D. (1987) 'Breaking the shell that encloses your understanding', *Journal of Management Development*, 6(2).

Friedman, M. (1970) 'The social responsibility of business is to increase profits', *New York Magazine*, 30 September.

Goldratt, Eliyahu (1994) *It's Not Luck*, North River Press.

Hirschorn, L. (1999) *The Workplace Within: The Psychodynamics of Organizational Life*, Boston, MA: MIT.

Honey, P. and Mumford, A. (1989) *A Manual of Learning Opportunities*, Maidenhead.

Hutton, J. (1988) *The World of the International Manager*, Hemel Hempstead: Philip Allen.

Korten, D. (1995) *When Corporations Rule the World*, London: Earthscan Publications.

Maalouf, A. (2000) *On Identity*, London: Harvill Press.

Pedler, M. (1983) *Action Learning in Practice*, Aldershot: Gower.

Revans, R. W. (1980) *Action Learning: New Techniques for Management*, London: Blond & Briggs.

Sabbagh, D. (2000) 'From boo(m) to bust in under two years', *Daily Telegraph*, 19 May.

Senge, P. (1993) *The Fifth Discipline*, New York: Doubleday.

Sloan, A. P. (1964) *My Years with General Motors*, Garden City, NY: Doubleday.

BUILDING A
GLOBAL
E-LEARNING
ENVIRONMENT

Cath Redman and Andrew Ettinger

CHAPTER 6

BUILDING A GLOBAL
E-LEARNING ENVIRONMENT

*G*lobalization demands the breaching of time and space limitations. Information technology is a key component of the transformation to a global business environment. It challenges our modes of operation. Not surprisingly, education and training, along with all elements of the global organization, are undergoing a major transformation. The last five years have seen significant growth in the delivery of training and development through corporate intranets, learning centres, and corporate and virtual universities, often referred to now as 'e-learning'. For example, the learning needs of Xerox's 19 000-strong European workforce, which includes people from 35 countries speaking 15 different languages, are met through a virtual university dubbed the Xerox Virtual Learning Environment. Xerox Europe's plan has been to move away from its 1998 ratio of approximately 88 per cent of training and development being delivered through classroom-based learning and 12 per cent through e-learning/distance learning to a 50/50 ratio by the end of 2001. The demand for alternative delivery methods for training and development is growing fast. According to recent research from IDC (McGovern, 2001), while e-learning is becoming well established in the US, the European market for e-learning products will also grow to $4 billion by 2004 at an annual growth rate of 96 per cent.

E-learning can be of particular benefit to the large multinational. It has the potential to train an entire workforce across the globe simultaneously, for example on the introduction of a new product or innovation, with immediate results. The notion that learning must occur in a single place at a single time no longer holds true. However, while creating many opportunities at the same time, e-learning presents many challenges. HR and training managers must now craft learning strategies on a global rather than a regional scale, which presents issues in terms of the suitability of learning materials for a culturally diverse audience.

Ashridge itself has experience of these challenges. Our clients are demanding more flexible ways of working with us in the delivery of management development. Over the last five years, but particularly from 1999 onwards, the marketplace for business and management education has become more global and the nature of the programmes is changing. The pressures of the new economy mean that managers are no longer able to spend weeks away from the office developing their leadership and management capabilities. This fact, coupled with Ashridge's increasingly international client base, has meant that more of our management development programmes are now being delivered with a modular approach. As a result, we are constantly developing our learning technology capability to support managers in their personal development. The most notable example was the launch in 1999 of the Virtual Learning Resource Centre (see Figure 6.1), which provides 'just-in-time' access to a range of management development materials and research tools through the World Wide Web. As well as supporting our programmes, the Virtual Learning Resource Centre is used by over 60 organizations, many of them global, as part of their corporate universities or other e-learning initiatives.

The 1990s saw the rise of the 'learning organization', a term that is now less frequently used and has instead been replaced with a new tidal wave of literature about the 'knowledge company'. The ability to leverage 'intellectual capital' is now seen as a key differentiator for successful companies. Ashridge has always believed in the importance

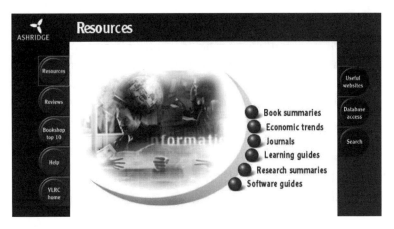

Figure 6.1   The Ashridge Virtual Learning Resource Centre.

of linking 'information' and 'learning' and through our learning resource centre we have always tried to create that vital connection. For example, course participants learn about strategic frameworks and this is made more effective by their using live information on their own companies and competitors to apply to those frameworks. We also have a strong belief in personal development and continuous learning. These themes are key to the development of global learning environments. Successful organizations of the future will be those that have made that crucial link between knowledge sharing and continuous learning on a global scale.

This chapter will explore some of the benefits, but also some of the potential pitfalls, in developing global learning environments. Using recent Ashridge research, we will explore the extent to which e-learning can or should replace more traditional forms of face-to-face classroom programmes. We will also look at the implications for the learner of introducing 'anytime, anywhere' or 'just-in-time' learning. For example, does it put pressure on them to learn in their own time? Are organizations taking the trouble to understand the needs of the learner and considering the cross-cultural issues that exist when trying to make learning a global phenomenon?

As we have already said, the demand for e-learning is growing rapidly. This has led to an extremely complex and fragmented marketplace, with many new players emerging alongside well-established ones. The chapter also explores the relationship between the traditional seats of learning and the new breed of corporate universities. Throughout the chapter we shall draw on Ashridge's experience to date, refer to best-practice examples and provide some practical guidelines for those attempting to develop their own global e-learning environment.

WHAT IS A GLOBAL E-LEARNING ENVIRONMENT?

One of the main reasons we can now talk about 'global' learning environments has to be because of the enormous advancements in technology, predominantly the Internet revolution. The World Wide Web has opened up many possibilities for virtual collaboration, the sharing of knowledge and learning.

The term 'e-learning' has become prevalent in the last two or three years and there is often confusion about its actual meaning and how it differs from other terminology that has been in existence for much longer. The glossary in Table 6.1 helps to explain some of this.

So how does e-learning differ from the above definitions? True e-learning makes use of Internet technologies to bring together knowledge, learning tools and interaction through the same interface. Interaction with an expert or fellow learner provides a more engaging learning experience. *This is where the real power of e-learning lies.* The Aberdeen Group use the following definition of e-learning:

> A knowledge, information infrastructure that leverages the power of the internet to provide timely, effective training and education in an increasingly fast-paced and rapidly changing world. (1999: 2)

Let us now consider what makes up a learning environment. If we think of the elements that constitute a traditional learning environment, such as a college, university or business school, we can perhaps think of certain common aspects associated with them all:

- Availability of knowledge experts, e.g. faculty.
- Provision of learning resources, library facilities.

Table 6.1 Glossary

Term	Definition
Distance learning or distributed learning	Any form of learning that is done away from the place of study, i.e. at home, at work. It may involve using paper-based, video or computer materials or the Internet. It involves two-way communication with tutors and other course participants
Just-in-time learning	Learning that occurs from dipping into pieces of information or interactive learning from self-guided tutorials or databases. It allows people to solve problems and perform specific tasks when they crop up. Most often applied to learning in the workplace and made possible by e-learning
Technology-based training (TBT)	Any training where technology is being used to transfer knowledge and learning, such as CD-Rom, computers, audio tapes, video tapes etc.
Computer-based training (CBT)	Training packages that make use of computers and computer networks. Typically of a linear nature with assessments prior and post course. Often few graphics or other media incorporated into these packages
Multimedia training	Training packages that use sound, video and rich graphics
Knowledge management	Exploiting existing knowledge within the organization and in the process creating new knowledge. It involves connecting people to people, expertise and vital information
Web-based training	WBT is essentially computer-based training that is only available through the use of Internet technologies. These include the Internet, intranets and extranets (part of an internal website that is made available externally via the Internet to select users). Often used interchangeably with e-learning

- Opportunities to practise skills through teamwork/simulations/ role play.
- Provision of personal coach or mentor for one-to-one feedback.
- Assessment of prior knowledge/skills/personality attributes.
- Testing or examination of skills and knowledge.
- Opportunities for socializing and networking.
- Face-to-face classroom-based teaching.

For the purposes of this chapter, an e-learning environment implies the use of Web technologies to re-create some, if not all, of these elements. For example:

'Anytime' tools (also termed asynchronous tools)

- Facilitated discussion areas, e.g. people can post up items for discussion that remain there for everyone to see and reply to in their own time. Items are arranged by topic area.
- Interactive Web-based courseware/pre-course tests/post-course assessments/pre-recorded Web-casts.
- Web-based libraries, including databases of full text resources/ knowledge bases.
- E-mail links to experts, e.g. tutors or in-company experts, where questions are posed and the expert replies within a set period of time but not necessarily instantly.

'Sametime' tools (also termed synchronous tools)

- Real-time chat rooms – several people are logged on simul- taneously and can e-mail messages and replies to each other.
- Virtual classrooms – the activities in a classroom are viewed live by participants in other locations who can participate in the class by e-mailing questions to the tutor.
- Video conferencing – either using the PC (one-to-one coaching or feedback) or full-scale video-conferencing equipment (for meetings and team collaboration).

- Live Web broadcasts or Web conferencing – real-time video and audio delivered to desktops.
- Web-based simulations – virtual teams use collaborative real-time tools to practise live situations.

What differentiates e-learning, if done properly, from what has gone before is that it creates a true environment for learning by providing linkage with knowledge bases and experts. There are many forces driving the integration of knowledge management and e-learning, as illustrated in Figure 6.2.

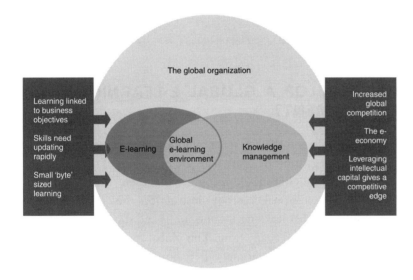

Figure 6.2 Forces for creating a global e-learning environment.

Clark Aldrich from the Gartner Group (Berry, 2000) points out that knowledge management and e-learning are essentially about knowledge acquisition. The process of knowledge acquisition in the knowledge management context is not so very much different from knowledge acquisition through self-paced learning. He points out that they can both encourage information sharing. Aldrich therefore believes that in the future e-learning will become a subset of knowledge management or vice versa. One could say that the extent to which an organization can call itself a 'knowledge-driven' or 'e-learning' company depends not just on the existence of e-learning and knowledge management strategies, but on the extent to which they are integrated.

While technology has 'enabled' this integration and the new ways of working and learning associated with it, it is important to remind ourselves that technology alone will not create a 'knowledge-driven' organization. Implementing e-learning and knowledge management initiatives often requires a huge shift in organizational culture. This can only be done with buy-in from above and champions who will drive the ideas forward. Further on in this chapter we look at some of these issues in more detail.

WHY DEVELOP A GLOBAL E-LEARNING ENVIRONMENT?

Internet technology is the key to a revolution in learning. Any effective e-learning strategy must be more than the mere sum of the content and technology. Although it should recognize that there are still a place and a role for some traditional classroom instruction, the crucial element to this revolution is that learning is continuous and should be available to anyone, anywhere and at any time. This global approach takes us out of the classroom and into the home, office, hotel or airport. The emphasis is now on performance rather than training. E-learning enables one to move from training to disseminating real-time information that supports performance. The knowledge may be through a third-party supplier or reside anywhere on your globally networked architecture.

Employees now want to learn when it suits them, not necessarily fitting in with the training provider's schedules and deadlines. Some will want accelerated learning, others need more time than is usual on a formal instructed course. Learning materials and resources are produced electronically online and continually updated, rather than the far more laborious process involved with paper or compact disc products.

E-learning is not just about using the new technologies for learning but is a completely new way of thinking about learning. It is also inextricably connected to knowledge management, as discussed above. One could argue that online learning and knowledge management are the two sides of the e-learning coin. Heads I learn, tails I get information. E-learning will not always be totally appropriate, however, and to get a complete learning architecture one should link it to classroom training. This should create a cultural glue. We will look at what kind of learning is best delivered through e-learning in the next section.

E-learning Benefits

Table 6.2 E-learning benefits

1. E-learning gives one the opportunity to provide a standard message to a large number of widely geographically dispersed people. This can also be customized to account for cultural difference

2. E-learning saves time and money, especially on travel and accommodation. Although there are development costs, these can be quickly recovered

3. Learning becomes more accessible. It's all about 'just-in-time' learning that makes for global learning. It is not location specific and can be used at any time

4. The material is constantly updated. It can be instantly updated and distributed. The content therefore stays fresh and relevant

5. With a learning management system (LMS) one can get data centrally on users or learners

6. It uses Web and browser technology with which most people are already familiar

7. It can be linked with discussion forums and chat rooms that enable people to share knowledge and learning

8. Many organizations have turned to e-learning in order to get global reach. They need to ensure that there is a consistent level of knowledge globally to deliver customers' needs. This often has to cross boundaries when catering for multinational clients. Here there are global plans but local execution

E-learning Problems

There are problems if the right approach is not taken. It can be thought of as a cheap alternative, often with no human interaction included. Motivating the learner in this scenario is difficult; this is covered in the following section on the experience for the learner. There have been many claims around the area of return on investment (ROI), especially in the US, but often these do not appear to be comparing like with like in the final equation. Merely giving thousands of employees access to a number of programmes via the Web is in no way comparable to classroom or other training initiatives. Online MBAs with individual tutorial support costs are some of the most expensive programmes in the world.

A quote from recent Ashridge research illustrates this well:

> For Duke, the online MBA is more expensive than its traditional offering. Partly through technology costs but also through the higher individual tutorial support costs. If a professor is e-mailed then a response is expected. Out to lunch is not an option! (Kernan, 1999: 5)

As we have already stated, e-learning requires a strategy that is more than technology or content. It needs to include leadership support and a learning environment and to be ongoing. Often this means that it needs to become part of a change management process and to be constantly tested against the mission and vision of the business. So we can see that merely putting content on an intranet does not ensure success. We will look in the final section at other issues around making global e-learning a success.

Benefits and Disadvantages of E-learning: Ashridge Research Results

Ashridge research (Wildsmith, 2001) showed that the overwhelming advantages of e-learning listed by managers were that they could work at their own pace, learn when it was convenient for them and do this anywhere. The pace seemed crucial to many of them and was often linked to not being disturbed or interrupted at work.

Other advantages listed included the ability to go back over key learning points, avoiding and gaining time on travelling and in a few cases that it was a cheaper training option. A typical response was, 'It needs proper skilled design and delivery. When that is present, I believe there will be few areas which don't find themselves suited.'

By far the main disadvantage of e-learning given by respondents was around the theme of no human interaction. They missed a me-to-me relationship, and personal communication and bemoaned the lack of the ability to discuss and play with ideas. For a significant number the process was boring and dull and often too slow. Another area of discontent was the lack of immediate help, although this does not have to be a drawback for all e-learning.

GLOBAL E-LEARNING – HOW DO YOU CREATE THE BEST EXPERIENCE FOR THE LEARNER?

There are plenty of sceptics around who believe that e-learning is 'training on the cheap' and can never replace the richness of the face-to-face classroom model of learning. Some would say that too much emphasis is placed on the return on investment (ROI) that can be achieved by implementing global e-learning environments and tales of savings that can be made on travel expenses and so on. Calculating ROI is a particularly popular topic in the corporate university sector in the US. The danger with this is that the needs of the learner can be neglected and there may be resistance among employees to using e-learning.

Arguably, however, if it is well designed and used for the appropriate purpose, e-learning can provide as positive a learning experience as classroom instruction, with the added advantage of the 'any time, anywhere' aspect. As its name suggests, e-learning puts the emphasis on learning rather than training and is learner led rather than tutor led, allowing the learner to pick and choose the learning appropriate to them at a particular point in time. Nevertheless, in the rush to jump on the e-learning bandwagon, have organizations really stopped to think about what is best for the learner? There are four main issues here:

- What material is best suited to e-learning?
- Technology should enable and enhance, not dictate, the learning experience.
- How can the needs of the global audience be addressed?
- When, where and how are learners expected to learn?

What Material Is Best Suited to E-learning?

Gaining the motivation of the learner is vital if e-learning is to be successful. Given the choice of attending a two-day presentation skills course off site in a hotel or logging onto the PC in the learning centre to complete an online course, I'm sure we can all imagine which would be the most popular option!

Many organizations have made the mistake of believing that e-learning will be the solution to all training and development needs. This is clearly not the case. The new medium clearly has its drawbacks, for example the lack of human interaction means that you can lose the non-verbal reactions of others, which is critical for soft skills development. It should therefore be viewed as another tool in the tool-kit. Some activities are still best done in the classroom, so organizations should aim for a 'blended' approach.

That said, how do we know what is most appropriately delivered through e-learning to give the best options to the learner? Results from a recent survey of middle and senior managers carried out by Ashridge (Wildsmith, 2001) ranked the following areas as being most suited to e-learning:

1. PC/IT software skills.
2. Knowledge areas/sharing of knowledge.
3. Transfer of facts, figures and processes.
4. Foreign language skills.
5. Financial and accountancy training.
6. Internet/e-business/e-commerce – new/fast-moving subjects.
7. Theoretical textbook-based knowledge transfer.

This ranking is borne out by the huge availability of e-learning in IT-related areas. Management development content, in particular the area of soft skills, has until relatively recently been absent. Acquiring these skills largely depends on practising through role play and interaction, which arguably is best done in the classroom. However, there seems an increasing consensus among training and development managers that most management theory and frameworks lend themselves to self-paced e-learning. An experiment carried out by Youngme

Moon of Harvard Business School on a group of managers from IBM (Lewis and Orton, 2000) revealed that managers reported a preference for classroom learning over e-learning. However, when Moon conducted post-programme interviews for specific reactions to the elements of an experimental e-learning course, she found that most said they preferred learning the informational material online from their home or office rather than in a classroom setting. Conversely, the managers preferred learning the behavioural skills material in a classroom environment.

Breakthrough solutions transforming the IBM Culture: Company adopts IBM Management Development blended *e-learning* model

From its inception, IBM Management Development (MD) has taught leadership and management in nearly every business and economic cycle. Its knowledge base derives from the greatest experts in business, and from its own experience in managing one of the most dynamic companies in the world. Its programs are designed and taught by successful managers with firsthand, first-rate knowledge of their field, and an ability to impart their insights in meaningful and compelling ways.

To promote effective training and development, IBM MD uses designs that link active learning with the business environment. One such design, which became fully developed and deployed throughout 2000, is its industry-acclaimed 'blended' *e-learning* model. In 2000, IBM MD took the lead within IBM to develop a model of leadership development that incorporates four distinct instructional approaches (tiers) to provide an array of technology-enhanced learning to support the standard classroom intervention. IBM managers now use this 4-tier *e-business* learning approach to master skills and behaviors that grow them as outstanding managers and leaders.

In 2000, **IBM Learning Services** adopted the IBM MD model, and other company divisions followed, such that enterprise learning initiatives now build core competencies via the IBM MD design: a web-based learning infrastructure, virtual collaborative tools, and interactive online simulators to augment face-to-face classroom instruction.

IBM MD's blended 4-tier leadership-development approach provides IBM managers worldwide an integrated process available 24/7, directly from their desktops or ThinkPads.

Tier 1. Information and just-in-time online performance support. These online resources primarily address an ongoing, immediate management concern. The manager with an existing problem accesses the relevant topic either via an index or the keyword search engine, and brings the material directly to desk top for online reading, printing to hard copy, or mailing to an e-mail account. Best thinking on over 50 leadership and people-management topics of concern to our managers are available, including ManageMentor provided by Harvard Business School Publishing. Tools – printable worksheets and checklists – are also available for specific action issues. Links to important external web sites are also highlighted. Because IBM teams globally, managers need to have access to policies and practices in different countries. Tier 1 offerings allow managers quick and easy access to all global HR material.

Tier 2. Interactive online learning. Managers further enhance their knowledge and personal development beyond the awareness level by engaging in immersive simulations of the issues presented in Tier 1. The online Coaching Simulation alone comprises 8 different scenarios, with over 5000 screens of actions, decisions points, and branching results. Twenty-six other simulations cover other Human Resources topics such as Business Conduct Guidelines, Multicultural Issues, Work-Life Issues, Retention, and Personal Business Commitments. *Going Global*, IBM MD's award-winning web site on multicultural business, features over 300 interactive Cultural Clashes. **A generic version of MD's '4 Tier e-Learning Model' is currently under patent and trademark nomination for IBM.**

Tier 3. Online collaboration. Brings *e-learners* together through technology. Through IBM products such as Team-Room, CustomerRoom and Lotus LearningSpace, managers team with other managers in virtual groupware spaces. Here they learn collaborative skills, and create and build real-life learning networks to enhance our company's own intellectual capital. Collaborative spaces using same-place, different-time communication enable a truly global learning environment, eliminating the problems of time zones and travel. This part of the learning process introduces the give and take of human dynamics – and uses the benefits of technology to transcend time and space. Management Development supports virtual teams with materials and consulting to maximize business results and learning at the same time.

Tier 4. Classroom 'Learning Labs'. For developing people skills, face-to-face human interaction is arguably the most powerful of learning interventions. Classroom activities provide immediate responses, are flexible to human needs, and can adapt as needed to different learners' styles. For leadership development, nothing quite duplicates face-to-face learning. In addition, a classroom of peer learners can provide added motivation, inspiration, and a community environment further stimulating interest and involvement. IBM continues to offer interactive classroom experiences. The in-class experiences require the learner to master the material contained in Tiers 1, 2, and 3 so that the precious time spent in classroom Learning Labs can target deeper and richer skills development.

Over the last two to three years Ashridge has begun to experiment with different ways of delivering learning. For example, participants on the Strategy and Leadership programme now have the opportunity to familiarize themselves with many of the common strategic tools by using an interactive learning package on strategic awareness, before attending the taught element of the programme. This allows more time for the application of real company issues in the classroom. They can also continue discussing issues related to the programme between modules using the discussion areas on the Ashridge extranet.

The practical realities of today's business environment are, rightly or wrongly, helping the push towards developing e-learning content not just in management theory but also in a variety of soft skills.

According to recent forecasts (McGovern, 2000) non-information technology training, including soft skills, sales, marketing and leadership, will grow almost to equal IT training, increasing from $222 million in 2001 to $1.8 billion in 2004. With this in mind, the second issue, how we use the technology, is very important.

Technology Should Enable and Enhance, not Dictate, the Learning Experience

According to Lewis and Orton (2000), many learners are put off e-learning because they do not have a deep enough understanding to make informed decisions about the relative value of a Web-based vs a classroom learning experience. Arguably, however, it is more likely that e-learning providers have not thought through the best way of using the technology to enhance the learning, which has resulted in bad experiences. We should be aware of how the technology can help the learner, not try to deliver exactly the same as in the classroom. Dobbs makes an interesting point:

> Very few e-learning outfits want to take a big step beyond the status quo. . . . It's much safer to package some PowerPoint slides from an existing classroom session and call the result a bold innovation. (2000: 86)

A global e-learning environment must provide the learner with more than merely page after page of text to read. An appreciation of learning styles is key to the development of e-learning as it is to any other form of learning delivery. People learn in different ways. For example, those of us who are what Kolb (Kolb, Rubin and McIntyre, 1984) would describe as 'active experimenters' will benefit from a high level of interaction and the ability to try things out through simulations. The level of instructor involvement here may be different to those of us who could be described as 'abstract conceptualizers', who like to derive their learning from concepts and build models to explain events. Visual learners, auditory learners and kinaesthetic learners can all be accommodated through the careful use of multimedia. E-learning has the ability to be individually tailored. If well designed, it should be able to help learners discover their preferred learning style and then allow them to select materials that most suit them.

Table 6.3 offers some hints and tips on good use of the technology for developing an e-learning environment. These can also be used as a checklist when evaluating e-learning suppliers.

Table 6.3   Tips for using the technology wisely

1. Use attention-grabbing interfaces. Full colour, graphics, voice-overs and animation. The use of pictures or short video can say a lot more than words while holding the learner's attention

2. Provide good navigation. If people can't find vital information after a few clicks they will give up. This is particularly important for just-in-time learning

3. Ask learners to enter data, prompt them with examples and reminders using simulations, exercises and case studies

4. Ensure the technology is robust – a learner who experiences long download times, choppy video or the necessity to download plug-ins will not be motivated

5. Decide on the specifications to ensure quality of design, e.g. maximum download time, maximum size of graphics etc.

6. Ensure technology is flexible enough to survive the future, e.g. International Data Corporation predicts that by 2004, while 600 million people will connect to the Internet through PCs, some 1.4 billion will connect through cellphones and other devices such as TV

7. Provide the learner with obvious links to expert/coach/tutor to allow them to obtain feedback and prevent feelings of isolation

8. Offer the opportunity to link to other resources, fellow learners and communities of practice for knowledge sharing and best practice

9. Allow the learner to break off and still have the ability to return to the place they left

10. Develop learning in small learning objects or 'learning bytes' that can be mixed and matched according to the needs of the learner

11. Pay attention to content. The differences in content require thoughtful decisions regarding design and delivery platforms. Graphics or photography easily represent cognitive concepts. These are especially conducive to technology-based presentation. Abstract concepts such as exercising judgement, building trust and resolving conflict are more difficult. These require written and spoken language as well as interaction and reflection

How Can the Needs of the Global Audience Be Addressed?

The e-learning revolution began in the US and while it continues to grow in Europe, the take-up in some countries has been slow. France and Germany in particular have not embraced e-learning to the same extent as the UK. One major reason for this could be obvious: language. The vast majority of e-learning content is still in English. The take-up of e-learning in European countries where English is widely spoken, such as the Netherlands or Sweden, is higher than in those where it is less prevalent. As well as language there are other cultural considerations. According to Martin Delahoussaye (2001), generally Europeans want more than linear learning and talking pictures, they want cultural references they can relate to and connect with.

Ashridge experienced the reverse of this problem when trying to introduce some learning modules to a US market. The fact that they contained mostly UK and European case studies made them unsuitable for this audience, as they felt they could not relate to the examples being given. In order for organizations to adopt e-learning globally, the challenge for those producing e-learning content is to get over the localization issue. Although language is less of an issue at the management level, where English is the common business language, when selecting e-learning providers it is wise to see to what extent they have developed material that is culturally acceptable and satisfies the whole of the organization.

When, Where and How Are Learners Expected to Learn?

While e-learning gives us more flexibility in terms of where we learn and the ability to deliver learning to the desktop, are we simply putting pressure on people to learn in their own time at home? In a typical busy open-plan office, how can learners concentrate on acquiring new knowledge? Surely the pressure of everyday work and the constant fire fighting will simply mean that learning is put to the bottom of the list of priorities. In a telephone survey of 50 organizations in Europe (Kernan, 1999) that are using e-learning, one respondent commented:

Our experience is that in order to learn someone must be removed from their desks . . . they need privacy above all . . . this is as true for a board member as for a mechanic. (1999: 6)

It is certainly true that there has been a resurgence of new learning centres within organizations to tackle this problem. British Aerospace recently set up 39 networked learning centres as part of a huge investment in e-learning. Giving employees somewhere to go to learn quietly may provide more of an incentive.

However, as more and more organizations are supporting remote working, e-learning most certainly benefits the learner who is on the road or working at home. An important consideration for the global organization is the issue of support. An infrastructure must be in place to provide 24-hour support to accommodate different time zones.

Arguably, a true 'knowledge-driven' company has to trust and empower its workers to organize their learning in such a way that it helps them to achieve their work goals more effectively, whether that means learning at work, at home or while travelling.

THE RISE OF THE CORPORATE UNIVERSITY

Some see corporate universities as the future of education, learning and training in the workplace. Others perceive them as a major threat to traditional seats of learning. We at Ashridge believe that they are an opportunity and are already working closely with several such universities or academies, such as Lloyds TSB, Xerox Europe and Volvo. This view is not universally shared, however, and they have been called 'corporate incest' (Anderson, 2000).

A good working definition of a corporate university appears in a DTI report: 'an internal structure designed to improve individual and business performance by ensuring that the learning knowledge of a corporation is directly connected to its business strategy' (Learning to Live, Campaign for Learning, 2000: 7).

From this we see that learning becomes integrated with information or, to use current jargon, e-learning meets knowledge management. The university would contain e-learning content, access to competitor intelligence, internal best practice and expertise and customer information. This is often housed and delivered by a combination of intranets and learning resource centres and can be shared with suppliers and customers. Some companies are now turning them into profit centres and selling them on to other organizations.

Some benefits claimed by advocates of corporate universities include:

- Faster adoption of new global strategies.
- Faster adoption of new technologies.
- Faster adoption of new practices.
- Stronger sense of corporate values in the organization.
- You can 'cherry pick' intellectual capital.
- Virtual learning leaves time for one-to-one.
- Training and development is easier to control and measure.
- One can demonstrate return on investment (ROI).
- It moves the agenda from training to learning.
- It manages cultural diversity.
- It has synergy with knowledge management in the organization.
- It is rooted in corporate strategy, not in human resources.
- It motivates and retains staff by offering lifelong learning.

There are certain issues that must be considered when setting up a corporate university. The first is that if one is not careful, one will finish up with a whole series of clones within the organization. Certain consultancies appear to have gone through this process already. Many organizations actually thrive on their slightly anarchic nature and too much control and corporate culture brainwashing may well stifle innovation and creativity. It is therefore essential that benchmarking is part of the corporate university agenda.

In this model senior managers are often the educators within the organization. Will they really replace tutors? There may well be commitment, energy and enthusiasm at the outset, but how long will this last? Partnerships with business schools will continue to develop. For a corporate university to succeed it most certainly does need leadership and commitment from the top as well as a culture of sharing values and best practice.

The main difference between the traditional training department and a corporate university is the shift to performance-based learning. This includes moving from a reactive to a proactive stance and from enrolling on a programme to just-in-time learning. The learner becomes king or queen.

KEY SUCCESS FACTORS FOR GLOBAL E-LEARNING ENVIRONMENTS

Now that we have looked at some of the issues surrounding e-learning, the following are what we believe to be some of the key factors to consider in order to make a success of building a global learning environment.

Develop a Learning Culture, Giving Time for Learning

Implementing e-learning must involve more than merely making the tools and technology available to people. It requires a culture change in the way people approach learning. A culture that encourages personal development and where learners are responsible for their own learning and development needs is vital to the success of any e-learning initiative. Learners must be helped to understand their learning styles and learning needs and introduced to new ways of learning. Technology alone will not change behaviour. Learners must be actively encouraged to learn at work and be given the time and space to do this wherever they are in the world. Whether in airports while waiting for a flight, hotels, learning centres or at the desktop, the opportunities must be there. They must not be forced to do their learning at home. Learning that is linked to business goals must be seen as strategically important and have support from the highest level. In our experience, those companies in the Ashridge consortium who had actively encouraged employees to take responsibility for their own personal development and supported them with a learning infrastructure have gained most benefit from access to the Virtual Learning Resource Centre and are in fact its biggest users.

Treat Technology as a Strategic Consideration

One of the major inhibitors to the growth and success of e-learning has been corporate bandwidth. Many organizations do not have sufficiently good Internet connections or intranet servers to allow the transfer of video, audio and complex graphics. Even within one organization, different geographical regions may have different capabilities. Organizations considering developing a global e-learning environment need to build possible investment into the infrastructure as well as expenditure on the e-learning materials themselves. Many believe it is impossible to overinvest in connectivity. At Ashridge we have adopted a flexible approach that enables organizations to use a combination of CD-Rom, Internet and intranet to access our materials according to their differing infrastructure needs.

Traditionally within large multinational companies it is likely that multiple people in different regions or parts of the business will be talking to a range of training and development providers about training solutions, including e-learning. As different e-learning providers use different technologies and these do not always talk to each other, signing regional deals is no longer a viable option when introducing e-learning into the global company. The organization needs to define the platforms it will support across the company; in other words, technology must be a strategic consideration.

We would also strongly recommend that HR and training departments involve their IT departments at an early stage in developing an e-learning strategy. The powerful combination of their skills can help to ensure success.

Don't Forget the Importance of Marketing

Internal marketing is crucial to the success of any e-learning initiative. It should not be viewed as a one-off activity, when e-learning is first launched, but as an ongoing exercise. At Ashridge we are particularly aware of the need to work with our customers in helping them market our e-learning products throughout the organization. Our own experience has been that the most successful adopters of e-learning are those who have integrated it into other training and development processes such as performance development reviews, personal development plans and appraisals, and where content has been linked to competency frameworks. The least successful adopters are those organizations that have simply provided a link from the corporate intranet to a range of interactive learning materials without backing that up by linking it to the core business strategy.

There is a need continually to 'drip feed' the organization with information on new features and benefits and to share success stories. Branding e-learning initiatives through a corporate university is an important way of raising awareness. Open days, presentations, brochures and newsletters can also help to reinforce the brand. Organizations should plan the marketing of their e-learning initiatives in the same way that they plan external marketing campaigns, because the same rules apply to both.

Do Your Research When Choosing Suppliers and Partners

Much of the intellectual capital, content and best practice needed for your e-learning environment may well reside within your own organization. Working with an e-learning solutions provider to build and design bespoke material may be an option for very specific content relevant to your business or industry. However, some areas in which you wish to develop your employees may be more generic, such as recognized technical and IT training and in some cases management skills. In this instance it may be more cost effective to use existing off-the-shelf solutions from organizations specializing in this form of content. The e-learning marketplace is very fragmented and still in its infancy. At present no single supplier has more than a 2 per cent market share. It is therefore essential to do extensive research on products and suppliers before selection to ensure that they meet your needs. The checklist in Table 6.4 provides some useful criteria to use to benchmark suppliers.

Table 6.4 Checklist for evaluating e-learning providers

CONTENT: quality/level – does it suit your audience? Will the case studies/examples cross international borders?

FLEXIBILITY OF DELIVERY PLATFORMS: e.g. intranet, Internet. Can the supplier offer different options and accommodate future changes?

BRAND: is it a well-established player in the market? There will undoubtedly be fallout in the marketplace over the next few years. Will the supplier survive this and still be around?

CURRENT CUSTOMERS: ask for a list. Are they similar organizations to yours? Can they provide any recommendations?

UPDATES: how often is the material reviewed and updated? Are the updates included in the price?

SUPPORT: is there any form of technical or learner support? Is it 24-hour support? Will they help with marketing it internally?

TRIAL PERIODS: does the supplier provide free trials? This can be useful and enable you to pilot the material on a small group and gain feedback

LINKS TO COMPETENCIES: how well does the material match with the corporate competencies and business goals?

PRICE: is it confusing? is it annual fee? can you purchase global licences?

EVALUATION OF USE: can the supplier provide feedback on use or will the material link with your in-company learning management system?

INDUSTRY STANDARDS: certain industry standards are emerging in the e-learning marketplace in areas such as the exporting of data and the categorization of content. These will become more important in the next few years. Does the supplier conform to these?

LEARNING STYLES: to what extent does the supplier appear to understand the importance of the learning experience? Is it catering for different learning styles and building in interaction and learning communities rather than pages of text-based material?

William M. Mercer

William M. Mercer is a global consulting firm that helps organizations use the power of their people to enhance business success.

We partner our clients in all aspects of strategic and operational human resource consulting and implementation. Our special areas of emphasis include HR strategy, employee benefits, compensation, communication and actuarial issues. We also advise on risk management and investment issues. With some 12 500-plus employees in more than 125 cities in 34 countries, we can develop seamless business solutions and deliver them to clients anywhere in the world. We have over 35 000 clients globally.

Intranet for Learning

Initially the advantage of using the intranet was seen merely as a means of delivering training and development information more effectively. Over the last three years, we have learned how to capitalize on the technology and develop fully integrated learning solutions.

In the UK a training and development intranet site was established at an early stage. The website was used to replace traditional training manuals. All training courses and services available were listed and individuals could use this information in the selection of learning opportunities and administration efficiency. Other general HR information such as internal vacancies and sales of former company cars were included on the site to arouse interest and increase traffic.

At the same time an open learning approach was developed and 12 learning resource centres were set up in the UK. Each site held a selection of computer-based training programmes, video and audio tapes and books covering topics such as PC skills, management skills and personal development.

Both the above initiatives were well received and, as our skills in Web writing and design improved, we developed the simple communication website into an integrated career development programme. This was aimed at all individuals within the organization, giving them the opportunity to develop in their present or for future roles. The site provided the individual with diagnosis of development needs linked to a broad range of learning solutions. These solutions included courses, coaching and open learning. Financial approval and booking processes were also included on the site.

Intranet for Intellectual Capital

Simultaneously to developing the intranet for learning, we were also developing its use for knowledge management globally with proprietary software to gather and disseminate knowledge. Knowledge management typically includes organizational processes, technical knowledge, best practices and professional standards.

Integration

A major leap forward occurred when the intranet and intellectual capital were brought together into a single brand called 'MercerLink'. For the first time we had a user-friendly intranet interface supported by a sophisticated knowledge management system. Additionally MercerLink was a truly global system, with a central global site and local geographical sites.

Globalization of Learning and Development

In response to demands from the business, human resources' contribution to globalization was the development of cross-geography behavioural competencies and technical knowledge (technical competencies). The competency framework provided a company-wide approach to performance management and supported the 'One Firm, Firm' philosophy. This in turn drove the need for global learning solutions. A global head of learning and development was appointed and early initiatives included the introduction of Knowledge Planet™, a proprietary product. Knowledge Planet is a Web-based product that enables individuals to plan their own short- and long-term learning strategies.

Features include:

- Online selection and booking of learning, e.g. courses, computer-based training and books etc.
- 'Click to run' multimedia and Internet-based training.
- Records of learning undertaken.
- Enhanced collaboration with supervisor, mentor on individual's development throughout the year.
- Provision of accurate management information.

Additionally a distance learning project team was briefed to recommend cost-effective and appropriate learning solutions on a global level. These solutions would need to be sensitive to cultural and language diversity. Members of the project team were selected to represent the broad spread of the organization.

Outputs to date have included an inventory of distance learning products worldwide, the introduction of access to the Ashridge Virtual Learning Resource Centre across all geographies, the production of a distance learning website for sponsors of learning and training practitioners to facilitate the introduction of appropriate distance learning approaches.

Lessons Learned

- Ensure that supporting the company strategy takes precedence over attractive new technologies.
- Involve internal communications at an early stage to assist with branding, creative publishing and in-house communication.
- Don't rely on using technology to encourage individuals to visit an intranet site, consider other media such as brochures.
- Give presentations at board meetings, management meetings and any other meetings you can find to deliver the message 'face to face'.
- Design simple documentation to reduce form filling and maximize managers' control of time and money invested in development activities.
- Involve people from the business continuously in the design and building of any programmes.
- Identify and train local training representatives who can explain to people 'face to face' how the site can be accessed to start their own development.
- Put in place measurement processes to enable monitoring of progress.
- Train in-house Web writers to produce intranet material quickly and cheaply.

- Keep checking with the business and make changes regularly to ensure that the contents of the sites are relevant and current.

Future Developments
- Continuation of the roll-out of the infrastructure to support 'Knowledge Planet' and distance learning to all geographies, particularly Australia and Canada.
- Closer integration of learning, knowledge and information to provide our consultants with the right knowledge, skills and information, at the right time, in the right place, to make a positive difference to the client relationship.

Source: Hesketh (2000)

References

Aberdeen Group Inc. (1999) *e-Learning in the Enterprise*, Boston, MA: Aberdeen Group.

Anderson, L. (2000) 'Business education survey – article on corporate universities', *Financial Times*, 23 October.

Berry, J. (2000) 'Traditional training fades in favour of E-learning', *Internet Week*, 800: 33–4.

Delahoussaye, M. (2001) 'European echo', *Training*, 38(1): 61–5.

Dobbs, K. (2000) 'What the online world needs now', *Training*, 37(9): 86.

Hesketh, B. (2000) *William M. Mercer Case Study*, London: William M. Mercer.

Kernan, M. A. (1999) *Ashridge On-Line Market Research Report*, Berkhamsted: Ashridge Management College.

Kolb, D. A., Rubin, I. M. and MacIntyre, J. M. (1984) *Organizational Psychology*, 4th edn, Englewood Cliffs, NJ: Prentice Hall.

Learning to Live, Campaign for Learning (2000) *The Future of Corporate Learning*, London: Department of Trade and Industry.

Lewis, N. J. and Orton, P (2000) 'The five attributes of innovative e-learning', *Training and Development*, June: 47–51.

McGovern, S. (2000) *European IT Training and Skills Management Services Market Forecast and Analysis 1999–2004*, International Data Corp.

McGovern, S. (2001) *Worldwide Corporate E-learning Market Forecast and Analysis, 1999–2004*, International Data Corp.

Wildsmith, H. (2001) *e-research @ashridge*, Berkhamsted: Ashridge Management College.

WORKING IN COMPLEX TEAMS: ARE YOU BUILDING GLOBAL CAPABILITY OR DESTROYING IT?

Karen Ward

CHAPTER 7

WORKING IN COMPLEX TEAMS: ARE YOU BUILDING GLOBAL CAPABILITY OR DESTROYING IT?

*T*eams have been a feature of the organizational landscape since the fashion for quality circles was adopted from the Japanese in the 1980s. In 1995, a survey indicated that 79 per cent of organizations considered that teams would be vital to their success in the next ten years (Herriot and Pemberton, 1995). So what has this got to do with globalization?

WHY TEAMS?

Many commentators believe that teams are particularly critical for organizations operating globally as they offer a unique way of building global capability throughout the organization, while simultaneously delivering the strategic priorities. The following quotes from leading globalization experts illustrate the importance of teams in the global environment:

- 'Effective, efficient international teams are central to future global competitiveness' (Rhinesmith, 1996).

- 'International teams are the engines that pull companies forward to success or failure in the global marketplace' (O'Hara-Devereux and Johansen, 1994).

- 'The evidence is compelling that teams contribute to improved organizational effectiveness' (Appelbaum and Batt, 1994).

Yet despite the evidence that teams enable organizations to build global capability, many companies are failing to capitalize on the promise of higher performance offered by effective teams. Too few global organizations actively manage the creation and maintenance of teams. Too often the ineffective, 'wait and see' or 'sink or swim' approach to the introduction of teams has been adopted, with disastrous human consequences and business results.

One of the reasons for this lack of progress is that many managers see teams in isolation, as something that can be created almost without reference to the wider organization. This could not be further from the truth. Teams are deeply embedded in their organizational context and their effectiveness is significantly affected by this context. Teams are microcosms of the wider organization and thus creating effective teams touches on *every* aspect of the globalization model outlined earlier (Figure 1.1).

Although most obviously situated in the 'organization' bubble – teams are after all an organization design choice – alignment with the other aspects of the model is critical for complex team effectiveness. As will be discussed later in the chapter, team purpose needs to be aligned with global strategic priorities (strategy); the performance management, recognition and reward systems need to be aligned for all team members across the world (processes); the nature and magnitude of diversity among team members must be explicitly explored and team working practices developed (culture); appropriate leadership must be developed to suit the task and the diversity of the team members, sometimes in contrast to the dominant style in the line functions of the organization (leadership); and last but not least, if the organization genuinely wants to build a sustainable global capability, it needs to develop ways of running these teams throughout the organization (learning).

Another factor that hinders managers from creating effective teams is the nature of teams within global organizations. The increasing complexities of commercial life in a global environment demand that individuals from different backgrounds and different nations collaborate in order to identify and resolve problems and take advantage of the opportunities. As a global player, you cannot afford to ignore talent, ideas or markets, just because you don't personally understand them. Building teams is one of the only ways organizations can sense new trends and spot new opportunities, irrespective of where they occur in the globe. This isn't about being touchy-feely and nice to each other. It is about spotting and exploiting opportunities before your competitors do, anywhere on the planet. To make this happen, teams in global organizations are therefore complex, and can be defined as:

> A group of people who come from different nationalities, functions and locations and work interdependently towards a common goal. These complex teams usually work apart across time zones for extended periods of time: they are dispersed or virtual.

Establishing these complex teams provides a unique opportunity for the organization to create a sustainable global capability, but it also presents a range of challenges not faced by local co-located teams. This chapter explores the actions that can be taken to enhance the performance of these complex teams and ensure that likely pitfalls are avoided. It draws on experience of working with complex teams in a range of global organizations over the last decade and on ongoing research into the factors that make these teams effective.

HOW TO CREATE SUCCESSFUL COMPLEX TEAMS

Few organizations have been prepared to make the necessary investment to gain the potential benefits that complex teams offer. Many organizations that have introduced complex teams have focused on the performance of these teams in isolation, yet experience and research has demonstrated that the organizational context into which international teams are introduced plays a key role in determining their effectiveness (Ward, 1997). There are a number of preconditions for organizations wanting to develop a diverse outlook and thereby be able to sustain effective complex teams:

- Valuing and widespread acceptance of cultural diversity.
- Low levels of prejudice.
- Positive mutual attitudes among cultural groups.
- Sense of attachment to the larger system.

Creating this context is not a quick fix; it is a long-term commitment. Organizations need to take a systemic view of operating globally rather than simply creating complex teams in a vacuum and assuming that everything else will remain unchanged. Introducing complex teams brings into sharp focus the way an organization operates and this can act as a catalyst for a fundamental review of these practices. Complex teams are not a miracle solution for effective global working, but used thoughtfully they can enhance organizational capability to operate successfully across the globe. As with any organizational design, they have their strengths and weaknesses, as illustrated in Table 7.1.

Given these challenges, what should global organizations be doing to ensure that their complex teams are successful? Much has been written about effective team processes in general and the first thing to state is that most of these guidelines also apply to complex teams in global organizations. It is now well established that any team will have a greater chance of success if the team as a whole has:

- A clear motivating goal.
- A strong sense of commitment and urgency.
- Interdependent work.
- Competent team members with complementary skills.
- Well-set ground rules and standards for good interaction.
- Good interpersonal communication and relationships.
- Culturally appropriate leadership.
- Appropriately rewarded interim and final goals.
- Control over its own resources.

Table 7.1 Advantages and disadvantages of complex teams

Advantages of complex teams	Disadvantages of complex teams
Enables global strategies to be created that are sensitive to local requirements	Individuals can feel torn between loyalty to the team and to their local manager
Enables the organization to benefit from a diversity of perspectives that more closely match the preferences of their client base	It can be difficult to reach consensus on a way forward
Increases organizational learning about the global market	Language and communication difficulties mean that it can take longer to reach an optimum level of effectiveness
More efficient use of resources – avoids duplication of effort	Remote working can feel very isolated and demotivating and harm family life; it is also easy to get distracted by local issues
High level of intrinsic rewards: learning from different people and different parts of the company, and developing alternative methodologies for tackling problems	Potential for increased conflict due to different opinions
Extends international development opportunities beyond 'traditional' expatriate manager	Certain cultural habits, such as talking about oneself, pointing, burping, and certain types of food, can be offensive to people from other cultures
Being 'special' can increase morale	These teams need high initial investment in people, training and technology to avoid very expensive mistakes
Team leaders and members usually increase their skills with communication technology	Poorly supported complex teams can 'burn out' key members of staff and reinforce national stereotypes
Enables broader targets to be set that will have an impact in many different countries simultaneously	It is a challenge to create equitable reward and evaluation processes

- Effective boundary management – team and organization.
- External support and recognition.

While these 'team basics' may have very different interpretations in different cultures, they are as important to international teams as they are to national teams. Consequently, companies that have already invested in creating good teamwork locally find it much easier to create effective international teams.

However, implementing these team basics is not enough to ensure sustained success. Research and experience have illustrated that there are six additional factors that have a marked impact on the performance of complex teams in global organizations, as highlighted below:

- The nature and magnitude of diversity within the team (cultural norms, commitment to these norms and cultural status).
- Organizational context.
- Geographical spread.
- Ability to manage personal boundaries.
- Different expectations of working practices, e.g. decision making, conflict resolution, performance feedback.
- Language fluency.

These factors must be acknowledged and actively managed throughout the life cycle of a team for that team to thrive. To help teams manage these factors, a model can be used based on four simple phases in a team's life cycle, as illustrated in Figure 7.1.

For anyone who has worked with complex teams, this model will intuitively be common sense. Whatever the composition and geography of a team and whatever their task, there is a time before teams interact: phase one. There is a time when the whole team first meets: phase two. There is a period of continuing to work together to get the task done: phase three; and a period of completing the task and passing on the learning: phase four.

Feedback from team sponsors, leaders, members and facilitators indicates that this four-stage model is easy to work with and can be tailored to suit varied circumstances. The model is cumulative. That is, the better each phase is managed, the more productive and less

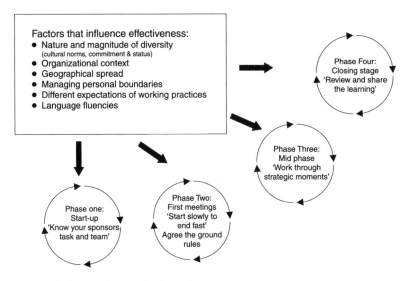

Figure 7.1   Life cycle model of complex teams.

troublesome the next phase will be. Similarly, the more mistakes that are made in each phase, the more likely your team is to fall apart.

BEST PRACTICES THROUGHOUT A TEAM'S LIFE CYCLE

Experience with teams in a range of organizations has demonstrated that there are a number of best practices that can be utilized throughout a team's life cycle to minimize process losses and thereby maximize performance. These are described fully below and illustrated in Figure 7.2.

Phase One: Start-up

This phase can be summed up as: 'know your sponsors, task and team'. The first useful step that team sponsors, leaders and relevant managers who will be setting up the team can take is to agree its purpose.

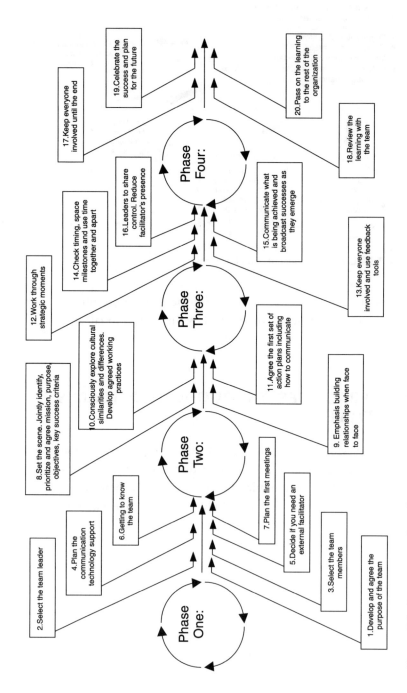

Figure 7.2 Best practices throughout the life cycle of a team.

1. Develop and agree the purpose of the team

There needs to be clarity and consensus about why the team has been established and what it is expected to achieve. In particular, how does this team contribute to overall global strategic priorities and choices? This happens best in one, or a series of, face-to-face meeting(s), but can be done in a series of teleconferences, e-mails or in a groupware discussion if necessary.

The team leader and sponsor(s) need to painstakingly clarify the mission, purpose, agenda, accountability, time frame, resources available, organizational barriers and key stakeholders. The sponsor(s) should lead this activity and ensure that all key stakeholders have the opportunity to influence this discussion. Inclusion of all key players at this stage facilitates rapid implementation.

Suppose that a new cross-regional team is being set up in an organization that has otherwise worked very nationally. The relevant country/line managers need to attend some of these design meetings, as they are the ones who will need to work out their new relationship to the team members, change the support systems and agree cross-regional budgeting.

2. Select the team leader

The team sponsors and key stakeholders need to be very clear about the challenge of leading complex teams and take care in selecting the best team leader available. There are two aspects to this selection process.

First, they must be able to define the team leader's role clearly. If an organization does not understand and cannot articulate the content of a particular role, it will have difficulty selecting someone for that position if it becomes vacant, and it will not know how to develop the individuals in the role to improve their performance. Agreed criteria create an international standard against which managers anywhere in the world can be identified, selected and promoted. This means that companies can increasingly act as large pools of interchangeable talent at senior levels. It also means that internal vacancies focus on objective criteria and potential, rather than a description of the person who just left, e.g. 'five years' experience with toothbrush sales'.

One of the first issues to resolve is whether the complex team leader needs in-depth technical knowledge of the subject or highly developed leadership skills. The fact is that for most technical experts, once an expert, always an expert first, even if they have been a director of an important international research organization for over a decade. It is very rare to meet a brilliant scientist or technical expert who has either the desire or the in-born skill to lead a complex team. Yet much of a complex team leader's time will be taken managing external boundaries, co-ordinating the workflow and the people, and accessing necessary resources.

Where should the balance lie between leader and expert? There is no single right answer. It has long been established that the answer to 'Should a leader have at hand the answer to any question asked by their employees?' will create very different statistical norms across different cultures (Hofstede, 1980; Trompenaars, 1993). In Sweden and America the answer tends to be no. In Japan, Indonesia and Italy it tends to be yes: 'If you do not have knowledge, you will not gain our respect.' This is related to differing preferences on two cultural dimensions: power distance and ascription/achievement. These dimensions explore how leaders gain status, respect and authority in the organization. The challenges this poses are illustrated in the following example.

A global player in the automotive industry had a history of ap-pointing technically brilliant engineers as leaders of their product design and development teams. This was seen as an important career development opportunity. When these teams were co-located in one country and the team members were primarily from similar technical backgrounds, this choice was not a problem.

Yet to bring a new vehicle to the global marketplace re-quires leadership of a complex array of players: many components of the end product are now outsourced to third parties; sales, marketing and brand managers have a close eye on the customer specifications of their market; and environmental lobbyists want cleaner and recyclable products, to name a few issues. To manage this complexity effectively requires far more than technical brilliance and a cleverly designed car.

The challenge is how to ensure these teams have the appropriate leadership without disenfranchising your key technical talent.

What can organizations do to resolve this dilemma? Wherever possible, it is best to involve the people concerned. Do some of them have willingness and potential to develop some of the other skills required? Could technical experts work in partnership with highly skilled process facilitators and coaches? Where it is not possible to involve the potential team members, then it should be clear that no one person can sanely handle both the necessary technical depth and the co-ordination of the team. If the team leader is the expert who will get deeply involved in the technical discussions, then they need to assign the role of managing the process to another person. If the team leader's main role is perceived as co-ordinating the process, then they will need technical experts on the team. This concept of shared leadership is critical for effective complex teams.

Having identified the criteria for an effective complex team leader, the second step is usually to select individuals from the existing workforce to take on the roles. Experience indicates that unless a well-thought-through and interactive selection process is applied, the leadership role will tend to go to the person perceived to have the most power and influence in the existing organization and this can seriously limit an organization's ability to respond to global challenges.

Often, the person selected is the headquarters person in charge of that issue, which again diminishes the contribution of significant numbers of potential team leaders in other parts of the organization. The problem is that if you use selection processes based on the way national line management has been selected and you limit your pool to the hierarchical status quo, you may be narrowing your potential field of talent. By challenging the existing selection norms, organizations often uncover hidden talent. In summary, the issues to bear in mind are:

- Challenge existing selection practices – are they appropriate?
- Be open minded about who can apply for complex team roles – personal motivation is very important.
- Be creative and design the selection process to meet the needs of the teams and the business.
- Be proactive – lack of a specific selection process will reinforce current political power bases rather than get the right person for the role.

3. Select the team members

Once the purpose of the team has been clarified and a leader has been appointed, the next step is to establish the team membership. The purpose of the team will determine the type of staffing and the skills needed. The strengths and weaknesses of the team leader may also influence the choice of other key team members. For example, if the team leader is a strong technical expert on the task, she may need to ensure she has members of the team with strong process skills. Alternatively, if the team leader has been selected for his ability to facilitate diverse teams, he may need a content expert among his colleagues.

The process by which the team members are selected will also have a powerful influence on the subsequent dynamics of the team. As with team leader selection, structured selection processes can overcome organizational biases such as dominant cultures (geographical, functional or professional) and gender biases, which can destroy team performance. Again, the sponsors and team leader must be clear of the balance between technical and process skills that is required to make the team effective.

There is also the question of who should have the main say in selecting team members. This should not be the role of the team sponsor, although they sometimes try to have a strong influence. Often it is only the team leaders who know who is, or has been, good on someone else's team and they want experienced people who are already very competent and available. On the other hand, line managers may not want to lose their best people on long-term secondments or to manage the consequences of overloading their best people on part-time assignments. They may want to use the team to create opportunities for training up-and-coming staff. The role of the sponsor is to facilitate resolution of these different perspectives.

Teams are a microcosm of the wider organization and will therefore reflect the underlying tensions present in the organization. These tensions will begin to emerge as the team members are selected and the sponsor(s) will need to resolve conflicts in the most culturally appropriate manner.

Throughout this setting-up process, the team leader will be gaining insights into the areas of similarity and difference between the team members and the tensions or points of cohesion that are likely to occur. For instance, if a young team leader has been selected on the basis of having broad project skills, older, expert technicians may feel resentful. This insider knowledge is vital. Without it, the team leader cannot start to consider how to make these issues conscious within the team in phase two of the team's life cycle.

4. Plan the communication technology support

Once the geographical location of the team members is established, the sponsors and the leader need to assess what communication technology will enhance the interaction of the team for the particular task they have been set. An expert from the information technology or services department usually needs to be involved, especially if the team is dispersed and this is a new phenomenon for the organization.

This is not necessarily the time to introduce or design new technology. Instead, you should appraise what means of communication currently exist within the organization, what is available on the market, what the team can benefit from, how much it would cost, how long it would take to introduce/train the team members and how much budget is realistically available. Then select the method that allows *all* team members to communicate as efficiently as possible. Don't go for high tech if it excludes any member of the team.

5.   Decide if you need an external facilitator – if you do, contract with the sponsors and team to clarify the boundaries of responsibility and the facilitator's role

All effective teams actively manage their process as well as the task on which they are working. This process/task balance will require active facilitation. So, as early as possible in the life cycle of a team, decide what level of facilitation skills is needed for that particular team and whether to use external or internal resources or to self-facilitate. The key issues to consider when making these decisions are:

- Are the team members coming with conflicting agendas where a neutral person would aid common agreement?
- Do the team leader and team members all need to be heavily involved in the detail of the task? This will make it hard also to attend to process.
- What is the level of experience and confidence of the team leader in managing a team with the particular mix of experience and backgrounds involved?

A facilitator's role should *not* be to get teams out of trouble. It is to develop teams' capability to manage themselves from the beginning so that they can progressively improve their performance throughout the life cycle and creatively manage differences and stalemates when they arise.

If facilitation and managing the processes of teams are very new to the organization, there can be a strong sense of resistance. 'We want to have a go at this first without outside interference' can be a typical response from teams in these organizations. The sponsors then need to decide whether they believe the team is capable of self-facilitating. Sometimes it is a question of risk. Can the sponsor risk a team learning on its own and making its own mistakes as it goes along? Or does the team need to deliver critical outputs within a tight time constraint with no room for learning from mistakes? What are the risks of 'imposing' a facilitator vs letting the team go it alone? The experience of teams who have tried to go it alone and discovered (often too late) that they needed external coaching is summed up best by this team leader's comment to their facilitator:

> We used you as a paramedic, when it was a life and death situation and we should have been using you as preventative medicine. We did not need to get sick in the first place.

Whatever the sponsor(s) and team leader decide, this must be clearly contracted with the facilitator and the team. An experienced facilitator will acknowledge this tension at the beginning of the relationship with the team and be able to establish quickly how to gain credibility to enable them to begin to add value.

Expense should not be the primary consideration in deciding whether to have a facilitator or not. Good facilitators will pay for themselves many times over if the team would otherwise have difficulties. Many teams have rejected a facilitator only to have to start again when they have reached a stalemate. This invariably costs the team and the organization far more than if a facilitator had been involved all along. There is no fixed single role for a facilitator and the most effective role will depend on the needs of the team. At least half of a facilitator's effectiveness depends on clearly defining the role that the facilitator will play, prior to working with the team, and then continually reviewing this contract throughout the life cycle of the team.

6. Getting to know the team

Once the team members have agreed to participate on the team, it is useful for the team leader to start getting them involved, prior to meeting face to face. This can be done through interviews or sending out a questionnaire to find out how much the team members already understand about the task, their attitude towards, or historical interaction with, each other and their level of commitment to the team. Some leaders and facilitators find it useful to ask would-be team members to fill in work style or team role questionnaires and to process these before the team first meets. Simplicity and cultural relevance are the key to any diagnostic tool. Teams can then employ the results of the questionnaires as a feedback tool to improve their own performance.

This kind of preparatory work is especially useful in organizations where there are high levels of cynicism or uncertainty. This could be due to previous cost-cutting or retrenchment exercises, previous weak management or because the organization is highly decentralized or dispersed. Team members can unload any potential frustrations one on one in advance, rather than bringing them, still burning, to the start-up meetings. The team leader (and/or facilitator) can then plan in advance how to acknowledge any outstanding issues relating to historical events before moving on to create a positive feeling about how this team can do things differently. These up-front exercises also send the message that each team member matters to the team as a whole.

7. Plan the first meetings

Team members, the leader and/or facilitator and key sponsors need to go through the agenda for the first meetings. They need to establish who will present what and check to see that any proposed team exercises or process activities will be culturally and organizationally relevant and at the right level of experience.

They then need to collate and distribute any necessary documentation and pre-reading and view and book the venue and the social and culinary arrangements. While these administrative details might seem less important, if they are done badly it can have a major impact on the start-up of the team. For instance, the timing on the first day needs to take jet lag into account. A Korean coming to Finland may well sleep through presentations on the first evening if he arrived that morning, which will be frustrating for the presenter and embarrassing for the new team member.

Phase Two: First Meetings – Start Slowly to End Fast, Agree the Ground Rules

Most teams in action-oriented cultures (e.g. American, British, Scandinavian) have a tendency to jump straight to the task. While this approach may appear in the short term to be very productive, in their

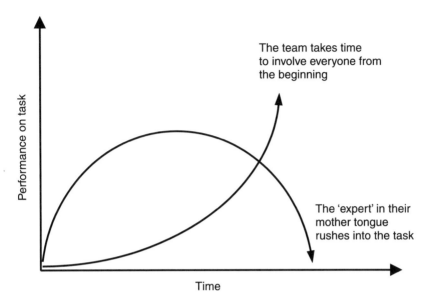

Figure 7.3   Start slowly to end fast.

rush to 'do' and be busy these teams often don't ensure that everyone is on board. The resulting conflicts and disagreements on what is to be achieved and how, which usually surface at key milestones or prior to implementation, mean at best that the team stalls, at worst it collapses. Not only does this lead to non-delivery of the task, but it potentially destroys staff's desire to work on these teams in the future, thus destroying the organization's ability to develop a global capability. The alternative approach illustrated is to take time in the early phases to work on task and process simultaneously. Although appearing to be less productive initially from a task perspective, productivity speeds up exponentially after the first phase of the life cycle, usually allowing the team to deliver superior performance in financial and time terms, while still having fun and learning (see Figure 7.3).

To illustrate this using a non-work example, if the task were climbing a mountain, then no team in their right mind would set out without carefully planning the route, allocating key responsibilities, identifying the ways in which they were going to avoid major pitfalls along the route and agreeing how they were going to communicate, especially if things started going wrong. For some reason, many people think you do not have to have the same kind of preparation for tasks in the corporate environment, despite these tasks often being as complex and risky as our metaphorical mountain climb. The common misconception is that it will all fall into place as soon as the team starts its journey. Often this is because everyone assumes that everyone else has the same ideas of how they should proceed. However, if the foundations aren't laid in phase one, when the team members encounter the first crevasse they flounder and start arguing about basic procedures that should have been clear right from the start.

Bringing all the different expectations and understanding of processes to the surface at the beginning of the life cycle and planning a common working approach are essential for the success of teams.

8. Set the scene – jointly identify, prioritize and agree the mission, purpose, objectives and key success criteria

Companies create teams for a variety of reasons, but usually the tasks they are required to complete cross a range of organizational boundaries. If team members have no sense or previous experience of the wider organization, it can feel like groping in the dark for an answer. It is critical that teams have a clear sense of the context within which they are working. Managing boundaries effectively is a key characteristic of successful teams. This context setting is the primary role of the team sponsor(s).

Experience has illustrated that it is more effective to gain commitment to a common direction for the team first, before exploring any differences that exist in the wider organization. However, it is important to surface and acknowledge these differences as early as possible in a team's life cycle, otherwise unchannelled differences can destroy a team's ability to deliver successfully.

Once the purpose of the team, within the big picture, is clear, then the team needs to identify what it wants to achieve, how it is going to do this and what it should look like when the team gets there.

When it comes to establishing how, the focus should be on accessing different expectations about what constitutes effective team work, including decision making, leadership, performance management, conflict resolution and so on.

9. Emphasize building relationships when face to face

Evidence indicates that trust is best established at the same time in the same place, i.e. when people are face to face. It is much harder across a distance. Trust is built in different ways in different cultures. For example, aspiring American presidents usually start poking fun at themselves and deriding their weaknesses in the last stages of a run-up campaign. In Hong Kong they would never get elected. For some cultures, the idea of establishing trust after only a few meeting is meaningless. Some Germans, for example, will wait to see the steadiness and quality of the work before trusting their colleagues.

In general, the following activities are best done when working face to face:

- Agree the overall vision, common goals and interim targets.
- Work through and integrate personal agendas.
- Lay the ground rules within which working trust and working relationships can be developed.
- Form personal aspects of trust, appreciation and understanding of different communication preferences.
- Work through difficulties, conflicts of interest and interpersonal problems.
- Argue through differing viewpoints and make important decisions, especially on value-laden, complex, non-technical issues.
- Evaluate and review overall progress.
- Jointly undergo some training.
- Introduce a new person or aspect of the work.
- If necessary, change values, policies and targets.
- Agree the patterns and styles of communication at a distance.
- Celebrate successes.

10. Consciously explore the similarities and differences and resulting strengths and weaknesses of the team – develop agreed working practices or ground rules

This is perhaps the most important process of all in complex teams, an in-depth understanding of who you are as a team. Having done this, you can decide how to best work together. Only then can you tap into the enormous potential that a team can offer. There are a range of tools (questionnaires, role plays, exercises) to help teams develop a greater awareness of their similarities and differences.

An international IT organization of French origin has been trying to ensure that non-French employees don't experience a cultural glass ceiling. On development programmes that have international participants, they run an exercise that explores what it is like to work in an organization with a dominant culture, in this case French.

Participants are split into two groups, one French, one non-French. The groups have to answer the questions in Table 7.2.

The two groups then share their responses and perceptions and together build an action plan to overcome any areas of conflict.

Colleagues from the human resources function should be able to advise on any questionnaires favoured within the organization. One

Table 7.2 Cultural questions

French group	Non-French group
What do you feel proud of in your culture?	What do you value in the French culture?
What would you change if you could?	What would you change if you could?
What have you never been able to explain to a non-French person?	What have you never been able to understand?

questionnaire that works well with teams, irrespective of the functional or cultural mix, is the Myers Briggs Type Indicator™ (MBTI). This will require a qualified coach to give feedback to the team, but the insights gained and the long-term benefits of enhanced performance are usually worth the initial investment in time and expense.

The critical issue to remember is that these questionnaires or checklists are tools/frameworks for facilitating a discussion among team members.

Two things are happening simultaneously during these discussions. First, the basis of awareness and sensitivity is being established, the team is legitimizing and appreciating its members' similarities and differences and assessing their strengths and weaknesses. By using an agreed framework, the team members will later be able to give each other feedback on behavioural issues without becoming personal. Second, the team is setting the 'ground rules' for how its members will best interact. Even though this is often up-hill work and some people may only agree reluctantly, establishing ground rules has the following benefits:

- Creates workable communication norms specific to the team.
- Creates a commitment within the team that all team members are responsible for generating the best interaction.
- Protects the views of minorities, which enhances the overall performance of the team.
- Enables the ground rules to be utilized as a neutral judge when conflict and destructive behaviour start to take over.
- Creates a much broader 'field' in which creative and constructive conflict can take place.

Some people are fascinated by these discussions and immediately see their relevance and others think they are a total waste of time, but later even they often begrudgingly admit that if they had taken these discussions seriously, they would not be encountering many of their subsequent difficulties. If team members and especially the team leader lack intercultural sensitivities or have not established clear ground rules, stereotypes and organizational norms will probably prevail and some very valuable members of the team are likely to be excluded from meaningful interaction.

Cross-cultural project team working in Hong Kong

Hong Kong is a vibrant city that is home to the Pacific Rim operations of many multinationals as well as large indigenous companies. Most of these organizations consist, in the management ranks, of numbers of local Chinese staff working alongside largely Anglo-Saxon (British, American and Australian) expatriates. Many of these organizations have also experienced problems in project team working due to cultural clashes. For example, Avon, the famous US headquartered home retailer, sources much of its product from China via its Far East buying office in Hong Kong. Senior management there noticed tensions and miscommunications between American head office staff, Hong Kong Chinese staff in the buying office and Chinese staff in China itself.

Standing back and reflecting on the situation, it is easy to see why such problems arise. Anglo-Saxon and Chinese cultural values are poles apart (see Table 7.3).

Table 7.3 Cultural values compared

Anglo-Saxon cultural values	Chinese cultural values
Individualism	Collectivism
Low power distance	High power distance
Universalism	Particularism and pragmatism
Rationalism	Contextualism and holism
Competition	Harmony
Guilt	Face and shame
Time focused	Time flexible

Anglo-Saxons tend to be more individualist; less concerned with hierarchy; believers in fair treatment; competitive; and very time focused. On the other hand, Chinese tend to be more family oriented; more concerned with hierarchy; more concerned with personal relationships; afraid of losing face; concerned with pre-serving harmony; and more flexible in terms of time (Kirkbride and Westwood, 1992).

Of course, it is not all doom and gloom. Both cultures can see positive aspects to the other culture, as can be seen from Table 7.4, which summarizes the views of both cultures in a Hong Kong multinational (HKMNC).

Table 7.4 Positive cultural aspects

Anglo–Saxons (as seen by Chinese)	Chinese (as seen by Anglo-Saxons)
Friendly	Industrious
Assertive	Family oriented
Open-minded	Clever
Innovative	Thirsty for knowledge
Informal	Harmony seeking

The darker side is unfortunately depicted in Table 7.5, which shows some of the negative attributions and frustrations. Obviously such an atmosphere is not conducive to good team work and co-operation within the organization!

Table 7.5 Negative cultural aspects

Anglo–Saxons (as seen by Chinese)	Chinese (as seen by Anglo-Saxons
Short-term results focused	Don't give clear answers to questions
Impatient and arrogant	Won't give bad news
Too direct and aggressive	Try to satisfy everybody
Inconsistent	Won't take personal responsibility
Lazy	Not creative

One large Hong Kong company (HKCO) was particularly concerned at the problems that Chinese and Anglo-Saxon staff were having in working co-operatively and productively together. It suspected that part of the problem was deep-seated cultural approaches to conflict management and interpersonal frictions. A researcher measured the approaches to conflict used by both groups using the well-known Thomas-Kilmann Conflict Mode Instrument (Thomas and Kilmann, 1974) and found the patterns of response, given in Table 7.6.

Table 7.6 Patterns of approaches to conflict

Style	Chinese managers	Anglo-Saxon managers
Competing	4.6	6.0
Collaborating	6.1	7.9
Compromising	7.9	6.1
Avoiding	6.7	5.2
Accommodating	4.5	4.7

As the table shows, the Anglo-Saxon managers tended to use the more assertive styles of collaborating, competing and compromising and rarely avoided confrontation, while the Chinese managers had a clear preference for compromise to preserve harmony and, if that was ineffective, fell back on avoiding, which really irritated the Anglo-Saxons.

Both HKMNC and HKCO decided to tackle these cultural blockages to team working by undertaking cross-cultural training sessions for mixed groups of Anglo-Saxon and Chinese managers and using a mixed Anglo-Saxon and Chinese training team. Both sides were encouraged to explore and question aspects of their own culture and to seek to understand aspects of the other culture. Indeed, sessions were held entitled 'Everything you always wanted to know about the other culture but never dared to ask!' These training interventions appeared to lead to greater understanding and an easier working relationship across the cultural divide. In fact, more than one expatriate remarked that they had learned more about Chinese culture and behaviour in one day that they had in the previous ten years.

Most groups derived some key lessons from the training sessions, which can be summarized as follows and which were often incorporated into ground rules for action:

- Examine and know your own cultural assumptions and values.
- Understand why you traditionally behave and act in a certain way.
- Understand your colleague's cultural assumptions and values.

- Be aware that your colleague's behaviour is perfectly logical when viewed from their own cultural assumptions/values.
- Predict how your colleague might prefer to do things differently.
- Jointly search for culturally synergistic solutions.

11. Agree the first set of action plans, including how to communicate

At this point, the team needs to agree what will be done, who will do it and by when before the next meeting. Most importantly, it needs to agree how its members are going to communicate, not only how they will use different technologies, but also the style of communication. Establishing a communication charter should specifically aim at managing the complexities of the team and its stakeholders.

This is where the information technology person from the design team can present their findings and the team can work through the options and formulate their needs. This process can prompt organizations to get serious about establishing cross-boundary e-mail or intranets and standard software packages.

By the end of this first set of meetings, the team should be clear about what it is doing and where it is going. Differences should have been opened up and explored only after a common understanding of purpose and goals has been established. The team should then work on the 'how' before the detail of the 'what'. Culturally different norms, different levels of language fluency, different working practices, leadership styles, geographical distances and status issues should have been made visible and integrated into a workable interactive process that best supports the task and incorporates each team member's individuality.

Phase Three: Work Through Strategic Moments

The middle phase of a team's life cycle is often characterized by bursts of activities followed by periods of stagnation and poor momentum in which problems arise. The hidden agendas missed at the beginning can emerge and create 'strategic moments'. Aside from working through difficulties and 'strategic moments', the team needs to renew, review and undergo relevant mid-term training. The frequency of strategic moments, the severity of discomfort and the implications of how they are handled by the leader or facilitator all seem to be far greater in complex teams, e.g. multicultural, multifunctional or virtual, than in homogeneous teams.

12. Work through strategic moments

To illustrate what is meant by 'strategic moments', let's look at a typical team meeting in a multinational organization.

> The European Product Development Team meets quarterly to review progress against product launch plans. At this meeting, a chart is drawn up listing current activities and responsibilities. The team members from the Spanish production plant do not want to reveal how far they have moved along with the marketing of a new product because they are convinced that the Germans from headquarters will steal their ideas and take the best markets. However, the company is racing against three other competitors to get to market. As the review progresses, the names of senior vice-presidents and the chief executive are being given for who is responsible for key activities, with no names from within the team being proposed. The German head of production beckons to the Spanish head of sales and storms out of the room, leaving the rest of the team in stunned silence.

The team has reached a strategic moment. What happens next could make or break the team. If the leader or facilitator knows the history, was expecting the stand-off and can lead the team through this moment, the likelihood is that old corporate patterns and years of antagonism and vested interests can be broken down. So while they may be extremely uncomfortable, strategic moments are also great opportunities for changing unworkable corporate habits. In fact, the team can be energized and enthused by the release of all the potential energy that was held in previous dysfunctional patterns.

Back to our team.

The facilitator pointed out to the remaining team members that two key people had left the room and proposed a break. She asked the team what it wanted to do after the 15-minute break. 'Oh, we want to discuss the product in general,' came the response. This was relayed to the two senior managers when they returned ten minutes later. The German head of production suddenly became very 'Spanish' and burst into an emotional tirade that if no one on the team was going to take responsibility for these launches, then he was walking out for good. A small Spanish voice came from the back of the room to explain that they feared what would happen if they were open about their progress and that they had been competing internally. The German head of production acknowledged that this had happened in the past, but that he was committed to a new way in the future. Suddenly the dam burst and everyone was looking for constructive ways of moving forward and stayed late into the evening.

It is the leader or facilitator's responsibility to get the team through such moments in the most constructive way possible. The form of a strategic moment can vary from highly charged, 'over the top' emotional discharges to complete stony silences that are equally hard to work through. Courage, persistence, humour and temporary diversion are all useful strategies that can be adopted. The strange combination of a personal thick skin and yet high sensitivity to what is going on is also very valuable. Emotional outpourings and frustrations can be met by quiet acknowledgement and gentle feedback about someone's perspective and values. Strategic moments can be very healthy indeed. The point is to be prepared for them through having done in-depth homework in the first two phases. This is the time when 'knowing your team', understanding the inequalities and having workable ground rules pays off.

A word of warning is called for here. The richness that leads to excellent outcomes can collapse at any moment and needs to be constantly protected from dominant inertia. However good your ground rules, the team has to have the will or energy to maintain and use differences. You cannot 'legislate' it into happening. In fact, many problems and poor results within organizations seem to arise from laziness, cynicism, inertia, wanting the quick fix, protecting your own turf or a lack of courage to venture into the unknown or stick one's neck out to change prevailing norms. Team leaders will often need to inspire, motivate, coerce, negotiate, cut deals or strategically get angry. It is a tough and emotionally exhausting job.

13.   Make sure that everyone is involved and uses the feedback tools established at the beginning

Equal involvement does not equate with having everyone speaking the same amount. The only way to find out if everyone is involved as much as they want to be is to ask. In fact, it is useful to carry out major 'health checks' every six months and to hold mini verbal check-ups throughout any face-to-face meetings. The main focus of a review is to establish that the pattern of interaction that has been set up is meeting the needs of the team and the task.

Major reviews are a good opportunity to 'initiate' new team members. These people can be shown all the records of the first meetings so that they understand the history and development of the team.

14.   Keep a check on the timing, space the milestones and use the time together and time apart to its full potential

It is helpful to spread out the milestones and keep a check on the timing. Don't plan too tightly or too far ahead if the project is emergent and ensure that regular reviews and updates take place to plan the next set of activities. Process reviews can be conducted in the lulls between bursts of activity on the task.

In general, the following activities are best done when working apart:

- Establish a disciplined and regular system of communication.
- Share output of face-to-face meetings.
- Have regular tele/video conferences.
- Update everyone on progress, e.g. weekly e-mail, establish chat files as well as technical files on Lotus Notes.
- Send each other motivating messages and comments on each other's work.
- Clarify goals and make suggestions.
- Implement agreed actions.
- Reach consensus on purely technical issues.
- Find, share, collate and edit information.
- Co-create documents, co-design products.
- Meet in subgroups.
- Prepare for face-to-face meetings in advance.
- Anticipate colleagues' questions and needs.

No complex team should ever spend expensive face-to-face time digesting, commenting on or re-editing information that they could have read before the meeting. Computer-based groupware technology can allow the exchange and manipulation of data and reports in different places at different times. These now give companies *no excuse* to perform any of those tasks face to face. One Swedish-based team commented, 'When we do get together, we seem only to get as far as sharing small parts of information, the time frame does not allow for more.' The time frame did allow more; they were using the time for the wrong reasons.

Using the time apart for such information exchange means that expensive time together can be devoted to resolving difficult decisions and interpersonal difficulties (although sometimes, time apart may allow people to cool down and rethink their approaches). Time together is also useful for 'just-in-time' training such as new problem-solving, decision-making and creative conflict techniques.

15. Communicate what is being achieved and broadcast successes as they emerge

Managing the external boundaries of the team at this point will determine the impact of the final outcome on the organization. This is the time to broadcast interim successes and send out concept papers of what your final results will achieve for both the organization and individual stakeholders. This can be done through lunchtime briefings, presentations to senior managers, newsletters, team pages on shared databases as well as one to one over lunches. What is important is to package the information in ways that people can access it.

Communicating successes as they arise can:

- maintain the interest and involvement of the sponsors
- enable some interesting and useful feedback
- encourage the sponsors to advocate for the team
- motivate the team members when they see interest being taken.

Broadcasting interim successes obviously puts extra pressure on the team members, especially those who feel that their reputation depends on coming up with a final polished product before letting the rest of the organization know about it. But the price of not broadcasting interim successes and priming key stakeholders for the output can be high.

Team leaders also need to do anything that will keep motivation up at this point, especially celebrate the interim successes. Publicly acknowledging team members' involvement in preparing a team leader's external management review, publishing interim results and highlighting individual and team developments can all help to maintain a sense of ownership and belonging in the team.

16. Leaders sharing control and facilitators reducing their presence

Facilitators should support the team in managing themselves and so need consciously to reduce their presence by this point. Similarly, if it is culturally appropriate, leaders should be controlling events as little as necessary by this stage and the team should be becoming self-managing and accountable.

Phase Four: Completing the Task, Review and Share the Learning

17. *Make sure everyone stays involved to the end*

There is a great tendency to let team work collapse as deadlines press and especially to decide that the cost of involving distant members in finalizing work is too great. This can undo much of the earlier team building efforts and breed cynicism in those who feel suddenly excluded. This is where groupware can really come into its own and prevent this kind of problem. If it has been introduced at the beginning, the team should be able to customize their work to suit their own needs.

18. *Review the learning within the team*

This is undoubtedly the most important part of wrapping up. Teams will only be able to work together better in the future if they can learn from their mistakes and share their successes. All the records of previous phases and the interim reviews should be available. The performance on the task will ultimately be judged by the wider organization, but immediate feedback can be actively sought from the sponsors.

The team needs to review its process in a formal way using all the background information to sort out what went well and what could be improved on, and to record specific intercultural problems and guidelines for other teams. Again, written questionnaires and checklists can be helpful, as people may write down, especially anonymously, what they will not say in public. The written record demonstrates that as well as the task, the interactive process was something concrete and agreed on and that it developed over time. This is important.

It can be valuable to include the sponsors in the review process as it occurs, rather than to collect their views and feed these back to the team. Many international team sponsors have not been part of an international team themselves and cannot appreciate the peaks of enthusiasm and excitement and the troughs of despair. By participating in the review process they can begin to appreciate the energy and commitment that the team have contributed to the task. This is turn makes them more able to sponsor future international teams effectively.

If you have worked with a facilitator throughout the life cycle of the team, it can be valuable for a different, 'neutral' facilitator to manage the review process. This enables the team facilitator to contribute to the content of the review and provide the team with insights from their perspective. It also enables the whole team to be constructively critical about their interactive processes and the role the facilitator has played.

19. Celebrate success and plan for the future

To close the team and bring its activities to an end, celebrate the achievements. This is critical even if the team is wound up early due to reasons beyond its control. After the celebrations, the team needs to lay out an action plan of how the results can be fully implemented, evaluated and broadcast through the company. The team also needs to think about what its members are going to do next and, if the project was longer than six months, how they are going to be reintegrated into the company and use the network that they have established in the team.

20. The team needs to pass on what it has learned to the rest of the organization

The team members need to brainstorm how they are going to communicate their learning in the most effective manner within their organization. Large formal gatherings attended by senior management are usually not conducive for sharing major mistakes, which are better shared informally. Other methods that teams have suggested have included electronic databases, with the attendant problems of how to codify the learning to make it accessible, update it and manage its relevancy. One company set up a best–practice office and all sorts of incentives for teams to share ideas. Social events and smaller–scale forums are sometimes arranged around the larger, formal reviews to which managers are already travelling. Newsletters, electronic whiteboards, mentoring schemes, a team leaders' network and lunchtime briefings all figure as suggestions.

The methods chosen will depend on the organization and probably the main national culture(s). Some cultures socialize easily out of hours, others do not. Some cultures will only take up what is passed on in person, others are happy learning from a computer. The chosen methods need to be multi-faceted. Even so, the most concrete passing on should come as skilled team members go on to act as facilitators or proactive team members when they join another team. Internal and external facilitators should only act as catalysts for a process that then spreads 'systemically' throughout the organization.

CONCLUSION

These 20 best practices summarize the key steps to creating successful complex teams. Each team is unique and the way in which the best practices are applied will vary for each team, but the more effort is taken to manage the issues discussed, the more rewarding and successful your teams will be.

Operating in the global economy is a complex challenge. Teams can be one way of building a sustainable capability to meet these challenges. Yet, as we have seen, creating and sustaining complex teams is no easy task. It requires a comprehensive review of the way your whole organization operates. If you want to embark on this journey:

- Consider each part of the globalization model and ask yourself: does our performance in this area help or hinder the creation of complex teams?
- Use the lifecycle model and the best-practice framework to review any existing or past teams you have created. What did you do well? What do you need to do differently in the future?
- Reinforce the positive – transfer the learning and develop an action plan to work on areas for improvement.

- Have a clear picture of the end game and communicate what is in it for everyone.

Then start out with some small steps and enjoy the ride.

References

Appelbaum, E. and Batt, R. (1994) *The New American Workplace*, Ithaca, NY: Cornell University Press.

Hofstede, G. (1980) *Culture's Consequences: International Differences in Work Related Values*, Beverly Hills, CA: Sage.

Kirkbride, P. S. and Westwood, R. I. (1992) 'Managerial behavior in Hong Kong', in Peterson, R. B. (ed.), *Managers and National Culture: A Global Perspective*, New York, Quorum, pp. 321–47.

O'Hara-Devereux, M. and Johansen, R. (1994) *Global Work: Bridging Distance, Culture and Time*, San Francisco, CA: Institute for the Future, Jossey Bass.

Rhinesmith, S. (1996) *A Manager's Guide to Globalization: Six Skills for Success in a Changing World*, San Francisco, CA: Jossey Bass.

Thomas, K. W. and Kilmann, R. H. (1974) *Thomas-Kilmann Conflict Mode Instrument*, Palo Alto, CA: Xicom, Consulting Psychologists Press.

Trompenaars, F. (1993) *Riding the Waves of Culture*, London: Nicholas Brealey.

Ward, K. (1997) 'Factors influencing the effectiveness of international teams in an organisational setting: an exploratory study', unpublished MSc dissertation, Birkbeck College, University of London.

DEVELOPING
GLOBAL LEADERS

Stefan Wills

CHAPTER 8

DEVELOPING GLOBAL LEADERS

*I*n 1993 the Ashridge *Management Across Frontiers* report was published (Barham and Wills, 1993), which was followed by an article in the *European Management Journal* called 'Being an international manager' (Wills and Barham, 1994). In this work it was suggested that there now exists a cadre of successful, international managers of global organizations, whose ways of operating and behaving cannot be adequately explained by lists of behavioural competencies. We felt at the time that if we are to really understand individuals who are managing across a number of countries/cultures simultaneously, we need to understand the core or 'being' of individuals who clearly have proven track records in this area.

The model we put forward suggested that there are three interlocking parts of a core of any successful international manager: cognitive complexity, emotional energy and psychological maturity. Cognitive complexity refers to the degree to which an individual is capable of complex thinking. More specifically, it comprises two primary components: differentiation and integration. Differentiation is the ability to perceive several dimensions in a stimulus rather than only one (i.e. several different ways of viewing a problem). Integration builds on this and implies an ability to identify multiple relationships among the differentiated characteristics. In other words, it is an ability to find patterns in what were previously thought of as unrelated phenomena.

In order to explore this fully in the context of international managers and globalization we went on to highlight and discuss a number of important characteristics in this area:

- Cultural empathy – being able to 'walk in the shoes' of people from different cultures.
- Active listening – allowing one to integrate both simple and complex information.
- A sense of humility – respect for others and a humble attitude of mind.

The area that we called emotional energy referred to the degree to which our sample of international managers knew themselves emotionally and the ways in which they were prepared to express these emotions in order to achieve a successful outcome for all concerned. Again, as a means of exploring and understanding this more fully, we broke it down into:

- Emotional self-awareness – knowing oneself emotionally.
- Emotional resilience – opening oneself emotionally to others and relating on this level appropriately to the situation.
- Risk acceptance – the self-confidence to accept some of the risks associated with the emotional domain.
- Emotional support of the family – a recognition of the holistic nature of one's life as well as of the family environment as a place to recharge emotional batteries.

Psychological maturity was a specific reference to an international manager's values and beliefs. It is the adoption of a sort of 'philosophy of life' that evolves from a clear, consistent and systematic way of seeing meaning in one's life. Successful international managers appear to have a unifying value system that helps them to formulate the dominant goals or themes that ultimately make their lives meaningful. Three specific core values appear to be significant:

- Curiosity to learn – an openness to seeking out the new and unfamiliar and an acceptance of the importance of lifelong learning.
- Orientation to time – an ability to put the past/present/future in perspective and make the most of the 'here and now'.
- Personal morality – clarity and a set of personal standards on what is right or wrong, good or bad.

Within this framework, we resisted referring to the core as a person's basic character structure or identity or even key aspects of their fundamental personality, due to the fact that this would have put too strong an emphasis on a person's internal psyche. Instead, we preferred labels that strongly implied that international managers exist as beings-in-the-world.

Having a cadre of international managers who are at the same time cognitively complex, emotionally resilient and psychologically mature is important for organizations that are either in the process of globalizing or already operate globally. As well as being able to conduct themselves in this way as individuals, these managers tend to act as role models for many others in the organization. They are key figures in the creation and sustenance of an organizational culture that values and promotes globalization.

What follows has not come about as a result of more applied research, talking specifically to so-called international managers specifically about this topic. It is more accurately described as reflections on working with these sorts of individuals on a wide array of international leadership development programmes and workshops run at Ashridge in the UK and other locations around the world. Such work allows me the great privilege of being able to 'rub shoulders' and work with international leaders and their respective organizations from a wide range of diverse cultures.

Rather than returning to the more diagnostic aspects of what constitutes a successful international leader, this chapter serves as a particularly timely update on developing into and 'becoming' one.

'BEING': DIFFERENCES OR SIMILARITIES?

An ongoing debate around what constitutes 'being' concerns whether we should be focusing on the cultural differences between international leaders from various parts of the globe or whether we should be attempting to recognize some of the similarities that contribute to their success. While recognizing the importance and usefulness of the work of people such as Gert Hofstede and Fons Trompenaars in the area of cultural differences, my position on this issue has not changed. As we continue moving at a rapid pace towards a more global business world, it is my belief that the differences in what both Hofstede and Trompenaars refer to as people's 'values' are very slowly being eroded.

This is not to say that cultural differences will ever completely disappear – what a bland, uninteresting world it would be if they ever did! But we have entered an era where the dominant ideology in terms of the creation of people's values, that of the United States of America, is experiencing such a powerful period of hegemony over other cultures and ideologies that it is able to gain a great deal of ground in transporting its values (particularly its business values) to all corners of the world. The degree to which a particular culture is either open or closed to this sort of influence will of course influence the degree to which this gets into and affects the 'being' of its people. Certain parts of the Arab world still contain what are probably the clearest examples of where this sort of influence is being most strongly resisted.

So redressing the balance away from cultural differences towards the continued search for similarities is both complementary and increasingly apt.

'BEING' AS THE HEAD/HEART/SOUL

What is this so-called core of an individual human being? In using the model of cognitive complexity, emotional resilience and psychological maturity subsequently in my teaching, it became apparent that what was really being referred to was a much more straightforward amalgam of the head, the heart and the soul. Now it seems ever more appropriate to question whether there really is such a thing as a person's essential core that can be explored and described by another. Following this, is it useful to attempt to discover and describe an ideal personality in the context of globalization?

To explore this properly we have to enter briefly into the philosophical merits of holism versus elementalism. The holist assumption is that human nature is such that behaviour can only be explained by studying persons as totalities. Holists maintain that the more one fragments the organism, the more one is dealing with abstractions and not the living human being. Conversely, elementalists assert that a full and complete understanding of human nature can only be reached by means of a detailed analysis of its constituent parts. In other words, it is perfectly feasible to pull out and comment on specific competencies of an individual, which may or may not relate to other parts.

It is important to recognize that there are major difficulties with lists of behaviours or competencies that encourage skill development in specific areas. Such studies are often both superficial and lead to a simplistic view of change and development. Of far greater appeal is the notion that underneath all of these behaviours is a core that is driving things and is much more difficult but not impossible to explore and develop. The intrigue of the whole is that it has to be both bigger and richer than the sum of the parts.

Here is the paradox. While stating categorically my allegiance to holism in 1994 and then moving on to find no alternative but to reduce the whole to a number of interlinking constituent parts, my position on this has not changed. While I am philosophically committed to a more holistic position, it is still difficult to move beyond describing the most pertinent issues in each of the areas now defined as developing the head, developing the heart and developing the soul.

DEVELOPING THE HEAD

The term 'the head' is a specific reference to an individual's thinking or thought processes. This is referred to by some as the 'left hand side of the brain', the place where language and communication with others reside. Working internationally is by its nature more complex than operating in a single culture, so it follows that individuals who are achieving success at working globally must be capable of greater degrees of complex thinking and hence are more cognitively complex.

To reiterate, they appear to have an ability to look at a problem or issue and perceive several dimensions to it rather than only one. Further to this, they are then able to find links in the different ways of looking at the issue in order to assist them in coming to a considered conclusion or judgement. Within the cultural differences literature, Fons Trompenaars (1993) draws what he calls a 'circle of reconciliation' (Figure 8.1) as a suggestion for people from differing cultures to work together and overcome their differing values – bipolar cultural values such as Individualism versus Collectivism. In my view,

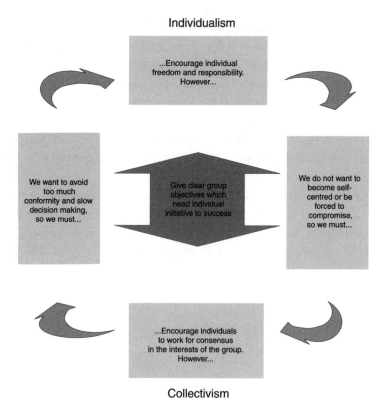

Figure 8.1 A circle of reconciliation.

practising this successfully demands that both parties are capable of high degrees of cognitive complexity.

Prior to focusing on how leaders might begin to develop qualities like 'cultural empathy', 'active listening' or 'a sense of humility', I would like to extend the concept of cognitive complexity to include an individual's basic stance or attitude to others and demonstrate some of the necessary interactive skills. In my work with international leaders, the difficulties that individuals have in listening and empathizing with others if they do not respect the other person/s has become an increasingly evident issue. No amount of practice or skill development will rectify what is first and foremost an attitudinal or values-based issue.

Where does having a humble attitude of mind and an ability to walk in the shoes of others come from? In a similar way to which an anthropologist might view people from cultures other than their own, successful international leaders are able to hold or bracket their assumptions about others, rather than rushing to judge or evaluate them. In other words, they are fair and equitable in how they treat others, indicating an extremely healthy attitude towards diversity.

A model borrowed from the race relations industry (Figure 8.2) suggests that when working with people who are distinctly different from oneself, it is tempting to enter into the 'cycle of superiority'. This begins with the process of stereotyping people from different cultures to our own, which, contrary to the view that only bigoted people

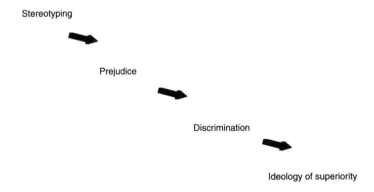

Figure 8.2 The cycle of superiority.

think in such ways, we all do from time to time, often without know-ing it. In fact, such thinking is part of a normal, natural process that helps us to some degree to make sense of the world. It is a sort of pattern recognition process. As the popular, but not well-accepted phrase goes, 'we have met the enemy of equality, and the enemy is us'.

In workshops on this topic, whenever groups of leaders stereotype other cultures, it is relatively easy to divide their responses into positive and negative assertions. So the judging or evaluating process has already begun. Negatively labelling others in this way and then automatically assuming that this is how people from this culture are likely to be and act, before any real attempt to understand them, runs the risk of turning into prejudice. Prejudice occurs if an opinion is formed before the facts are known. Successful international leaders have the ability to hold or bracket their assumptions before the onset of prejudice; however, they are not immune from ultimately adopting a prejudiced stance.

Beyond the prejudiced attitude, it becomes possible to take ac-tions towards others that show a partiality or prejudice based on their differences. This can lead to the creation of policies directed against the well-being and welfare of groups or cultures being prejudiced against. As the 'cycle of superiority' gains momentum, prejudiced actions be-come discrimination.

Finally, the individual or group practising the discriminating can come to believe that they are actually superior to or better than the group being discriminated against. It is a deep-seated arrogant stance with little or no sense of humility towards others. Experience has taught us that individuals or groups can spread and contaminate others with this type of attitude, leading to the setting up of whole cultures with an assumed ideology of superiority. The history of the world is rife with examples of how this can happen.

From a development perspective, helping leaders become more cognitively complex about their treatment of others who are different from themselves has to begin with this type of awareness raising. In the context of working cross-culturally, as opposed to race relations, it can have the effect of shocking some leaders. As an accompaniment to the showing of a classic video about racial discrimination called *A Class Divided*, the model provides a good platform to demonstrate the often deep-seated nature of the sorts of changes that are required to trigger development in this area.

It is only after this type of awareness raising that individuals are ready to start considering their own attitudes to people different from themselves and to what degree they are able to empathize with people from other cultures. They begin to realize how difficult it is to escape completely the 'cycle of superiority' and achieve genuine empathy with another human being on an issue that is close to that person's heart.

Breaking out of this cycle involves:

- the capacity to communicate respect
- the capacity to be non-judgemental
- the capacity to accept the relativity of one's own position
- the capacity to display empathy
- the capacity to be flexible
- the capacity for turn taking (during discussions)
- a tolerance for ambiguity

In conclusion, having an ability to empathize with another person requires an important cerebral component that for me is essentially about communication. As a concept, empathy also brings together and integrates the head, the heart and the soul. Linking back to my previous assertions that to really understand 'being' an international leader one has to understand the individual as a totality, empathy also involves understanding another person's feelings and core values.

It is this second aspect, the heart, to which I now turn.

DEVELOPING THE HEART

My interest and passion in developing this area come primarily from a deep-seated belief that within the world of leadership development, we overemphasize all things to do with the 'head'. The origin of this stems from the influence science and the scientific method have had on the design of organizations, particularly in the western, Anglo-Saxon world. A major consequence of this paradigm in terms of how we develop and grow our organizations and the individuals in them has been the overwhelming predominance of rational-objective models. In other words, the head has had potency over the heart. This has undoubtedly had a knock-on effect on a whole range of issues, from crafting strategy to leading change to working in international teams.

Stephen Fineman (1993) provides an indication of the extent to which this paradigm is capable of affecting the life of people in organizations:

> Frederick Taylor and Elton Mayo were influential in the design of industrial organisations at the turn of the century. They were both from middle-class families where a nineteenth-century form of anger control was dominant. They were appalled by the level of open anger they witnessed among workers, but failed in their early attempts to curb it. By the 1940s human relations training was well in place, aimed at assisting 'well-controlled' managers and professionals to hear, diffuse and smooth the angers and anxieties of workers. Today, the rhetoric of emotional control is still in place. (1993: 11)

In the context of leading change in organizations with which many international leaders are faced, they are conscious of the fact that it is a process that is fraught with both excitement and frustration. Excitement because it is new and challenging, frustration because there are usually numerous blockages or resistors. Interestingly, in most of the surveys conducted regarding the obstacles to implementing change, fear regularly comes top of the list as can be seen from Table 8.1.

What is fear? It is of course an emotion! So, to be able to understand and act on what is happening during change processes, international leaders have to be able to understand the more emotional aspects.

Table 8.1 Common obstacles to implementing change

Obstacles	% of respondents who mentioned
Fear factor and human resistance	92
Complacency and low sense of urgency	82
Insufficient dedicated time set aside	75
Poor communication	73
Late systems and technology	62

Source: Vandermerwe, 1991

From the perspective of their own development, in much the same way as it is difficult for them to be able to understand and empathize with others if they do not know themselves, it is difficult for them to be able to understand and act on organizational phenomena such as fear, if they do not understand their own emotional self.

At the individual level there are a number of basic assumptions about our emotions that need to be stated. The first is that we must be open to the possibilities of personal change in both the intellectual and the emotional domain. Given the motivation to do so, change is possible in both the degree to which a particular emotion is felt and the way in which it is expressed. Following on from this, it is possible to take the view that we must develop emotions that enhance our lives and change those that do not. Convincing some leaders that changing and developing one's emotions is possible isn't always easy.

Secondly, emotions are not universal across cultures. There are many examples of cultures that experience refinements of an emotion that other cultures do not possess. To take just one example, Spanish speakers have two subtly different ways of saying and expressing 'I love you': *te quiero* and *te amo*. The latter version has a much more romantic and deeper intent than the former. The final assumption that needs to be stated is the assertion that change begins with an awareness that our emotions are our own doing. In other words, we can to some extent choose to live the kind of emotional life we live, it does not just happen to us as a result of outside factors (a *fait accompli*). Once it becomes clear that we are choosing, that we do have an influence on the ways in which we are expressing ourselves emotionally, change becomes a much more feasible option.

As a consequence of it being largely sidelined, the whole area of emotions as a subject has been characterized by the generation of mystification and myths (Averill and Nunley, 1992). Interestingly, a myth is defined as being a popular belief or tradition that has grown up around something or someone, especially one embodying the ideals and institutions of a society or segment of a society. Myths are unfounded or false notions. In terms of their direct relationship to 'truth', most myths contain 'small truths', something that begins as a 'truth' but then gets distorted, no longer remaining totally factual.

Following Averill and Nunley, numerous myths have been created around our understanding of emotions. Some of the most common are described below.

The Myth of the Passions

We are gripped, seized, overcome by our emotions – they are ultimately out of control. The incident at a UK football match several years ago in which Eric Cantona lost his temper and attacked a spectator is the sort of event that nurtures this particular myth. There is some interesting gender difference research around this myth suggesting that when expressing anger men do not have a wide range of choices, hence the tendency to resort to aggressive behaviour. In contrast, women appear to have a much wider repertoire of choice (often using language creatively) in the ways in which they express this particular emotion.

This is a myth. Our emotions are not out of control; indeed, control can be considered to be an emotional response. The stimuli for control are often the signals for possible adverse consequences.

The Myth of Innocence

We are not fully responsible for our behaviour during emotional expressions. The most obvious example of how this myth has come about is of course the crime of passion. In some countries it is still possible to plead not guilty on the basis that 'the situation that led up to it left me so angry I had no choice but to'.

This is a myth. Emotions do not just happen to us. They occur inside us and lead to our actions – our passions do not make us innocent. Our behaviours and our emotions are of course intimately connected. When a child is having a tantrum, behaving very badly, as a parent we try to change both the behaviour and the emotion.

The Myth of Primary Emotions

The heart of one emotion is actually another (e.g. depression is really all about anger). Following on from this, there are basically few core or primary emotions: the most common number advocated is four (mad, glad, sad and afraid).

This is a myth. There are roughly 500 words in the English language describing emotional states. Interestingly, two-thirds of these have negative connotations, suggesting that (for those whose mother tongue is English) there are more ways to be unhappy than happy. There are in fact only 38 words describing states of happiness, but in terms of what we feel more generally there are endless possibilities.

The Myth of Childhood

Most, if not all, of our emotional development occurs during infancy and childhood. Once into adulthood the 'die has already been cast', making it very difficult to change our basic emotional disposition.

This is a myth. There is now wide acceptance of the idea that one develops and changes one's intellectual capabilities well into old age. Why should our emotional development be any different? There is huge potential for change in one's emotional make-up whenever we experience traumatic life events.

The Myth of Equality

All people within a particular culture are able to express themselves emotionally in much the same way.

This is a myth. Personality differences (of which emotions are a part) exist in all cultures, so, for example, extroverts develop their own repertoire of emotions, whereas introverts develop a different repertoire. To be creative is to be different – each person is different in their own way.

In working with international leaders on opening up their potential to work with their emotions, one has to begin by raising their awareness about the importance of the topic. A mixture of stories, symbols and pictures is useful for achieving this. The following is a typical story.

The Most Important Thing in the World

Peter Larking at first enjoyed his work as a marketing director of a large cosmetic company. He liked the social life and the high salary he earned; he travelled all over the world staying in expensive hotels. But it was a burning ambition to head the multinational parent company that drove him to work all hours of the day and night. The weekends he spent thinking solely about business or on the telephone to colleagues or customers. At 56 years old, the year he gained a seat on the main board, his wife divorced him and he had his second ulcer. Next year he had a coronary, and on doctor's advice he had to give up his sole remaining pleasure of mountain climbing. Just before he was 58 he was so busy managing a takeover bid that − if successful − would almost certainly secure him the coveted job of chief executive, he did not have time to visit his 18-year-old son in hospital after contracting a serious illness. The day after Peter got the top job his son died. 'Although I never had much time to spend with the boy,' he said to his secretary, 'he was the most important thing in the world to me.' Was he?

It is only when leaders are fully tuned into the emotional domain (i.e. their heart is engaged) that they are ready to consider the notion that emotions can be changed and developed.

This begins at the level of repressing internally (see Figure 8.3). Some individuals appear to have been socialized into completely suppressing any degree of emotional expression. This is the classic 'little boys don't cry' phenomenon so familiar to us in the West. For some leaders, the situation has become so extreme that they are no longer able to answer the straightforward question: 'How are you feeling right now?' What they consider to be the taboo world of emotions has been extricated from the way they interact with others and operate more generally. For some this is particularly true for their work persona, for others it has implications for the whole of their life.

Four levels of emotional expression:

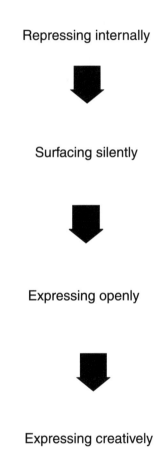

Repressing internally

Surfacing silently

Expressing openly

Expressing creatively

Figure 8.3   What is emotion?

People at this level of emotional expression often describe their lives as following a rather static and stable momentum with few real ups and downs. A common misconception is that they have become skilled at controlling their emotions. Control is an emotional reaction that stems from making a proactive choice. A lack of emotional expression that can be traced back to repression in an individual's history is quite different.

Level two in the model is characterized by people who with some encouragement are able to answer the question 'How are you feeling right now?' but are most reluctant to 'take their emotions out' in normal circumstances. From the perspective of the outside world, they are still prisoners of the early socialization process.

Individuals who are expressing their emotions openly are living their lives knowing how they are feeling and are expressing these feelings in everyday interactions with others. They are so used to expressing their emotions openly to others that there are occasions when it becomes inappropriate. To take the example of anger, there are people who express their anger so openly that it results in them using highly expressive body language or even resorting to banging the table at the merest sign of frustration or anger. This state almost sounds as if the connection between the logical brain and the feeling heart has in some way become obstructed. Those around them get so used to the fact that they are so outwardly expressive that it reduces their impact and effectiveness.

As mentioned earlier, the Eric Cantona incident at a UK football match is a clear example of an individual inappropriately expressing his emotions openly.

In helping international leaders work with this model, they are encouraged to attempt to move towards a state of emotional creativity: to be in touch with how they are feeling, to be able to take their emotions out and express them in an appropriate and creative way. So again using the example of anger, there is a time to express anger by banging the table and there is a time when this degree of expression needs to be controlled. This is not a new idea. As Aristotle is known to have said:

> Anyone can become angry – that is easy. But to be angry with the right person, to the right degree, at the right time, for the right purpose and in the right way – this is not easy.

Emotionally creative individuals have an extensive 'kit-bag' of different ways of expressing themselves and are masters of timing. The scene at the end of the film *A Few Good Men* in which Tom Cruise confronts Jack Nicholson is a wonderful example of an individual (Tom Cruise as a lawyer) expressing anger with the right person, to the right degree, at the right time, for the right purpose and in the right way.

From a practical, developmental perspective emotional creativity is a more usable and richer concept than the more popular emotional intelligence (Daniel Goleman, 1996). As psychologists are only too aware, the term 'intelligence' has never travelled well across cultures. What is deemed to be a measure of intelligence in one culture isn't necessarily interpreted the same way in a different culture. Emotional creativity does not evoke the same degree of bias and prejudice.

In conclusion, international leaders need to be encouraged to become more emotionally creative in the following ways:

- Attending more to their own and others' bodily reactions. The body often remembers what the head chooses to forget or ignore.
- Observing more carefully others' emotional reactions. We often act as mirrors to each other. Emotionally creative people pay close attention to how their behaviour affects others, rather than focusing too much on themselves.
- Listening more carefully to what words are saying emotionally. When expressing emotions verbally, we often do it indirectly through the use of metaphor ('I feel like shit').
- Identifying the social and personal rules that surround emotional expression in different situations. Like the rules of grammar, they are not easy to identify but once they are, they can be the dos and don'ts of behaviour.
- Setting goals in this area similar to other aspects of personal development. Such goals have to be woven into the total fabric of a person's life.
- Taking care to practise in low-risk environments. At first developments in emotional creativity may seem artificial, but with practice the experience of the feeling and its expression will become integrated.
- Being particularly flexible and patient with regard to tangible changes, expecting lots of trial and error and the realization that we learn more from failure than success in this area.

■ Using their imagination more fruitfully. We don't have to always experience the expression of an emotion directly in order
to practise it. Top-class sports stars or musicians often use their
imagination to rehearse encounters. Doing this effectively requires large amounts of self-discipline and conscientious effort.

The biggest challenge in helping international leaders develop the heart
remains convincing them that they can choose and do something about
becoming more emotionally creative if they have the will and the
desire to incorporate such transformational change into their whole
being. As Mahatma Gandhi said, 'You must be the change you wish to
see in the world.'

Discussion of their whole being brings me finally to developing
the soul.

DEVELOPING THE SOUL

The original title for the final piece of the three interlinking parts of the
core, psychological maturity, placed a heavy focus on an individual's
core values. My thinking during the last few years has continued along
this vein, flirting with various other concepts but for the moment
settling on what is undoubtedly the most unifying and holistic of all
possible defining concepts: spirituality. Successful international leaders
care enough about their soul to be conscious of their own higher-order
values and overall purpose in life, particularly how it connects with
others. What I refer to as 'being-in-the-world', Mitroff and Denton
(1999) usefully describe as 'interconnectedness' and go on to say that:

> Spirituality is inextricably connected with caring, hope, kindness, love and op-
> timism. It cannot be proved logically or scientifically that these things exist in the
> universe as a whole. Spirituality is the basic faith in the existence of these things.
> Faith is exactly the thing that renders their strict proof unnecessary. (1999: 89)

Perhaps not surprisingly, this is the area where I have made least
progress in creating materials designed to assist international leaders in a
developmental context and therefore my thoughts and ideas are still to

some degree embryonic. Where I have made progress is in opening up an awareness of this issue as being of fundamental importance. As a means of getting these sorts of issues out into the open, many international leaders have begun thinking about and debating the meaning and importance of an aspect of their lives that again unifies the head, the heart and the soul – happiness. As well as having an obvious spiritual component, this is a state that for the most part appears to come from inside through introspection, and for many it is one of the primary emotions, along with anger, sadness and fear.

When considering their lives, learning and what the future may hold, international leaders can often get caught up in the apparent hype and gloss of the world in which they live. It is fruitful from time to time to encourage them to return to questions surrounding some of the basics of life and the core of their being, questions such as:

- Are you happy/unhappy?
- Is happiness a relevant topic for your personal developmental plan?
- Do happier people perform better at work?
- Do unhappy people make worse leaders?

This inevitably leads to discussions around what happiness is and how we will know if we are in that 'place' or not. We know that happiness is to some degree a physiological reaction that sets in motion tiny neurotransmitters that circulate around the body. At a more fundamental level, being in such a state suggests that the individual is no longer driven and plagued by uncontrollable forms of desire. Beyond the rather transient state of being happy, we also know that happiness consists of feelings that are attached to special moments in one's memory. Its transient nature is such that the so-called ups and downs are what really give it meaning. The impermanence and incompleteness of happiness could be considered to be two of its greatest virtues. Through this we come to realize that a brief moment of happiness doesn't make a person entirely happy, or as Aristotle so wisely said, 'One swallow does not make a summer.'

According to an old Chinese proverb, happiness consists of three things: someone to love, something to do and something to hope for.

James Kouzes and Barry Posner asked General Stanford of the US Army how he would go about developing leaders in business or the military. This is what the enlightened general said:

> I have the secret to success in life. The secret is to stay in love. Staying in love gives you the fire to really ignite other people, to see inside other people, to have a greater desire to get things done than other people. A person who is not in love doesn't really feel the kind of excitement that helps them to get ahead and lead others and to achieve. I don't know any other fire, any other thing in life that is more exhilarating and is more positive a feeling than love is. (1992: 479)

In the same article, Rodney Ferris defines love specifically in an organizational context as:

> A feeling of caring or deep respect for yourself and others, of valuing and believing in yourself and others, and of helping to achieve the best of which everyone is capable. It means finding a sense of purpose, fulfilment and fun in your work and helping others to find these qualities in their work as well. Without these feelings, leaders fundamentally are taking advantage of their constituents. (1992: 480)

Following on from this, happiness via someone to love is clearly connected to sharing with others. This comes about through occasionally learning to forget ourselves in the quest to make others happy; yet more confirmation of just how important the human need for interconnectedness or being part of a community really is.

Leaders who are willing to explore this aspect of their lives come to realize that there are a number of significant others who play a major part in bringing this to fruition. For most people, a partner relationship serves as a basic building block for both self-understanding and the understanding of others. Beyond partnership, rearing children can often be a catalyst for 'teaching' us that happiness comes through giving rather than receiving. And finally, friends who are willing to play the role of 'containers' or confidants encourage us to learn the significance of reciprocity and genuine empathy with others.

Finding something to do is another cornerstone of life that inevitably engages us in social activity. For most people, more than any other feature of life, it is work that really ties them to the human community. Work that is sufficiently enjoyable, challenging and rewarding helps give our lives a rich sense of purpose and meaning.

Leaders who feel like this about their work don't view it as work at all. They are fond of saying things like, 'When you love what you are doing, you never have to go to work again.' Work becomes highly aligned with their life purpose, vision and values, and ultimately a major part of why they exist. Gorky summed this up well when he said: 'When work is pleasure, life is a joy. When work is duty, life is slavery.'

The final piece of the Chinese proverb giving us a perspective on the keys to happiness is something to hope for. To a large degree, hope is a natural part of the human condition. Without it we stagnate and shrivel up. It drives us on to explore and embrace all sorts of change in our lives. From a more practical perspective, I encourage international leaders to explore this aspect of their lives by getting them to consider and talk about their dreams. Some of them are able to frame their dreams as possibilities, which they can choose to use all their talent, energy and courage to work towards fulfilling. Ultimately, this sort of exercise encourages them to be proactive about their life rather than sitting and waiting for things to happen. Put another way, it enables them to be free agents, capable of choice. Creating a trusting and safe environment in which to do this is of course of paramount importance. Dreams are like delicate flowers: they are easily crushed and normally shared with only a few others.

Manfred Kets De Vries (2000) gives us his thoughts on what makes happiness. Commenting on his own rich experience in international leadership development, he recommends leaders to live the Chinese proverb by achieving balance in their lives, finding 'playtime', living a healthy lifestyle and regularly engaging in introspection.

Balancing someone to love, something to do and something to hope for is one of the greatest challenges many international leaders face. It is my experience that when faced with such difficult questions many choose either to confuse happiness with outward success (wealth, position and power) or merely to delude themselves.

Finding the most appropriate amount of 'playtime' and living a healthy lifestyle are equally important aspects of practically living out the proverb. Laughter can often be seen to connect both of these. As well as being an essential component of an individual's mental and physical health, when working cross-culturally the ability to laugh is often viewed as the perfect antidote to arrogance and pomposity. As Ethel Barrymore once said, 'You grow up the day you have the first real laugh at yourself.'

Finally, the thread holding many of these principles together is the ability and the courage to regularly look introspectively at the quality and nature of one's life. Sogyal Rinpoche (1992) put this beautifully when he said:

> Looking in will require great subtlety and great courage. We are so addicted to looking outside ourselves that we have lost access to our inner being almost completely. We are terrified to look inward because our culture has given us no idea of what we will find. We may even think that if we do, we will be in danger of madness.
>
> So, we make our lives hectic to eliminate the risk of looking into ourselves. In a world dedicated to distraction, silence and stillness terrify us. We protect ourselves from them with noise and frantic busyness. Looking into the nature of our mind is the last thing we would dare to do. (1992: 52)

Being introspective in this way must be thought of as a continuous journey. It is not about seeking a final destination; on the contrary, it is the way in which we travel and what we choose to focus on along the way. Put another way, happiness is not something a person searches for – they choose it. Being a successful international leader in this new age of spirituality, demands enlightenment, along with the knowledge that the greatest happiness you can have is knowing that you do not necessarily require happiness.

References

Averill, J. R. and Nunley, E. P. (1992) *Voyages of the Heart: Living an Emotionally Creative Life*, Toronto: Free Press.

Barham, K. and Wills, S. (1993) *Management Across Frontiers*, Berkhamsted: Ashridge Management College Report (AMRG 929).

Fineman, S. (ed.) (1993) *Emotion in Organizations*, London: Sage.

Goleman, D. (1996) *Emotional Intelligence: Why It Can Matter More Than IQ*, London: Bloomsbury.

Kets De Vries, M. (2000) 'The business graduation speech: reflections on happiness', *European Management Journal*, 18(3) June: 302–11.

Kouzes, J. M. and Posner, B. Z. (1992) 'Ethical leaders: an essay about being in love', *Journal of Business Ethics*, 11: 479–84.

Mitroff, I. I. and Denton, E. A. (1999) 'A study of spirituality in the workplace', *Sloan Management Review*, Summer: 83–92.

Rinpoche, S. (1992) *The Tibetan Book of Living and Dying*, London: Rider.

Trompenaars, F. (1993) *Riding the Waves of Culture*, London: The Economist Books.

Vandermerwe, S. (1991) 'Making strategic change happen', *European Management Journal*, 9(2): 174–81.

Wills, S. and Barham, K. (1994) 'Being an international manager', *European Management Journal*, 12(1), March): 49–58.

LEADERSHIP AND THE GLOBAL ORGANIZATION

Phil Hodgson and Randall P. White

CHAPTER 9

LEADERSHIP AND THE GLOBAL ORGANIZATION

A company-wide scheme to harness and promote innovation globally is shelved after less than 18 months in operation. Questions are asked internally and externally if the organization's leaders really want it to be seen as a first-to-market, innovative producer.

A global supply chain system – designed to deliver major cost savings around the world – is consistently and systematically evaded by senior regional executives. The reason: local managers have made special deals with local customers and these contracts will be adversely affected by the global system. In addition, executives, fearing a decline in their regional results thus depressing their yearly bonus, helped to subvert the system.

The relaxed and fairly easy-going new CEO of a global fmcg company is stunned to learn from two of his most trusted operations directors that they feel he is cramping their style. Why? Because in his drive to learn more about the organization – he racked up 100 000 air miles in his first six months – he was sitting in on operational meetings. At the meetings he asked penetrating questions, which were interpreted, in many of the countries he visited, as him taking command away from his local operations director. He believed he was simply getting his 'hands on' and understanding what the real issues, opportunities and problems were in the company.

GLOBAL LEADERSHIP: WHAT'S NEW?

In each of the examples above, people trying to be effective leaders in global organizations were initiating schemes and taking actions designed to benefit the entire organization. But something somewhere – an unintended consequence? – made a good idea turn sour and not release its full potential. Why didn't these ideas work? What contributed to their demise? If we are to believe colleagues and the leadership literature, many leadership initiatives fail because organizations are so much more complex today than yesterday. Yet when we examine the great civilizations of the past – the Romans, Chinese, Incas, Aztecs – they all were global (at least as far as they could reach), complex organizations of enormous dimensions and enormous power. The rulers of those empires influenced the lives of huge numbers of people and they did it using approaches that are still valid today. Think of it in these terms: these values are vastly complex (in their time), remote, multicultural problems that resulted in management and leadership control issues.

In order to be effective, global leaders prize three areas of clarity:

- *Clarity of purpose.* The effective global leader and global organization have to be clear on its purpose. Purpose gives energy, allows the leader to assess success, and gives motivation and drive to followers. The Romans clearly saw as part of their purpose the acquisition of vast areas of land, but they still confined themselves, in central Europe for instance, to the boundaries of the Rhine and the Danube as the limit of their territory. Today financial commentators get distinctly edgy if they see a company they are tracking making an acquisition in an area that is not obviously linked to the existing strategy and for which there is no onboard range of competencies. Sticking to the knitting – a phrase made popular by Peters and Waterman – is still an important part of maintaining a clarity of purpose.

- *Clarity of external operation.* Those age-old empires all had very clear views on how they would treat the populations of other countries, tribes and religious groups. It was with various levels of tolerance of course, but there is an analogy to, say, late 1970s IBM, where there was a clear attempt to differentiate IBM sales people in their famous dark blue suits with white shirts from any other kind of technology sales person. They even had their own company song to give them succour.

- *Clarity of internal operation.* The successful global organization needs to have a clear set of rules of behaviour – a clear culture, something that sets norms for standards and styles of behaviour. Even the most unruly internet start-up still has unwritten rules about the style of dress that its people wear. The dress-down Friday that has gripped various organizations over the last decade only serves to highlight the norms and counter-norms governing appearance that we set ourselves in organizations. It doesn't seem to matter what the norm is, as long as it is consistent.

So we see these three leadership clarities as having existed for a long time and we expect that this will probably be true for global organizations of the future. However, in recent times organizations operating globally – and that must include everyone, whether they understand that or not – have faced an extra dimension. This isn't a fourth clarity, it's a *lack* of clarity.

One of the signal features of the last decade or so is that information, communication and transport technologies have made the number of choices facing executives and managers hugely greater than ever before. Materials can be sourced from anywhere on the globe, specialist advice can be hired from anywhere, decisions can be made anywhere and communicated to anywhere. The retailer IKEA has 2000 suppliers based in more than 50 countries. Whereas once there were head offices and clear regional centres in organizations, now position doesn't matter at all. You can be anywhere to do anything and do it at any time. While apparently this offers much greater freedom to the modern global executive, in practice it offers a vastly increased level of ambiguity for almost everything that that executive wishes to do.

Unfortunately managers and leaders have not been trained or educated in coping with ambiguity. So often it has simply been assumed away. Most of the evidence of the past 50 years has been devoted towards reducing ambiguity or avoiding it. The research described in the rest of this section is about the behaviours necessary to cope with and even thrive with ambiguity.

- *Ambiguity* is what exists in the environment.
- *Uncertainty* is what you feel as a result of facing that ambiguity.

Most leaders report increased levels of uncertainty. In fact, there seems to be a general principle that the more senior you are in an organization – the more responsibility you carry – the more uncertainty you face (see Figure 9.1). An entry-level manager generally is given reasonably straightforward tasks to achieve and has a reasonable number of rules and ideas about how to achieve them. As a first-line supervisor, their big discovery is that people are a problem, and that those people are often the ones they grew up with and were previously colleagues with. If they meet an issue or difficulty that they are uncertain about, if they cannot solve it themselves, they pass it on upwards.

Figure 9.1 As you go up the hierarchy, skill sets change.

At the mid-manager level the key emotional issue is giving up technical mastery on any given issue and learning that directing and motivating people is the key input that leaders make. Not only solving problems, but defining which of the problems should be handled by you and which are the problems that can be ignored is also critical to success at this level. However, if you meet something that you can't handle because you are uncertain about it, you tend to pass that upwards as well.

At the most responsible level (it is here that we have called the general manager level) the tasks are:

- To be strategic – to gaze into a crystal ball and decide where the organization and the industry are going.
- To delegate effectively, not just the stuff you don't like, but also some key parts of your responsibility – to realize that you can't do it all and that you need the team.
- To handle uncertainty and ambiguity – there are multiple right answers, and just because something works today does not mean it will work tomorrow.

The strategy and delegation tasks are obvious – it's what being a senior manager is all about. But why ambiguity? Because you are sitting at the top of what is in effect a very powerful ambiguity pump. Most organizations of whatever shape (they don't have to be hierarchical) act as ambiguity pumps and the person who receives most of the ambiguity is the person with the greatest responsibility.

Now we get to the hardest issue. How can leaders in organizations that are global operate in such a way that they thrive on the ambiguity rather than running from it or avoiding it, or more likely pretend that it is not there?

Surely effective exploitation of ambiguity is a contradiction in terms? Take a look at Figure 9.2. The left side of the frame describes how difficult something is to learn to do in your organization. The higher up the chart, the more difficult it is. The bottom of the frame is how valuable doing that thing will be to your organization. Now ask yourself a question: where do you think your organization is at the moment? Follow this up with a second question: where should it be? If you – like many – say bottom right, then you are going to be in an organization where the strategy can only be to follow on. You can be a fast follower, but you won't lead. You are going to do things that are of high value to the organization but are not difficult to learn. If they are not difficult for your organization to learn, they are easy to copy and all your competitors can do so. Some people put their choice in the top right box. This has been described to us as the *Star Trek* strategy. That is, you are always 'boldly going where no one has gone before'. This is the strategy of most start–ups and most biotech organizations. Their overall aim is to be first or best in the market and to gain advantage from being there early.

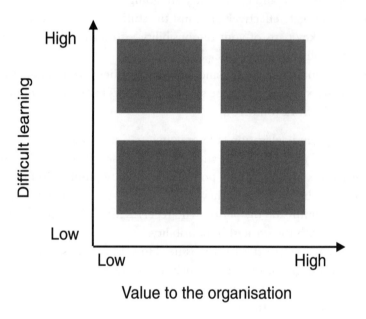

Figure 9.2 Leader as learner.

So let us ask another question: where do you head for if you want to find areas of difficult learning? Is it the things that you already know a lot about? Or could it be the things about which you have lots of uncertainty and for which there is lots of ambiguity? Our argument is that organizations and their leadership have been consciously moving towards a constructive approach to ambiguity and letting go of certainty. Heading into areas that are frighteningly ambiguous and uncertain requires a high capability from a leader and organization to do the necessary difficult learning. If you can learn to make the most of a situation that other organizations shrink from and are not paralysed by fear of failure, you will have created competitive advantage. Although the e-commerce world is awash with examples of failed dot-com start-ups, there are still some very successful ones who are now thriving. For the most part the Amazons and e-Bays got into the business early and were able to demonstrate learning in translating the ambiguity they faced into significant business opportunities.

What are the behaviours that matter to global leaders facing high levels of uncertainty? And how can they develop them? Our research has identified eight specific behaviours that contribute directly in helping leaders operate effectively when faced by higher levels of ambiguity and consequent feelings of uncertainty. We call these behaviours enablers, because they allow people to cope with ambiguity in the world and feel less uncertainty while doing so. In no particular order, the eight are:

- Being motivated by mysteries
- Being risk tolerant
- Scanning ahead
- Tackling tough issues
- Creating excitement
- Being flexible
- Simplifying
- Being focused

BEING MOTIVATED BY MYSTERIES

People who are motivated by mysteries – we call them seekers – are very curious people who are attracted to areas and problems about which they know very little. They are often difficult to work with because they question a lot, they want to know what is behind things, and they are always seeking to increase their own and other people's understanding. Often this exploration is of a playful nature. These people experiment, delight in testing things, and usually want to try something different each time they tackle a problem. Seekers are attracted by the unknown and almost take a delight in bringing the unknown into everyday activities. You thought you were going to a meeting to agree the new sales plan, but actually you end up in a debate about how the product could be modified and how a new market could be explored. Seekers seem to get energy from not knowing; the less they know the more energy they put into finding out. Even though they have a solution, they will look for a second solution, and another.

The entrepreneur James Dyson is a seeker. In struggling to make a vacuum cleaner that did not require a paper or cloth bag, he made more than 5000 prototypes before finally achieving the level of performance for which he was searching. Having made his first production model he carried on developing and that curiosity to improve on what was already improved continues to this day. Seekers are drawn instinctively to the edge of their knowledge rather than the centre of it. For this reason we believe that being motivated by mysteries may well be one of the fundamental skills underlying the ability to handle ambiguity and uncertainty. These habits seem to be built in at an early stage. Think back to when you were at school and you were offered 'facts' by your teachers. Was your instinct to accept them, learn them, move on to the next thing? Or did you question? In today's information-drenched society, who knows if the information you're being offered is true, partially accurate or completely wrong? Seekers are prepared to leave their comfortable and safe centre ground of accepted 'truth', and are therefore more likely to discover what the real situation is.

How Do You Enhance Your Seeking Ability?

- Deliberately take on a project or a task that is outside your area of expertise. Choose something that is not too high a risk for your first experiment, so that you don't need to worry too much about a completely successful outcome. When you face some of the unknown aspects of the project, make time to ask yourself why you find these things worrying. How could you make them more interesting, even enjoyable? What is it you are reacting to? If you can understand the process, you are well on the way to finding a way of more effectively facing the unknown.

- Relearn to question. Ask the question 'why?' as often as you can. Model yourself on the way children behave, particularly small children who are very good at asking deep and insightful questions. Children for the most part seem not to be worried by mysteries, in fact they seem to be attracted to them. See if you can be a little more child-like (not childish) in your behaviours.

BEING RISK TOLERANT

People who are risk toleraters can take decisions when necessary, despite incomplete information. They have learned to tolerate the risk of failure. They don't hamper themselves by the fruitless pursuit of data that will never provide them with what they need. These are not people who are unaware of the risk in their decisions; quite the reverse. They are acutely aware of the risks they are taking, but are comfortable with doing so in order that decisions can get made and progress can continue. It is a curious commentary that many societies now – particularly in the West – have chosen to move towards legislation and litigation in order to reduce risk. Yet the same citizens protected by their litigation voluntarily seek extreme sports to increase the apparent risk in their lives. Perhaps we all have a preferred level of overall risk under which we wish to live?

How Do You Improve Your Risk Tolerance?

- Usually people who are poor at risk tolerance 'cushion' themselves by demanding huge amounts of data before they will make a decision. If you are one of these people, then think back over a recent decision you made that turned out well, and using hindsight analyse exactly how much information was really needed to make the decision – go for the minimum. If a similar decision is needed in future, what is the least information you could 'get away with' to make a reasonably certain outcome?

■ Try making a decision purely on gut instinct. We know that feels uncomfortable, but try it nonetheless. If necessary, make your gut instinct decision tuck away the answer and go about your normal decision process. Once the decision has been made and you are in a position to assess its effectiveness, go back and assess your gut decision. How close were you? If you regularly compare your gut instinct with the more formal process, you will find that there are many occasions when your gut instinct was at least as good and much faster. How will you know when to use your gut instinct in future?

SCANNING AHEAD

People who are scanners link two skills. They gaze into the future and imagine the possibilities of a new idea or a new product, but they also drill deep: they are curious about the implications of a new idea and what that may do to what they already know. By drilling deep they can ask penetrating questions of people who know much more than they do about a particular subject. When you give up technical mastery over a given area, followers will know more about the technical aspects than you will. In a sense they have worked through the logic and applied it at a different level. We know of one top manager in a global publishing organization who when hearing presentations from members of his division, hardly ever hears the whole presentation through before interrupting with brilliant questions about the implications of what has been told so far. His staff acknowledge that sometimes it is a little off-putting – even irritating – but they are just as often impressed with the depth of this executive's perception and the quality of his questions. He always improves the debate when he is present.

Scanners are curious and inquisitive, and also they are aware of what has and what has not happened. They have a tendency to make connections between apparently disparate areas and then integrate what they know into a new concept, product or idea. Sherlock Holmes had that uncanny knack of probing deeply for data that was available, but then was also able to spot the absence of data – the dog that didn't bark – and appreciate its significance. Scanners can also be disturbing because they have ideas that may not fit into current thinking and they are not ashamed of them. In fact, they are prepared to argue a very coherent logic based on a complete supposition.

How Do You Improve Your Ability to Scan Ahead?

- When turning out an old filing cabinet, or reviewing old files on the hard disk, have a look at what you and others were saying five years ago about the future of your organization. How did it actually work out? How accurate were your predictions? Now make some predictions for the next five years. Keep and review them from time to time. Compare your ideas with your colleagues.

- Take an assumption about your organization, perhaps one that is somewhat far fetched, and then work through the logic of what life would be like if that assumption were to occur. Assume an interest rate of huge proportions, or perhaps the invention of a new product by a competitor. What would your organization do? What would you do? It is by practising thinking through the unthinkable that you become more flexible in both drilling deep and scanning ahead.

TACKLING TOUGH ISSUES

The chief executive of a major UK public regulatory body was speaking at his retirement. 'I just loved the fights,' he said. 'I think it's great when people are challenging us and we can challenge them back.' Certainly his tenure as chief executive was not without incident, and yet he could never be accused of ducking a situation or trying to smooth things over rather than resolving them. He was excellent at tackling tough issues, especially those where the solution was not apparent to anyone at the beginning of the process. He was a tenacious challenger and although he didn't spend his entire life fighting, certainly it was one of the attractions of the job that there would be continual challenge both to him and from him. He was seen by his colleagues as rather a gentle man, a person who could be very gracious and extremely polite. However, when a conflict arose he was the man to be there. Organizations need tenacious challengers, both to apply themselves inside the organization where old customs tend to get enshrined and not reviewed and challenged, but also outside the organization where new ideas, new opportunities and new threats are continually being presented.

Tenacious challengers know that they are going to face many setbacks and unforeseen problems on the way. They have some kind of in-built sense of determination and perseverance that allows them to keep going when other people have decided it is not worth the effort. Of course, when overdone, this can seem like obsessive behaviour. At times it is often difficult to make a distinction. The hallmarks of a tenacious challenger are when the going gets tough the motivation increases, and they really do view every problem as an opportunity.

How Do You Enhance Your Ability to Tackle Tough Issues?

- You have probably tackled a number of tough issues in your time already. Make a list of some you can think of and then review what was it that allowed you to be so tenacious and tough in those situations, compared with some equivalent situations where you have felt you were less tough.
- Are there problems or issues in your organization that are recognized by many but voiced by no one? The unmentionables? What would be the action steps that would be needed to get some of the unmentionables mentioned? And then tackled?

CREATING EXCITEMENT

We have always known that people in leadership roles have had considerable personal energy. High levels of responsibility are burdensome and energy is needed to keep leaders working through long days and wilting travel schedules. However, in these times of greater ambiguity our research has demonstrated that effective leaders in areas of ambiguity must also be part of the supply of energy into the system. They are people who energize other people too. These effective leaders invigorate the rest of the team. Why is this so important? Handling uncertainty is often quite tedious. It involves doing a great deal of trial-and-error work, which can be extremely boring. Just for an instant, imagine that you have arrived in a city where you don't speak the language, you haven't got a map and you can't find a taxi. But you must find a particular road. You've got to do a lot of trial-and-error walking. It's the same when facing uncertainty. You need to do a lot of walking to find the road you are looking for. Much of that walking is tedious, so the leader who can make it more fun for the people in the organization, who can bring a sense of enthusiasm, fun and energy to the task, is much more likely to get the task done well.

How Can You Be Better at Creating Excitement?

- Review what makes you enthusiastic. Sit down and think about when you get really enthusiastic. Ask your colleagues. Now do an analysis of yourself. Why are you enthusiastic about some areas, but not others? How can you broaden the range of areas about which you can generate enthusiasm? Don't forget, we're not asking about your own personal energy, but where you can enthuse other people to be as energetic.
- Think of some people who have invigorated you. How did they do it? What were they doing? Could you borrow some of their ideas or styles?

BEING FLEXIBLE

Anyone can be randomly flexible, but the person who is confidently flexible is the kind we are talking about here. People who are the most confident when the need for flexibility arises are usually those who have had the greatest range of experience. They've been in large and small organizations, they've started businesses, they've closed businesses, they've been experts, they've been generalists. They've worked for great and for lousy managers. Contrast these people with other equally intelligent and able managers who have only worked for one boss in one organization, doing one thing. Who would you bet on to find the more appropriate and flexible response for a new situation? But these people are not just flexible in themselves, they are able to persuade other people who are involved in the situation of the need for flexibility too. People who are flexible in this way do not have an internal sense that there is 'only one right solution to any problem'. Because they can shift their approach when necessary, they are also able to admit their own mistakes when they make them. They acknowledge what has worked and what hasn't worked, and learn from that. They also acknowledge the importance of other people's ideas.

How Do You Learn to Be More Flexible?

- Find an issue that is of relatively low importance. Now work with someone else to come up with a different solution from the one you would normally use. It doesn't matter how the difference emerges. Now implement that solution and look at the results. Review for yourself how it feels to do something differently from the way you would normally tackle it. What can you learn? How could you apply what you have learned?
- Watch how other people sell the need for change. When someone is trying to persuade you, what methods are they using? What works? What doesn't? Let someone persuade you on a matter that is relatively trivial. How does it feel?

SIMPLIFYING

With organizations and events moving faster and faster, with life becoming more complex and with greater uncertainty, the person who can convey their ideas simply, clearly and briefly is going to have a head start over the rest. People who are good at presenting ideas simply (and we don't mean simplistically) but with the necessary depth usually have three aspects to their simplifying ability:

- They are good at understanding the fundamentals, the essence of something.
- They are good at clarifying a message so that it is in the right not the wrong order.
- They can act as interpreters, using symbols and metaphors and images that resonate with their particular audience.

People who can simplify in all three areas are going to take complex and confusing ideas and present them in a way that makes them quickly understandable to a wide audience, thus speeding acceptance and implementation of novel ideas. (See the top right box in Figure 9.2.)

One of the great tests of simplifiers is whether a child could understand what they are talking about. Try this test. Imagine you are going to explain to a group of 11-year-olds the strategy of your organization. Could you do it? Our suggestion is that unless you can find a way of explaining those things so that 11-year-olds can understand them, we wonder if you are clear enough yourself. Certainly we wonder if all of your colleagues are as clear as they need to be.

Let us be clear, when we talk about simplifying we are not talking about sound bites. The sound bite scrapes a thin layer from a deeper argument and presents itself as the complete argument simplified. It often has the reverse effect: it can obfuscate as often as it illuminates.

Simplifiers are able to get to the essence of something. They can communicate it to others in a simple way that is appropriate to aid the listener in a deeper understanding of the subject.

How Do You Improve Your Ability to Simplify?

- Rewrite an important memo as a telegram in 25 words or fewer. It's going to be hard, we know, but keep working at it until you get it down to that magic 25 words.

■ If you have to present an idea to people, tell it as a story, not as a set of bullet points. Use the normal conventions of story telling with a beginning, a middle and an end, possibly also a moral. Ask your audience how they felt about hearing the thing as a story rather than as a series of overhead bullets.

■ Before you write your next report, spend a moment phoning two or three of the report's customers – the readers. Ask them what questions they want answered in their report and how they would like those questions phrased. Do your best to incorporate their wishes in your report.

BEING FOCUSED

Focusers are able to keep an eye on a few specific objectives, no matter what else may be going on. In the modern organization with so many priorities and so many concurrent activities, people who can focus on what the real issues are can become very valuable. Trevor Bayliss, the British inventor and entrepreneur, spent 12 years perfecting a clockwork radio. He was interested in many other things as well, but those 12 years spent developing and finding markets for a product demonstrate a considerable level of focus. In the beginning no one believed that there was a market for a clockwork radio, yet in countries where reliable supplies of electricity are unavailable there has turned out to be a huge market. In the US, Corning Glass executives talk about the 'critical few', their constantly reviewed list of four or five key issues, the key strategic tasks and initiatives that everyone in the organization must be aware of and must in some way subscribe to.

Of course there is a downside. The person who is over-focused can be accused of being narrow and blind to other possibilities. Much like the tenacious challenger, they can be perceived as obsessive. We wouldn't want to deny the difficulty of being focused as well as behaving flexibly and being curious and motivated by mysteries. However, the effective leader of a global organization, facing unprecedented levels of uncertainty and ambiguity, must balance all of these skills.

How Do You Become Better at Being Focused?

- Go back over a project or assignment you have recently completed. If you could start the whole thing again from the beginning using the benefit of hindsight, where would you focus your energy and attention? Was it where you put your energy initially? Have you learned something by doing the project that would allow you to know where to focus your attention more efficiently in future? Review a number of your projects, activities and tasks, and see if you can identify a pattern of how you tend to focus when faced with the problem for the first time, and how you would shift that focus when you review it with the benefit of hindsight.

CONCLUSION

Global leadership is never going to be easy. It is always going to be filled with contradictions, difficulties and challenges. It demands special people with special skills if it is going to be done well. The key discovery from our own research is that there are skills for handling uncertainty. These skills are not unknown but are not widely known or practised. All of the eight enablers we have described have been utilized by leaders in the past, but typically have not been explained to people wishing to emulate their skills or learn to be better leaders for themselves. These are private skills that tend not to be passed on from one leader to the next. They seem to be discovered anew each time. Perhaps we can now acknowledge that the skills of handling ambiguity need no longer be hidden.

In our view, as organizations are facing greater levels of ambiguity it is not just the few select leaders who need to deploy these skills, but everyone in the organization who needs to be enabled to handle ambiguity.

To lead their organizations into the unknown and create success by methods and routes that are as yet undiscovered, global leaders will need to lead their organizations effectively towards uncertainty. This ability to define that uncertainty and make it attractive and inhabitable for their organizations is perhaps the most important clarity of all.

How Do You Become Better at Being Focused?

CONCLUSION

GRIPPING THE ROAD TO ROAD TO GLOBALIZATION: DEVELOPING LEADERSHIP COMPETENCIES AT PIRELLI

Paul Kirkbride

GRIPPING THE ROAD TO GLOBALIZATION: DEVELOPING LEADERSHIP COMPETENCIES AT PIRELLI

*I*n Chapter 1 we introduced the 'six-ball' model for global organizations, which delineated the key components of strategy, organization, process, culture, learning and leadership. We argued that to be considered a global organization, any organization would have to have developed global strategies, a structure for globalization, globally focused processes, a global culture and a global leadership style. In terms of the latter dimension, we posed a number of questions that organizations wishing to be truly global would have to ask. These included:

- Have you created a clearly defined cadre of global leaders or a global leadership system within the organization?
- Are your global leaders looking forwards or backwards?
- Is your leadership style aligned to both your global competitive environment and to your local market requirements?
- To what extent is your global leadership style clearly communicated throughout the organization and owned by employees worldwide?
- Are your leaders open to feedback and change from anywhere in the globe?

Chapters 8 and 9 considered aspects of these questions from a theoretical and a general perspective. In this chapter we will take a practical and specific approach by considering in detail how one such large organization has begun to consider and deal with these questions and the interaction between leadership and the other organizational components. We will examine how Pirelli is attempting to improve its global leadership capability through a worldwide leadership initiative.

THE PIRELLI GROUP

The Pirelli Group (Pirelli S.p.A.) is headquartered in Milan, Italy. The group is divided into two business sectors: cables and systems, and tyres. Cables and systems accounts for around 51 per cent of total sales, while tyres accounts for 49 per cent. Worldwide sales are distributed as follows: Europe 55 per cent (of which Italy is 15 per cent), North America 14 per cent, Central and South America 22 per cent, and Australia, Africa and Asia 9 per cent. Pirelli has around 70 factories worldwide and has affiliated companies in around 20 countries. The total Pirelli workforce is around 40 000 employees (Pirelli, 1999).

The Pirelli mission statement includes the following:

> In all parts of the world, tyres and cables are essential to national economies in the areas of transportation of people and goods, and transmission of energy and information. Pirelli's business is centred on those key markets in which we are among the world leaders and innovators.
>
> For more than a century we have grown as a truly multinational corporation, deeply rooted in local markets throughout the world and building upon our two core product sectors.
>
> Our technological and research capacity in terms of professional skills and resources will continue to be a great source of our strength. This, coupled with close involvement with customer requirements, enables us to manufacture and market good value, high quality products and to operate successfully from our bases around the world.

The cables and systems sector has around 17 000 employees in 52 plants in 19 countries and over US$3 billion in annual sales. In recent years Pirelli has grown the business by acquisition or merger, including the acquisitions of the energy cables divisions of Siemens and Metal

Manufacturers, Australia as well as the merger with BICC. Pirelli produces and markets a series of integrated components (products, systems, engineering and installations for global turn-key projects) for customers in the telecommunications and power transmission sectors.

The tyre sector has 21 factories and around 21 000 employees in Argentina, Brazil, Germany, the UK, Italy, Spain, Turkey, the US and Venezuela, as well as a marketing network covering over 120 countries around the world. Pirelli is one of the world's top six tyre manufacturers with sales of over US$3 billion. Pirelli Tyres produces tyres for cars and motor cycles (standard, high performance and motorsport) and tyres for trucks, buses, agricultural vehicles and earthmovers.

THE PIRELLI LEADERSHIP PROGRAMME

In 1999 the Pirelli Group launched a worldwide leadership initiative entitled 'Effective Leadership: A Path for Development and Improvement'. This was organized by the group management development function at group headquarters in Milan, but was to be rolled out in affiliates and subsidiaries worldwide during 2000/2001. The leadership initiative was to be co-ordinated by Professor Bruce Avolio of the Centre for Leadership Studies, University of Binghampton, New York, co-author of the 'Full Range Leadership model', one of the most researched and validated leadership models in the world today (Bass and Avolio, 1998). Local consultants were sourced in each of the countries in which Pirelli operates based on either their skills in leadership training and coaching and/or their familiarity with the Full Range Leadership model. Pilot programmes were run in Italy using both US and Italian consultants and then training workshops were held in Milan for selected consultants who were unfamiliar with the model. The Leadership Path was rolled out into the affiliate companies. For the purpose of this chapter we will examine in more detail the roll-out process in the UK.

What were the reasons behind the decision to launch this leadership initiative? First, and perhaps most importantly, were the strategic and environmental pressures facing Pirelli businesses. For example, the tyre business faces massive competition on a global scale. On the one side the customer base, the global car companies, demands reduced prices, forcing cost cutting and reduced margins, constant technological improvement and increased integration into their own businesses in terms of modularity of supply. Here tyre companies will increasingly have to agree to supply integrated modules of tyres and wheels and perhaps even brake assemblies or axles. On the other side are increasing numbers of low-cost Far Eastern competitors who are making inroads into the basic tyre market as well as gradually improving their technological capabilities. In order to meet these pressures, the major western manufacturers (Bridgestone/Firestone, Michelin, Goodyear, Continental and Pirelli) will, in some way, have to transform the industry in order to compete successfully.

Pirelli has gone some way towards achieving this transformation via the forthcoming launch of its 'Modular Integrated Robotised System' (MIRS), which analysts predict will revolutionize the industry. MIRS reduces production costs per tyre and through total automation of the tyre-making process improves productivity by up to 80 per cent. An additional advantage is that its small scale will free the industry from the confines of large-scale production and will allow tyre production to be done alongside car assembly lines.

Coincidental with this technological revolution Pirelli is also seeking a revolution in leadership. It argues that the new strategic demands of the marketplace require new leadership skills and approaches and admits that some of the old leadership styles will not work in the future environment. Pirelli acknowledges that the current standards of leadership in the group need improvement and the senior management team in Milan is convinced that leadership is a key lever for the achievement of future business success in a changing marketplace.

As Warren Bradley, director of personnel for the UK tyre operations, put it:

> There is no doubt in my mind that the longer-term survivors in many of our UK and global industries will be those that achieve real competitive advantage through the actions and behaviours of their managers and leaders. In many cases, this means shaking off the traditional approaches that may have worked well in

the past, and installing those that will rapidly develop and transform our organizations to meet the emerging demands of the global market.

Thus, based on a successful pilot project in Italy, the group decided to involve all Pirelli managers worldwide in a training path aimed at strengthening their skills in leadership and at establishing a common framework of appropriate leadership behaviours across the whole group. This was to be achieved by encouraging a process of reflection by managers on their own leadership styles based on 360° feedback from bosses, colleagues and subordinates.

Martin Hughes, training and development manager, Pirelli Tyres (UK), commented:

> Line managers regard the leadership initiative as a continuous development process, aimed at bringing about a change in their leadership style. It was important that they recognized the strategic importance of the programme and not to view it as an isolated training event.

THE FULL RANGE LEADERSHIP MODEL

The 'core' of the Pirelli Leadership Path is the Full Range Leadership model (Bass and Avolio, 1998; Avolio, 1999). Bernie Bass, perhaps the doyen of leadership research, was one of the first to argue for a new transformational style of leadership to replace transactional forms. Put simply, transactional leadership encompasses fairly traditional managerial styles where managers or leaders gain compliance and performance by either offering rewards or punishing deviations from standards. These styles are useful for stable-state situations, but are less useful for organizations undergoing environmental turbulence or rapid change. Here transformational styles are required. Transformational leadership involves the provision of a compelling and clear vision; the mobilizing of employee commitment through personal identification and involvement; and the institutionalization of organizational change.

The Full Range Leadership model, as the name suggests, attempts to depict the whole range of leadership styles, from non-leadership to the more transformational styles (see Figure 10.1). The leadership styles identified are as follows (and see Figure 10.2):

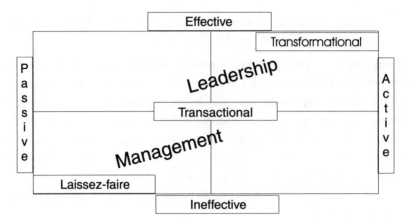

Figure 10.1 Full Range Leadership model 1.

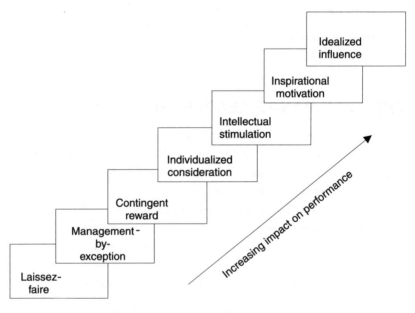

Figure 10.2 The Full Range Leadership model 2.

- *Non-leadership* – laissez–faire
- *Transactional leadership* – management-by-exception (passive); management-by-exception (active); contingent reward
- *Transformational leadership* - individualized consideration; intellectual stimulation; inspirational motivation; idealized influence

Laissez-faire

The laissez-faire leader is essentially a non-leader. This type of manager tends to withdraw from the leadership role and offer little in terms of either direction or support. They are often 'absent' or indifferent to the needs of their followers. As a result, followers are often in conflict with each other regarding roles and responsibilities, try to usurp the leader's role, or seek direction and vision from elsewhere in the organization. Key indicators of this style would be:

- Avoids making decisions.
- Abdicates responsibilities.
- Diverts attention from hard choices.
- Refuses to take sides in a dispute.
- Lets others do as they please.
- Shows lack of interest in what is going on.
- Is disorganized in dealing with priorities.

Management-by-Exception (Passive)

Management-by-exception (MBE) refers to the process of paying attention to the exceptional rather than the normal. Thus MBE leaders tend to be relatively laissez-faire under normal circumstances, but take action when problems occur, mistakes are made, or deviations from standard are apparent. Passive MBE leaders only intervene when the exceptional circumstances become obvious. Thus they tend to have a relatively wide performance acceptance range and poor performance monitoring systems. Key indicators of this style would be:

- Takes no action unless a problem arises.
- Avoids unnecessary changes.
- Enforces corrective action when mistakes are made.
- Places energy on maintaining the status quo.
- Fixes the problem and resumes normal functioning.

Management-by-Exception (Active)

In contrast, the active MBE leader pays very close attention to any problems or deviations and has extensive and accurate monitoring and control systems to provide early warnings of such problems. Followers subject to this style often learn to avoid mistakes by 'burying' them. MBE-A is negatively related to innovation and creativity in the organization. Even when done well, this style only tends to produce performance of a moderate standard. Key indicators of this style would be:

- Arranges to know if something has gone wrong.
- Attends mostly to mistakes and deviations.
- Remains alert for infractions of the rules.
- Teaches followers how to correct mistakes.

Contingent Reward

Contingent reward (CR) is the classic transactional style. Here the leader sets very clear goals, objectives and targets and clarifies, either openly or by inference, what 'rewards' can be expected for successful completion. By rewards we do not simply mean financial or pecuniary rewards, not least because many managers have little ability to offer monetary bonuses or to vary salary levels. Rewards in this case refer to the whole range of non-financial rewards, ranging from the more tangible (extra holiday, preferred work, time off) to the less tangible (praise, visibility, recognition). The CR leader then monitors performance and provides (or exchanges) the reward and recognition if the performance targets are met or exceeded. If done successfully, this style will produce performance at the required levels. In effect, followers will perform up to the objectives and targets that are specified. However, to get employees to 'walk that extra mile' it is necessary to use the transformational styles. Key indicators of this style would be:

- Recognizes what needs to be accomplished.
- Provides support in exchange for the required effort.
- Gives recognition to followers when they perform and meet agreed objectives.
- Follows up to make sure that the agreement is satisfactorily met.
- Arranges to provide the resources needed by followers to accomplish their objectives.

Individualized Consideration

Individualized consideration (IC) is the first of the 'transformational' styles, or the 4 Is as they are often known. The IC leader demonstrates concern for followers, treats them as individuals, gets to know them well and listens to both their concerns and ideas. When managers are asked to relate the behaviours exhibited by their best leader to date, the majority list some form of this style at the top of their list. Key indicators of this style would be:

- Recognizes differences among people in their strengths and weaknesses, likes and dislikes.
- Is interested in the well-being of others.
- Is an 'active' listener.
- Responds to followers with minimal delay.
- Assigns projects based on individual ability and needs.
- Encourages a two-way exchange of views.
- Keeps followers informed.
- Promotes self-development.

Intellectual Stimulation

Intellectual stimulation (IS) essentially involves the leader stimulating the followers to think through issues and problems for themselves and thus to develop their own abilities. It is a style that parents often use with their children, but is often less frequent in organizations where many managers favour a 'telling' approach to a questioning one. Key indicators of this style would be:

- Re-examines assumptions.
- Recognizes patterns that are difficult to imagine.
- Is willing to put forth or entertain seemingly foolish ideas.
- Encourages followers to revisit problems.
- Creates a 'readiness' for changes in thinking.
- Creates a 'holistic' picture that is imaginative.
- Modifies the context to support the vision.
- Encourages a broad range of interests.
- Encourages followers to use intuition.

Inspirational Motivation

The inspirationally motivating (IM) leader has the ability to motivate followers to superior performance. Such leaders tend to be able to articulate, in an exciting and compelling manner, a vision of the future that the followers are able to accept and strive towards. Such leaders can also often succeed in elevating the expectations of followers so that they achieve more than they, or others, thought they could do. Key indicators of this style would be:

- Re-examines assumptions.
- Recognizes patterns that are difficult to imagine.
- Is willing to put forth or entertain seemingly foolish ideas.
- Encourages followers to revisit problems.
- Creates a 'readiness' for changes in thinking.
- Creates a 'holistic' picture that is imaginative.
- Modifies the context to support the vision.
- Encourages a broad range of interests.
- Encourages followers to use intuition.

Idealized Influence

The final I stands for the leader who has become an idealized influence (II) or 'role model' for those around them. Such leaders are regarded as a role model either because they exhibit certain personal characteristics or 'charisma', or because they demonstrate certain moral behaviours. Such leaders are often seen as being high on morality, trust, integrity, honesty and purpose. Key indicators of this style would be:

- Has demonstrated unusual competence.
- Engenders faith in followers.
- Celebrates followers' achievements.
- Appeals to the hopes and desires of followers.
- Creates a sense of empowerment.
- Addresses crises 'head-on'.
- Demonstrates a high activity level.
- Uses power for positive gain.

- Eases group tension in critical times.
- Shows dedication to followers.
- Offers radical solutions.

Bass and Avolio (1998) point out that all managers and leaders will exhibit all of these styles. There are times when all of us exhibit laissez-faire behaviour. Thus this approach is not simply a typology, but what counts is the frequency with which we exhibit these behaviours. Detailed research has looked at the effectiveness of each of these styles (Avolio, 1999). Many studies correlate the presence of these styles with the performance of the leader. Obviously these correlations can run from a totally negative correlation (−1.0) through the absence of correlation (0.0) to a totally positive correlation (+1.0). A meta-analysis by Coleman *et al.* (1995) found the following correlations from 27 studies:

- Transformational (IC, IS, IM, II)   + 0.45–0.60
- Transactional (CR)   + 0.44
- Management-by-exception (active)   + 0.22
- Management-by-exception (passive)   + 0.13
- Laissez-faire   − 0.28

Thus ideally a leader's profile should show higher scores on the transformational styles and lower scores on the management-by-exception styles and laissez-faire. Or, to put it another way, good leaders engage in the transformational styles more than they do the transactional or non-transactional styles (see Figure 10.3).

This model and the associated styles were developed from detailed research and by a process of factor analysis. The Multifactor Leadership Questionnaire (MLQ) was then developed and validated/tested to measure the Full Range Leadership behaviours. Recent research has shown that leaders who are rated high on the MLQ transformational items perform better as leaders on the job. An example of such a study was recently conducted in the Israeli Army with platoon commanders. Research has also shown that managers can be trained to improve their ability to engage in the transformational leadership styles (Dvir, 1998).

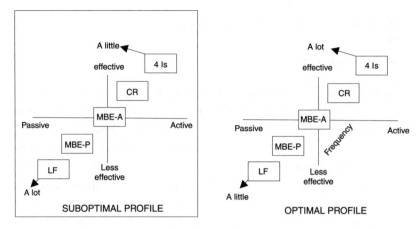

Figure 10.3 Contrasting Full Range Leadership profiles.

THE PIRELLI TYRES (UK) PROGRAMME

We can now examine how the Pirelli Leadership Path was rolled out into the local affiliates by looking in more detail at the process in the UK. Having decided to roll out the Leadership Path in early 2000, and thus becoming the first Pirelli business in the UK to do so, Pirelli Tyres (UK) had to select a partner supplier. Full Range Leadership Limited (www.fullrangeleadership.com) was chosen after tender, partly because of its extensive experience in using the chosen leadership model. Pirelli Tyres (UK) worked with Full Range Leadership to design a pro-gramme structure that would mirror the overall Pirelli leadership path while being tailored to local conditions and needs (see Figure 10.4).

The programme began with a series of launch briefings lasting between one and two hours each. These were held at both Burton (Pirelli Tyres' headquarters) and at Carlisle, where the main factory is located. The launch briefing for the senior management team was facilitated by the external consultant, while subsequent briefings were facilitated by Pirelli HR staff. The briefings were used to explain the structure of the leadership initiative and to issue the Multifactor Leadership Questionnaires (MLQs), which managers were to complete themselves as well as getting their bosses, colleagues and subordinates to

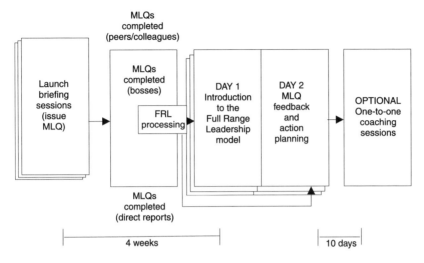

Figure 10.4 The Pirelli Leadership Path.

complete them. Time was taken to assure managers about issues of anonymity and confidentiality. The contract between Pirelli and Full Range Leadership specified that the MLQ forms would be faxed directly back to Full Range Leadership by individual raters. In this way the MLQ forms would not be seen within Pirelli Tyres and individuals could be assured that their evaluations had not been seen by the manager whom they were evaluating. Also the final individual reports for managers were only to be supplied to the managers concerned. The agreement with Pirelli specified that all Pirelli would receive would be a group report that contained only anonymous aggregate data.

The initial reactions to the Leadership Path were varied. Some appeared to take it in their stride and appeared unfazed by the prospects. As one senior manager put it:

> My reaction was 'Oh, here's another initiative' – and you pigeonhole it for a while until you get to hear more about it. And then as you learn more about it your interest and involvement increases and you pick it up from there.

Others were more sceptical. Pirelli Tyres has downsized markedly in recent years and some wondered whether this initiative could perhaps be connected with yet another round of reductions. Others felt that they had seen a number of similar initiatives, but this one seemed to have some unusual features. As one junior manager explained:

> I was surprised that all the managers were going on it. That was something that Pirelli hasn't done before. It was refreshing to see everybody, from the top to junior managers, going through the process. That was a surprise.

After a suitable gap to allow for processing of data and the production of individual reports, a series of six workshops was held in both Derby and Carlisle in 2000, attended by a total of 87 Pirelli managers. These workshops were two days in duration and in outline terms focused on exploring the Full Range Leadership model on the first day and receiving 360° feedback from the MLQ on the second day.

THE WORKSHOPS

The workshops began by using strategic tools to analyse the competitive environment of Pirelli Tyres (UK). This was extremely important in the overall design of the workshops. It was seen as essential to link the leadership styles to the strategic realities of the business, rather than let it be seen as just another HR initiative. Thus the trainers used a number of common strategic tools, including PEST (political, economic, social and technical factors) analysis, five forces analysis and turbulence models, to involve the participants in analyses of Pirelli's external environment and competitive pressures and threats. The output of these exercises was an understanding of the turbulent nature of the competitive environment facing Pirelli and thus the need for change-focused leadership at all senior levels in the organization. Participants were then introduced to the Full Range Leadership model and the concepts of transactional and transformational leadership styles, before exploring the seven styles of the model in more detail by using practical examples.

The second day of each workshop started with an introduction to the concept of 360° feedback and familiarization with the format of the MLQ report. Participants were then issued with their own 50-page MLQ report and given time to read and digest it. They then met in pairs to 'walk and talk'. Each participant reported in plenary on the following:

- One strength identified in their report.
- One weakness identified in their report.
- One development activity they intended to pursue.

The reactions to the MLQ report were virtually uniformly positive, with comments such as:

- 'Certainly an eye-opener.'
- 'Frightening but stimulating.'
- 'Enlightening feedback.'
- 'Very revealing, some unexpected findings.'

As one of the most junior managers put it:

> I'm not an emotional person, but I was close to tears, because out of all the managers there I was the most junior, and yet to read the positive things my peers thought about me left be dumbstruck. However, the report was not all positive and it highlighted two key areas of weakness which were very useful to me.

The reactions to the six workshops were excellent, with comments such as:

- 'Informative and stimulating.'
- 'Highly effective.'
- 'Very useful and thought provoking.'
- 'Relevant and beneficial.'

As Dennis Taggart, director of OE sales, put it when he reflected on the experience:

> Well, I thought it was interesting and informative. The most useful part was probably working with colleagues. Putting us into situations where we had to work together across functional boundaries that don't come with the normal routine.

Or, as Denise Williams, sales office manager, recalled:

> I liked the workshop because it was informal. Normally nobody has the confidence to speak up. With this workshop it was cleverly constructed so that you could discuss situations that were agitating you at work knowing that you had top managers there, but that it was a safe environment.

PERSONAL COACHING

At the end of the workshops participants were offered the opportunity of a one-and-a-half-hour coaching interview with a specialist coach, to be held at either Burton or Carlisle between one and three weeks after the initial workshop. There was no resistance to this process and over 90 per cent of the participants signed up for a coaching session; in most cases where they did not, this seemed to be the result of real diary pressures.

The coaching sessions were designed to be the most important and powerful part of the whole leadership intervention and this appears to be the experience of many of the participants, despite a lack of any clear expectations since they had never experienced the process before. Dennis Taggart's experience was probably quite common:

> I didn't really expect to get a lot from it. I just thought of it as a post-mortem discussion. However, I was pleasantly surprised. The coach managed to hone in on particular areas and was able to draw out more about what the data means, what it could lead to and what might be done about it. As we talked things fell into place. I could see a common thread. I was very pleased.

Others were even more positive:

> I found the coaching very interesting. I found it the most interesting part of the whole process, I really did. In a way it was also a little frightening. Here was a guy who I had never met and after 15 minutes he knew me. It was uncanny. The coach pointed out two or three areas to work on and also identified how I could work on them. He was excellent. I thoroughly enjoyed the one and a half hours.

Martin Hughes comments:

> The one-to-one coaching sessions were perceived by the participants as being the most valuable part of the process. They were amazed at how well the coach really knew them from the MLQ data. This helped them focus their action plan, and it was not uncommon for individuals to ask the coach to contact them if an extra slot became available.

For many the power of the coaching was amplified by the fact that it was seen as following up on an initiative properly, something that the organization had not always done. As Denise Williams commented:

> I thought it was an excellent idea. I felt as if my coach was all for me, on my side. She gave me some good pointers to walk away with. I needed to know if I was

doing what a leader needs to do. I'm a new manager so I'm quite fresh and can adapt. So I needed to know how I was doing. It was excellent timing for me and I found it very helpful.

FOLLOW-UP ACTIVITIES

The leadership initiative of the workshop plus personal coaching appears to have gone well, but as several participants have pointed out, this is only the beginning of a longer process. Following on from the successful launch in Pirelli Tyres, other Pirelli businesses in the UK (Cables and Construction) began to roll out the initiative in Autumn 2000 and Spring 2001.

Pirelli Tyres discussed the best way to take the initiative forward to the next stage and is now offering its managers short, skill-based workshops to offer help to managers and leaders who need to improve on their transformational styles. Workshops are being offered on a number of topics including the following, over a two-year period, each relating to a transformational style:

- Creativity and innovation (intellectual stimulation)
- Coaching and development (individualized consideration)
- Visioning a compelling future (inspirational motivation)
- Understanding individual differences (individualized consideration)

Pirelli Tyres is also considering a repeat of the MLQ 360 after two years. Perhaps Dennis Taggart best sums up the power of this initial part of the intervention:

> It was a worthwhile intervention. Time well spent. But unless we do follow it up, then it won't have been a waste of time, but we won't have derived full value. I've drawn many things from it and I still think about it now when I'm in certain situations. I think about being enthusiastic; about trying to motivate people; about trying to involve people. Thinking about what a situation means to other people and what they are thinking.

Of course, as we have seen, leadership is only one of the organizational components that have to be geared towards globalization. Even if the

intervention is successful, the new global leadership model and behaviours will have to be supported by the other four 'balls' of the
model, that is, by global organization, global culture, global processes,
and global strategy. Pirelli is currently working in a number of these
areas to ensure that the new leadership behaviours are supported and
reinforced.

EVALUATING THE INTERVENTION: IS THE MODEL CULTURE BOUND?

Obviously, it is too early to evaluate fully the outcome of the initiative
as it is still in progress. However, we can consider the initiative in terms
of its intended objectives and the likelihood of success.

Pirelli launched the initiative in order to help the organization
achieve transformation in an extremely competitive and turbulent set
of markets. Obviously, another objective was to establish a common set
of leadership competencies and behaviours worldwide for Pirelli. To
date the initiative appears successful in terms of alerting managers to the
needs for transformational behaviours. It has also successfully demonstrated to managers that their leadership behaviours may need improvement in certain areas and the follow-on work is supporting them in
developing some of these new leadership styles. If we return to the
questions we posed at the start of the chapter, we can see that Pirelli has
made progress on a number of these. It is creating, through the roll-out
of the Full Range Leadership model, a global leadership system in the
organization. As the model explicitly focuses on transformational behaviours it can be said to be forward, rather than backward, looking. It
is also being clearly communicated through processes of training,
feedback and coaching.

However, given that this process is being rolled out in cultures as
diverse as Argentina, Germany, Turkey and the UK, to what extent is
culture a potential barrier to this process? It is well known that many
leadership models have failed to travel cross-culturally and that considerable national and cultural differences have been found in basic

leadership behaviours. Take some of the classic leadership dichotomies, such as:

- Autocratic vs democratic
- Participative vs directive
- Task oriented vs relationship oriented
- Structure vs consideration
- Active vs passive

One can see from a number of research studies that these behaviours are particularly suited to certain cultures and not suited to others. For example, Haire, Ghiselli and Porter, in a classic early study (1966), found that subscription to, and acceptance of, democratic leadership was particularly high across the 14 countries they studied. However, as Bass (1990) notes, compared to US managers, managers elsewhere indicated little acceptance of what would be required for such democratic leadership, such as agreement that employees as well as supervisors have the potential to exhibit initiative, share leadership, and contribute to the problem-solving process in organizations (1990: 789). Thus democratic leadership only works fully in low power distance cultures (Hofstede, 1984). Haire, Ghiselli and Porter went on to conclude that introducing democratic leadership at that time (mid-1960s) into other countries with different (high power distance) cultures would be 'a little like building the techniques and practices of a Jeffersonian democracy on a basic belief in the divine right of kings' (1966: 130).

What about the more recent dichotomy between transactional and transformational leadership that forms the bedrock of the Full Range Leadership model? Is this equally culturally dependent or does it transcend cultural boundaries? The research evidence appears contradictory. Earley (1984, 1988) has noted that the contingent reward style has some important cross-cultural differences, both in terms of effectiveness and approach, in the American, English and Ghanaian cultures. Similarly, Yokochi (1989) has noticed problems with this style in Japanese culture. However, Yokochi also notes the close 'fit' for transformational styles, particularly at the higher levels of Japanese management.

Bass himself (Bass 1996, 1999; Bass and Steidlmeier, 1999) makes a case for the universality of the concepts of transformational and transactional leadership:

> Although the original theory, model, and measurements emerged in the individualistic United States, it appears equally or even more applicable in the collectivist societies of Asia. Collectivist cultures provide the leaders with ready-made opportunities to become transformational leaders. Most subordinates in collectivist cultures already have respect for their leaders. Transformational leadership is more likely to be enhanced further by the centrality of work in life and the high level of group orientation among followers. (Bass, 1999: 16)

Bass also argues that what distinguishes transformational leadership is the 'moral core' that sets it apart from mere lists of leadership or managerial behaviours:

> The point is this: for transformational leadership to be 'authentic', it must incorporate a central core of moral values. Yet the 'practices' (in Hofstede's terms) of such values are highly culturally relative. Further, even when a set of core values, such as friendship or honesty, may be found in all cultures their ordering and relative importance may also vary by culture . . . Rather than simply leading to the affirmation of ethical relativism, such global diversity of values underscores the need of transformational leaders at all levels of human society. At the core of all leadership . . . one finds a value core . . . Perhaps the greatest challenge of leadership is precisely to bridge ethical relativism by forging a platform of common values and stimulating alignment and congruence of interests. What is required of the authentic transformational leader is not a blueprint for all to follow but a sort of Socratic commitment to the process of searching out moral excellence. (Bass and Steidlmeier, 1999: 210–11)

Whether we agree with Bass or not is perhaps a little academic. As he notes, a key consideration in the 'elasticity' of leadership is how far you are culturally going to stretch it. In the Pirelli case, the cultures are probably close enough for this model to be relatively transportable. Certainly the evidence to date appears to support that assertion. Whether Pirelli manages to develop a truly worldwide leadership style and approach that are acceptable to all its affiliated companies around the world remains to be empirically tested over time.

However, the initiative does provide Pirelli with a number of advantages. It offers a common language throughout the organization with which to discuss and debate leadership problems and issues. This, in and of itself, can help an organization comprised of different nationalities using different national languages to represent difficult conceptual problems such as leadership by using terms that everyone in the organization understands. Second, it also provides a conceptual framework that enables people to discuss potential cultural differences. For example, Pirelli managers can now easily discuss how their approaches to 'inspirational motivation' may differ slightly across cultures. Finally, it is important to note that the Full Range Leadership model itself explicitly addresses cultural difference and cultural sensitivity through the concept of 'individualized consideration'. It is explicitly acknowledged that 'staff' will be different and need to be led differently. In this respect, the Full Range Leadership model is a long way from 'one size fits all' approaches. If in the implementation of the training and feedback initiative, Pirelli and its consultants continue to 'live' the model and use individualized consideration, this will allow the freedom and space to take cultural differences into account in terms of making the model work locally. Only if the initiative were to be implemented in a 'management-by-exception' style would the model itself become a potential barrier and be seen by other cultures as yet another imposition from headquarters in Italy. To date, this is emphatically not the experience of the author from his involvement in the initiative.

References

Avolio, B. J. (1999) *Full Leadership Development*, Thousand Oaks, CA: Sage.

Bass, B. M. (1990) *Bass and Stogdill's Handbook of Leadership: Theory, Research and Managerial Applications*, 3rd edn, New York: Free Press.

Bass, B. M. (1996) *A New Paradigm of Leadership: An Inquiry into Transformational Leadership*, Alexandria, VA: US Army Research Institute for the Behavioral and Social Sciences.

Bass, B. M. (1999) 'Two decades of research and development in transformational leadership', *European Journal of Work and Organizational Psychology*, 8(1): 9–32.

Bass, B. M. and Avolio, B. J. (1998) *Manual for the Multifactor Leadership Questionnaire*, Redwood, CA: Mindgarden.

Bass, B. M. and Steidlmeier, P. (1999) 'Ethics, character, and authentic transformational leadership behavior', *Leadership Quarterly*, 10(2): 181–217.

Coleman, E. P., Patterson, E., Fuller, B., Hester, K. and Stringer, D. Y. (1995) 'A meta-analytic examination of leadership style and selected follower compliance outcomes', unpublished manuscript, University of Alabama.

Dvir, T. (1998) 'The impact of transformational leadership training on follower development and performance: a field experiment', unpublished doctoral dissertation, Tel Aviv University, Israel.

Earley, P. C. (1984) 'Social interaction: the frequency of use and valuation in the U.S., England and Ghana', *Journal of Cross Cultural Psychology*, 15: 477–85.

Earley, P. C. (1988) 'Contributions of intercultural research to the understanding of performance feedback', paper, Society for Industrial and Organizational Psychology, Dallas.

Haire, M., Ghiselli, E. E. and Porter, L. W. (1966) *Managerial Thinking: An International Study*, New York: John Wiley.

Hofstede, G. (1984) *Culture's Consequences: International Differences in Work Related Values*, abridged edn, London: Sage.

Pirelli (1999) *Pirelli: the Group in Figures*, Milan: Pirelli S.p.A.

Yokochi, N. (1989) 'Leadership styles of Japanese business executives and managers: transformational and transactional', doctoral dissertation, United States International University, San Diego, California.

GLOBAL ORGANIZATION DIAGNOSTIC QUESTIONNAIRE

Complete the following questionnaire, ideally in consultation with colleagues, and then turn to the scoring key in Appendix B. Remember, try to describe your organization as it really is currently, rather than as you would want it to be or as the organizational hype and hyperbole say it is.

1. To what extent can the essence of your global strategy be described in less than five minutes?

1	2	3	4	5
Low extent		Moderate		High extent

2. To what extent would you describe your organizational culture as being strong and cohesive?

1	2	3	4	5
Low extent		Moderate		High extent

3. To what extent are the activities of your different strategic business units/affiliates well co-ordinated?

1	2	3	4	5
Low extent		Moderate		High extent

4. To what extent are tasks/activities requiring global integration executed efficiently and economically?

1	2	3	4	5
Low extent		Moderate		High extent

5. To what extent does your organization have a common leadership style among global senior managers?

1	2	3	4	5
Low extent		Moderate		High extent

6. To what extent do you proactively review any new activities in your global markets?

1	2	3	4	5
Low extent		Moderate		High extent

7. To what extent do organizational members understand your organization's global source of sustained competitive advantage?

1	2	3	4	5
Low extent		Moderate		High extent

8. To what extent do you have a formalized and written statement of your organizational values?

1	2	3	4	5
Low extent		Moderate		High extent

9. To what extent has your organization got a clear and easily understood global structure?

1	2	3	4	5
Low extent		Moderate		High extent

10. To what extent is the global quality of your products or services outstanding?

1	2	3	4	5
Low extent		Moderate		High extent

11. To what extent does your organization have an agreed set of global leadership competencies?

1	2	3	4	5
Low extent		Moderate		High extent

12. To what extent do you know why you have been successful in your most profitable markets?

1	2	3	4	5
Low extent		Moderate		High extent

13. To what extent does your global strategy articulate what is unique about your organization?

1	2	3	4	5
Low extent		Moderate		High extent

14. To what extent is the 'way we do things around here' clear and similar around the world?

1	2	3	4	5
Low extent		Moderate		High extent

15. To what extent do employees clearly understand the goals and purposes of different organizational parts of your global structure?

1	2	3	4	5
Low extent		Moderate		High extent

16. To what extent do employees understand the key global processes in your organization?

1	2	3	4	5
Low extent		Moderate		High extent

17. To what extent does your organization train managers in appropriate global leadership behaviours?

1	2	3	4	5
Low extent		Moderate		High extent

18. To what extent are you clear about why some of your global opportunities and initiatives have not delivered value?

1	2	3	4	5
Low extent		Moderate		High extent

19. To what extent do your global planning processes seek to take into account potential future discontinuities in your marketplace, environment or geography?

1	2	3	4	5
Low extent		Moderate		High extent

20. To what extent is your global culture future oriented and proactive in addition to honouring past successes?

1	2	3	4	5
Low extent		Moderate		High extent

21. To what extent does the worldwide structure you now have anticipate your future needs?

1	2	3	4	5
Low extent		Moderate		High extent

22. To what extent are you successful in bringing new global products/services to market more quickly than your competitors?

1	2	3	4	5
Low extent		Moderate		High extent

23. To what extent is the top management leadership style of your organization oriented towards future change?

1	2	3	4	5
Low extent		Moderate		High extent

24. To what extent do you spot opportunities in emerging markets before your competitors?

1	2	3	4	5
Low extent		Moderate		High extent

25. To what extent do your global planning processes utilize future-oriented techniques such as scenario planning?

1	2	3	4	5
Low extent		Moderate		High extent

26. To what extent does your organizational culture encourage creativity, innovation and learning?

1	2	3	4	5
Low extent		Moderate		High extent

27. To what extent are your global structures flexible enough to respond to the changing demands both of the global economy and local marketplaces?

1	2	3	4	5
Low extent		Moderate		High extent

28. To what extent do you constantly benchmark process best practice both within and outside your industrial sector on a worldwide basis?

1	2	3	4	5
Low extent		Moderate		High extent

29. To what extent do global leaders in your organization talk about the future rather than the past?

1	2	3	4	5
Low extent		Moderate		High extent

30. To what extent can you transfer your insights about trends in one market to other parts of your business?

1	2	3	4	5
Low extent		Moderate		High extent

31. To what extent are you setting out to add new global competencies, beyond those that already exist?

1	2	3	4	5
Low extent		Moderate		High extent

32. To what extent is 'failure' treated as feedback?

1	2	3	4	5
Low extent		Moderate		High extent

33. To what extent does your organization, on a global scale, have a good track record in innovation?

1	2	3	4	5
Low extent		Moderate		High extent

34. To what extent do you understand what additional global processes your organization will have to develop to succeed in the future?

1	2	3	4	5
Low extent		Moderate		High extent

35. To what extent do leaders in your organization seek to 'manage the present from the future'?

1	2	3	4	5
Low extent		Moderate		High extent

36. To what extent does your global organization (HQ) mobilize appropriate resources when a new opportunity is spotted in a local market?

1	2	3	4	5
Low extent		Moderate		High extent

37. To what extent do various strategic business units within your organization share a common strategic orientation, particularly in relation to globalization?

1	2	3	4	5
Low extent		Moderate		High extent

38. To what extent does the informal culture of your organization correspond with the formal espoused culture?

1	2	3	4	5
Low extent		Moderate		High extent

39. To what extent does your organization have a high level of co-operation across internal boundaries (product, country, region etc.)?

1	2	3	4	5
Low extent		Moderate		High extent

40. To what extent do you invest senior management time and money in improving the global processes most important to your future success?

1	2	3	4	5
Low extent		Moderate		High extent

41. To what extent does your prevailing leadership style match the informal culture of the organization?

1	2	3	4	5
Low extent		Moderate		High extent

42. To what extent are your corporate staff in HQ sensitive to the cultural differences of local markets?

1	2	3	4	5
Low extent		Moderate		High extent

43. To what extent is your global strategy responsive to competitor threats and environmental shifts?

1	2	3	4	5
Low extent		Moderate		High extent

44. To what extent does your global culture have relevance in the national cultures in which you operate worldwide?

1	2	3	4	5
Low extent		Moderate		High extent

45. To what extent can your structure respond rapidly to changes in customer requirements on either a global or local scale?

1	2	3	4	5
Low extent		Moderate		High extent

46. To what extent has your organization eliminated non–essential activities on a worldwide scale?

1	2	3	4	5
Low extent		Moderate		High extent

47. To what extent does your organization have a top management leadership style that is appropriate to both global environmental and local market conditions?

1	2	3	4	5
Low extent		Moderate		High extent

48. To what extent have you been able to transfer local successes on to a global scale?

1	2	3	4	5
Low extent		Moderate		High extent

49. To what extent is your global strategy responsive to customer needs?

1	2	3	4	5
Low extent		Moderate		High extent

50. To what extent do senior managers model the global behaviours you are trying to encourage?

1	2	3	4	5
Low extent		Moderate		High extent

51. To what extent does your structure facilitate the implementation of your global and/or business-level strategy?

1	2	3	4	5
Low extent		Moderate		High extent

52. To what extent are your global customer satisfaction levels and the quality of your relationships with global customers constantly monitored?

1	2	3	4	5
Low extent		Moderate		High extent

53. To what extent does the leadership style most prevalent in the organization support the global values and behaviours you wish to encourage?

1	2	3	4	5
Low extent		Moderate		High extent

54. To what extent can local employees influence activities on a global level?

1	2	3	4	5
Low extent		Moderate		High extent

55. To what extent does your organization have a formal written global strategy?

1	2	3	4	5
Low extent		Moderate		High extent

56. To what extent do you spend time communicating your global culture widely throughout the world?

1	2	3	4	5
Low extent		Moderate		High extent

57. To what extent do your employees have a strong feeling of being part of a global team?

1	2	3	4	5
Low extent		Moderate		High extent

58. To what extent are your global processes transparent both at the centre and at the periphery?

1	2	3	4	5
Low extent		Moderate		High extent

59. To what extent do top leaders in your organization regularly communicate directly to all staff worldwide?

1	2	3	4	5
Low extent		Moderate		High extent

60. To what extent do all employees understand the sources of business and technical expertise worldwide?

1	2	3	4	5
Low extent		Moderate		High extent

61. To what extent can staff in your organization clearly articulate its global strategic orientation?

1	2	3	4	5
Low extent		Moderate		High extent

62. To what extent do employees in your organization support your global value system?

1	2	3	4	5
Low extent		Moderate		High extent

63. To what extent do strategic business units/affiliates in your organization feel that their contributions are recognized?

1	2	3	4	5
Low extent		Moderate		High extent

64. To what extent are your internal and external global processes clearly documented (i.e. as in ISO9002 etc.)?

1	2	3	4	5
Low extent		Moderate		High extent

65. To what extent can your staff describe the goals of your organizational leaders?

1	2	3	4	5
Low extent		Moderate		High extent

66. To what extent can your customers access the best person in your organization worldwide to solve their problem?

1	2	3	4	5
Low extent		Moderate		High extent

67. To what extent does your organization encourage regular global strategic discussions and conversations?

1	2	3	4	5
Low extent		Moderate		High extent

68. To what extent can your staff clearly describe the formal espoused culture?

1	2	3	4	5
Low extent		Moderate		High extent

69. To what extent do strategic business units/affiliates/product groups understand how they link together for effective global product/service delivery?

1	2	3	4	5
Low extent		Moderate		High extent

70. To what extent are your staff trained to think in process terms?

1	2	3	4	5
Low extent		Moderate		High extent

71. To what extent are your staff satisfied with the current leadership style in your organization?

1	2	3	4	5
Low extent		Moderate		High extent

72. To what extent do you have a global 'knowledge management system' (IT based or not) that really works?

1	2	3	4	5
Low extent		Moderate		High extent

73. To what extent do you regularly revisit and challenge your global strategy and vision?

1	2	3	4	5
Low extent		Moderate		High extent

74. To what extent are personal and organizational values openly discussed in your organization?

1	2	3	4	5
Low extent		Moderate		High extent

75. To what extent is 'best practice' quickly transferred from one part of your organization to another?

1	2	3	4	5
Low extent		Moderate		High extent

76. To what extent are the internal and external global processes you have now qualitatively different to those you had in the recent past?

1	2	3	4	5
Low extent		Moderate		High extent

77. To what extent do leaders in your organization encourage debate, dissent and challenge?

1	2	3	4	5
Low extent		Moderate		High extent

78. To what extent do the leadership of your organization (HQ) proactively seek feedback from all parts of the world?

1	2	3	4	5
Low extent		Moderate		High extent

79. To what extent do you explicitly encourage 'devil's advocates' to challenge the global strategy?

1	2	3	4	5
Low extent		Moderate		High extent

80. To what extent has your global culture changed markedly in the last five years?

1	2	3	4	5
Low extent		Moderate		High extent

81. To what extent do you make changes to your global structures in light of feedback from global customers or suppliers?

1	2	3	4	5
Low extent		Moderate		High extent

82. To what extent do you have customer/supplier feedback mechanisms that lead to regular process change?

1	2	3	4	5
Low extent		Moderate		High extent

83. To what extent does your organization have formalized mechanisms of upward feedback and 'bottom-up' communication?

1	2	3	4	5
Low extent		Moderate		High extent

84. To what extent do processes exist to enable a local employee to challenge the dominant mindset of the organization?

1	2	3	4	5
Low extent		Moderate		High extent

85. To what extent do you look for competitors from 'outside the box' (i.e. beyond your 'traditional' competitors)?

1	2	3	4	5
Low extent		Moderate		High extent

86. To what extent do you regularly measure and monitor your worldwide culture/ climate by means of surveys or other instruments?

1	2	3	4	5
Low extent		Moderate		High extent

87. To what extent has your global structure been changed in recent years as a result of customer feedback or environmental change?

1	2	3	4	5
Low extent		Moderate		High extent

88. To what extent does your organization regularly revisit and review business processes using business process re-engineering (BPR) techniques or other approaches that develop radical as well as incremental improvements?

1	2	3	4	5
Low extent		Moderate		High extent

89. To what extent do your global leaders receive regular feedback on the effectiveness of their leadership style?

1	2	3	4	5
Low extent		Moderate		High extent

90. To what extent does your organization regularly bring in customers and suppliers to proactively challenge your assumptions about your business?

1	2	3	4	5
Low extent		Moderate		High extent

Now transfer your scores to Appendix B.

GLOBAL ORGANIZATION MODEL SCORING SHEET

Enter your scores on each question in the space provided and total each set in the space provided.

Strategy	Culture	Organization	Processes	Leadership	Learning	
1.	2.	3.	4.	5.	6.	
7.	8.	9.	10.	11.	12.	
13.	14.	15.	16.	17.	18.	
_____	_____	_____	_____	_____	_____	Clarity
_____	_____	_____	_____	_____	_____	
19.	20.	21.	22.	23.	24.	
25.	26.	27.	28.	29.	30.	
31.	32.	33.	34.	35.	36.	
_____	_____	_____	_____	_____	_____	Future orientation
_____	_____	_____	_____	_____	_____	

Strategy	Culture	Organization	Processes	Leadership	Learning	
37.	38.	39.	40.	41.	42.	
43.	44.	45.	46.	47.	48.	
49.	50.	51.	52.	53.	54.	
___	___	___	___	___	___	Alignment
___	___	___	___	___	___	
55.	56.	57.	58.	59.	60.	
61.	62.	63.	64.	65.	66.	
67.	68.	69.	70.	71.	72.	
___	___	___	___	___	___	Communication
___	___	___	___	___	___	
73.	74.	75.	76.	77.	78.	
79.	80.	81.	82.	83.	84.	
85.	86.	87.	88.	89.	90.	
___	___	___	___	___	___	Feedback and change
___	___	___	___	___	___	

Now transfer your scores to Appendix C.

GLOBAL ORGANIZATION MODEL RESULTS SHEET

Enter your scores from Appendix B into the grid below. In our training courses and consulting work, we use a 'traffic light' system where a red light indicates a potential problem area. As a rule of thumb, a score of 3–7 indicates a red light; a score of 8–10 indicates an amber light; and a score of 11–15 indicates a green light.

To what extent	Global strategy	Global culture	Global organization	Global processes	Global leadership	Global learning
Have you got clarity?						
Is it oriented to the future?						
Is it designed globally and locally?						
Is it communicated and owned?						
Is it open to feedback and change?						

AUTHOR BIOGRAPHIES

THE EDITORS

Paul Kirkbride BA, MSc, PhD, FIPD, FHKIPM

Paul Kirkbride rejoined Ashridge in 2000 as Research Fellow reporting directly to the Chief Executive, having previously been from 1991–94 a Faculty Team Leader responsible for Change, Leadership and HRM programmes. Paul is also a Visiting Professor at the University of Hertfordshire and Managing Director of The Change House Ltd. and Full Range Leadership Ltd.

Paul has been, over the years, an HR professional, a researcher, a 'proper' academic, a trainer, a consultant, a businessman and a life-long Carlisle United supporter. From 1989–91 he was British Aerospace Professor of Organizational Change and Development at British Aerospace (Commercial Aircraft) and the University of Hertfordshire. He has taught in universities in Oxford and Hong Kong and has been a Visiting Professor at the Australian Graduate School of Management (AGSM), the Fuqua School of Business at Duke University, North Carolina, and the University of Maryland.

In his consulting work Paul specializes in advising top management on change processes; developing strategic leaders; building new cultures in mergers and alliances; and developing and delivering project-based management development programmes. He has lived, taught or consulted in many countries including Argentina, Australia, China, most of the countries in the European Union, Hong Kong, Macau, Malaysia, Mexico, Philippines, Singapore, South Africa, Taiwan and the United States.

His current research interests include the post-modernist organizational change and structural inertia theory as well as the more pragmatic areas of leadership, strategic human resource management, international/cross-cultural management and organizational culture. He has published over 60 journal articles, 15 book chapters and four books. His research work has been published internationally in journals such as *Asia Pacific Human Resource Management, Industrial and Labor Relations Review, International Journal of Human Resource Management, Journal of Industrial Relations* and *Organisation Studies*.

Paul gained a degree in Business Studies and a Master's in Personnel and Industrial Relations before completing his PhD at the Centre for Organizational Change and Development, University of Bath. He is a Fellow of the Chartered Institute of Personnel and Development and a Fellow of the Hong Kong Institute of Human Resource Management.

Karen Ward BSc (Hons) Msc MCIM

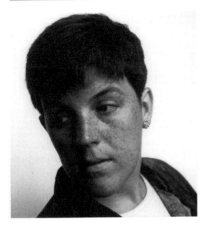

Since January 2000, Karen has been working in an associate capacity with Ashridge after being a full-time member of faculty for three years. Prior to Ashridge, Karen had a range of management and organization development roles within organizations in the pharmaceutical and financial services sectors. She began her career with PA Consulting Group, where she worked across both the private and public sectors.

Karen teaches and consults with a range of global organizations on issues related to the effective implementation of strategic choices. Her work focuses on organizations trying to work across boundaries, whether national, functional or organizational.

In particular Karen has extensive experience of the integration issues of mergers, acquisitions, joint ventures and strategic alliances in a global context. She led part of the Integration office during the merger of GlaxoWellcome and has subsequently consulted to a number of organizations on integration issues.

Her book, *Leading International Teams* (McGraw Hill), draws together her academic and consulting experience of enabling organizations to develop global capability through the successful creation and maintenance of complex teams. Her broad research interest lies in effective implementation of global strategies, i.e., how do organizations really make things work, and she has published articles and chapters particularly on the role of HR in global organizations; the impact of organization design as an implementation vehicle and the use of large group interventions in the development of a global Strategic Intent.

Karen was educated in the UK and Germany and has subsequently lived and worked in Nigeria and the USA. Her work has taken her to most European countries and Mexico and South Africa. English is her mother tongue and she speaks fluent German. Having gained a degree in International Business Studies, she then completed a MSc in Organizational Behaviour at Birkbeck College, University of London. Her professional qualification is a Diploma from the UK Chartered Institute of Marketing.

CONTRIBUTORS

Andrew Ettinger BSc, DipLib, FIInsSc

Andrew joined Ashridge in 1985 and is Director of Learning Resources. He is responsible for Ashridge's unique multi-media Learning Resource Centre and all of Ashridge's learning offerings. He also organizes and lectures on courses for several professional bodies in the UK and abroad and is an external lecturer at several universities. He has completed consultancy projects in India, Poland, Zimbabwe and the UK.

After graduating at London University, he completed a post-graduate diploma in Information Science and then worked at the North East London Polytechnic before moving to London Business School, where he worked for 7 years.

He is particularly interested in managers' use of information and how they learn and is currently leading a team that has recently launched the Virtual Learning Resource Centre, a web-based resource that includes a variety of internally and externally generated learning and information products.

Andrew has spoken at and chaired many conferences and amongst recent articles he has written are: 'The Shift from Information to Total Quality Learning', 'Benchmarking and Learning Resources' and 'Building a virtual world-wide learning environment'.

He was made a Fellow of the Institute of Information Scientists in 1996 and was European Business Librarian of the year for 1999.

Phil Hodgson BSC, MSc, MIPD, Cpsychol, AFBPsS, FRSA

Phil has worked full time at Ashridge since 1983. He is co-director of the Action Learning for Chief Executives Programme, and co-director of the Executive Coaching Service. He is a major contributor to Ashridge's strategic management and leadership programmes. He is client director for organizations in healthcare, financial services, fmcg, publishing, and manufacturing. He teaches, consults, researches and writes in the areas of leadership, change, handling uncertainty, and top executive learning and development.

Before joining Ashridge, Phil worked in real jobs for nearly 15 years as a manager in a variety of service and transport industries, where he was involved in management and organizational development roles. After leaving university his first work was as a volunteer social worker in the Solomon Islands, West Pacific, and before he completely grew up, he spent some time as a software engineer. His degrees are in psychology and industrial psychology, and he is a Master Practitioner in NLP.

His earlier books are: *A Practical Guide to Successful Interviewing – on assessment and interviewing techniques*, published by McGraw Hill; *Effective Meetings*, published by Century Business for the Sunday Times; *Making Change Work*, published by Mercury Books. He has written two books on leadership: *What High Performance Managers Really Do with Stuart Crainer*, published by Pitman in 1993, looked at how leaders implement strategy. His fifth, *The Future of Leadership*, with Randall White and Stuart Crainer, published by Pitman in 1996, explored and researched the skills needed for effective future leadership in the face of unprecedented change and uncertainty.

He is currently working with Randy White on a follow-up which, they hope, will shed some light on how managers handle uncertainty and ambiguity in their roles as leaders and influencers of strategy.

Samreen Khan, BA, MSc

Samreen joined Ashridge Consulting in 1998. Her consulting is informed by her particular interest in creating space in organizations where individuals are encouraged to reflect on, explore and share personal value sets, culture and experience in order to conceive learning communities that can build tacitly rich organizations. She is also fascinated by the e-world and the implications its rapid development and maturity will have for the 'organization' as an organic and human system.

Samreen's previous experience was in research in overseas government, editorial and marketing within the publishing industry and international portfolio management. Since joining Ashridge, she has worked with the National Health Service focusing on waiting list reduction initiatives, conflict and change and programme/project management using Theory of Constraints Methodology. Medical bodies she has worked with include Norfolk & Norwich Healthcare Trust, Radcliffe Infirmary, Wiltshire Health Authority and Southampton University Hospital. She has worked with Novartis Animal Health, Pharmaceuticals and Corporate divisions on the development and organizational ownership of a coaching culture. Samreen has dedicated significant time, however, to helping clients unleash hidden learning potential within their organizations. Clients within this context include Prudential Portfolio Managers, Infinium and Novartis.

Samreen did an MSc at City University in London. This degree introduced her to techniques such as Soft Systems Methodology and Object-Oriented Analysis and Design, as well as Project Management and IS Strategy. Her undergraduate degree was in Political Science and was gained at Colgate University in Hamilton, New York. Samreen is half Venezuelan, half Indian, and has lived in Europe and America in recent years. She is bilingual in Spanish and English and has a basic conversational background in French.

Paul Pinnington MA (Oxon)

Paul is a member of the Ashridge board and leads the strategic management and director development activity stream, a group of tutors concentrating on senior-level strategic and international management programmes. His current clients include Electrolux, PricewaterhouseCoopers, Royal and Sun Alliance and ICL, for whom he designs and runs highly tailored global programmes.

He is particularly interested in marketing and business strategy and is currently researching, developing and implementing strategy in a global context.

Prior to Ashridge, Paul worked for Stauffer Chemical Company (now part of Zeneca) in sales and marketing management positions, first covering the UK and Eire operations. Then based in Geneva as marketing manager for Europe and Africa, he held a short-term 'troubleshooting' assignment for the Johannesburg-based operation and managed several pan-European product launches.

His earlier career after Oxford University was spent with Massey Ferguson and Fisons in both sales and marketing management positions and with Marketing Improvements Ltd as a senior consultant responsible for training and consultancy assignments in Europe and South-East Asia.

Paul has experience in many industries including chemicals – especially petrochemicals, pesticides and pharmaceuticals – white goods, retail and technology. He has worked for Ashridge throughout Europe and Japan, and is a visiting professor at Babson College, Boston, USA, teaching business strategy on tailored programmes.

Cath Redman BA(hons) PG Diplib

Cath is the product manager for Ashridge's virtual learning offerings and has worked extensively in the area of technology based training. She played a key role in the development of a series of 40 learning guides on CD-ROM. Her most recent project was the development of the Ashridge's Virtual Learning Resource Centre, A web based service which was launched in May 1999. Cath delivered a paper at the Online Exhibition in London in December 1998 which dealt with project management issues associated with setting up the Virtual Learning Resource Centre.

In addition to the project management skills she has substantial experience of sourcing materials for projects using a range of web based and other electronic sources. Cath's other roles include training managers to use information sources, running presentations and workshops introducing Ashridge's Learning Resource Centre and the range of learning materials available.

R. I. Westwood BA (Hons), MA, PhD, APS

Bob Westwood is a Faculty member of the Australian Graduate School of Management, based in Sydney Australia. He was educated in the UK, where he received a BA (Hons) in Philosophy and Psychology, an MA in Occupational Psychology – both from the University of Sheffield – and a PhD in Management from the University of Bath. Since 1983 he has worked at universities in the Asia Pacific region where he has taught principally at the graduate level. Bob spent some time in the private sector, in publishing, prior to this departure from the UK.

He has researched and published widely in the areas of cross-cultural and international management, the sociology of work, and aspects of organization theory. Bob has published over 50 articles, books and book chapters in these areas. He was editor and chief contributor to *Organisational Behaviour: A Southeast Asian Perspective*, published by Longman in 1992. He is co-editor, with Professor Steve Linstead of *Language and Organisation*, to be published by Sage in 2001. He is also co-editor, with Professor Stewart Clegg, of *Point/Counterpoint: Central Debates in Organisation Studies*, which will be published by Blackwell in 2002. He has latterly developed an interest in creativity and innovation in organizational settings. He teaches an MBA course in that area and is developing research and consultancy interests.

He has consulted to a range of international companies including Procter and Gamble, Coca-Cola, Hong Kong Shanghai Banking Corporation, Avon Corporation, Eli Lilly, the Asian Productivity Organisation, the Malaysian Institute of Management, and the Mass Transit Railway Corporation. In addition Bob has presented seminars and paper at conferences around the world, including the UK, France, Finland, Ireland, the USA, Singapore, Hong Kong, China, Philippines, Malaysia, Mexico and Bermuda.

Randall White AB, MS, PhD

Dr Randall White is a principal in the Executive Development Group LLC, Greensboro, NC, and an adjunct professor at the Fuqua School of Business, Duke University. He also teaches MBA students and executives at the Johnson Graduate School of Management, Cornell University.

Randy's work in leadership development regularly takes him to Europe, South America and Asia-Pacific. He is a frequent speaker for a variety of industry groups, including the Conference Board of the US and Canada, the Human Resources Planning Society, the American Society for Training and Development, and the Institute for Management Studies. He maintains an affiliation with the Centre for Creative Leadership, where he spent 12 years developing programmes and research on leadership. His list of current consulting clients includes M.D. Anderson Cancer Centre, Siemens, Aetna, ABB, Morgan Stanley, Thomson, Eaton and Kennametal.

Randy's interest is in where leaders come from, how they develop, and their eventual success is borne out in his writing. As co-author of *Breaking the Glass Ceiling* and *The Future of Leadership*, he has had a major impact on the way women are viewed as leaders and the importance of less easily measured leadership skills like dealing with uncertainty. He has written in both popular and scientific outlets on leadership. He currently has a critically acclaimed piece on different types of leadership coaching (first published in the *Consulting Psychologist*). Due out in Spring 2001 will be his latest book, co-authored with Phil Hodgson, titled *Relax, It's Only Uncertainty* (London: Financial Times). He is currently working with Rick Gilkey of Emory University on a book tentatively titled *From Clinician to Coach*.

He serves on the editorial board of the *Journal of Leaders and Leadership* and in 1997 was a Salzberg Fellow on Women's Issues. Randy holds an AB from Georgetown, an MS from Virginia Tech, and a PhD from Cornell.

Stefan Wills BA, MSc, CPsychol

Stefan is a chartered organizational psychologist who joined Ashridge in 1991. He is a Programme/Client Director with responsibility for the 4-week 'General Management Programme' and a range of tailored clients (including Stinnes and Investors in People). His major activities include teaching and writing in areas such as high performing teams, leading change, emotional creativity, self-development and international management. His recent publications include articles on how managers learn, leadership and cross-cultural issues.

After serving a craft apprenticeship at Rolls-Royce Aeroengines, Stefan spent seven years as a mechanical engineer (HNC in mechanical engineering). As a mature student he gained a first-class honours degree in Social Sciences from Wolverhampton Polytechnic. He then went on to complete an MSc. in Organizational Psychology at UMIST. Immediately following this he worked as a teacher in the Middle East. Prior to joining Ashridge he worked as a Higher Occupational Psychologist in the Civil Service at an Employment Rehabilitation Centre where his major responsibilities were to assist disabled, unemployed persons back into employment or training.

INDEX